Barcelona

Jews, Transvestites, and an Olympic Season

Barcelona
Jews, Transvestites, and an Olympic Season

Richard Schweid

TEN SPEED PRESS
Berkeley, California

TEN SPEED PRESS
P.O. Box 7123
Berkeley, CA 94707

Cover design by Fifth Street Design
Text design by Ralph Fowler

Library of Congress Cataloging-in-Publication Data

Schweid, Richard, 1946–
  Barcelona : Jews, transvestites, and an olympic
season / Richard Schweid
      p.   cm.
  Includes bibliographical references (p.   ).
  ISBN 0–89815–578–9 — ISBN 0–89815–585–1 (pbk.)
    1. Barcelona (Spain)—Description and travel.   2. Spain—
History—Miscellanea.   3. Schweid, Richard, 1946–
—Journeys—Spain—Barcelona.   I. Title.
DP402.B25S39   1994
946'.72—dc20   93–34508
                                                                CIP

FIRST PRINTING 1994
Printed in the United States
1   2   3   4   5 — 98   97   96   95   94

For Carmen Martínez Gómez

Contents

Acknowledgments

When I called the newspaper library at the daily *El Periódico*—an upstart, post-Franco, colorful tabloid with short articles—a librarian told me that it could only be used by *El Periódico*'s reporters, good-bye.

When I called the library at *La Vanguardia*, Barcelona's staid, morning newspaper, published by the same family since 1881, the director of documents, Carles Salmurri, had only to hear that I was a journalist and he offered me the run of his well-organized files of newspaper clippings. We never discussed the exact nature of my work, but he and his staff were unfailingly cooperative and helpful in providing me information on a number of subjects, and I owe them deep thanks.

Neither they, nor the people below who helped me with this book in one way or another, bear any responsibility for its errors, mistakes, or ill-considered conclusions. Those all belong to me.

Thanks to: Montse Bea; Carlos Bosch; Daniel Capella i Samper; Marcelo Cohen; Ferdinand Crespo;

Sara Epstein; Rebecca Evarts; Phyllis Frus; Luciano Galli; Mike Golden; Jeff and George Judd; Sue Katz; Pablo Klimorsky; Silvia Komet; Andrée Akers Lequire; Susan Linnée; James and Heidi Lowenthal; Enrique and Dolores Majoral; Cailin Mankin; Domingo Marchena Martín; Dolores Martínez Gómez; Pilar Martínez Gómez; Elisabet Rodergas; Jay Sapir; Adele Schweid; David Schweid; and John Seigenthaler.

Thanks to Christine Carswell, whose editing made this a better book. My gratitude is also, and especially, due to all of the people in the book who were kind enough to grant me interviews, and put up with my poor Spanish grammar.

# Introduction

Sunday, September 1, 1991

Rents are higher here than in New York City, but after a week of searching I have finally found living space I can afford, a fifth-floor flat in Barcelona's central residential district, a huge grid of more than five hundred blocks called l'Eixample in the Catalan language, and el Ensanche in Spanish. From this base, I'll explore the city during its Olympic fever, and take a reading of its temperature. I've been to Barcelona before, but always in transit. Now it's time to stop here, to enter the city and have it enter me.

Occasionally over the past three decades, when I needed some place very cheap to stay for months at a time, I went to live on the Catalan island of Formentera. Life there is no longer inexpensive, but for many years $100 a month was enough to cover the rent on an old stone house (with a well and no running water), food, and drink. It is the smallest of the four Balearic islands in the Mediterranean—Majorca, Menorca, and Ibiza are the others—sitting out about two hundred miles southeast of Barcelona.

The cheapest way to get to Formentera in those days was by ship from Barcelona. I passed through the city many times en route to the island, usually spending a few days in a rundown hotel close to the port. The city always seemed like a liveable one on those brief visits. It was a visual repast to walk through, surprising the eye with beautiful buildings, narrow cobblestone streets teeming with people, and laundry hanging out over balconies. It was a constant delight to walk up and down the Ramblas, or through the back streets. I spent long hours sitting on a wooden bench in the beautiful, sunlit Plaza Real, as flocks of white pigeons banked through the air around the palm trees. I remembered the food as solid and tasty; large, cheap, flavorful meals in small restaurants tucked away in the twisting maze of streets near the port.

In fact, I was on Formentera ten years ago, in 1981, when the event occurred that heralded the new Spain. The nation had its first attempted coup in forty-five years, the first since General Francisco Franco Bahamonde led one in 1936 that plunged the country into civil war and almost forty years of dictatorship. This time, it was a snatch at the post-Franco, democratic government by right-wing military and police. They marched directly into Las Cortes, the congress in Madrid, on the afternoon of February 23, 1981, brandishing automatic weapons, firing into the air. They held the legislators hostage, while in the city of Valencia rebel soldiers rumbled through the streets in tanks. The king, Juan Carlos de Borbón y Borbón, saved the country and Spanish democracy when he stood firm and retained control of most of the military.

The monarchy had been restored only twelve years before, but King Juan Carlos, forty-three, did not buckle under pressure, as the right-wing coup leaders believed he would. As the titular head of the military, he went on nationwide television the night of the takeover in full military uniform to denounce the coup's leaders. He is a tall man, and on television that night he sat ramrod straight and unyielding behind his desk. In less than twenty-four hours, the armed men inside the Cortes surrendered and were taken off to jail.

The king's defense of democracy endeared him to his subjects, and affected the future of the country as nothing had since Franco's death in 1975, after almost forty years of dictatorship. It was clear that democracy was going to have a long run in Spain, and that there would be no more coup attempts in this generation. Spain was demonstrably stable enough to link its destiny to the rest of Europe's, as a full partner. In the 1982 elections, the socialist party won a large victory at the polls. For the first time since the Republicans were in power during the five years preceding the Spanish civil war, Spain had a left-of-center government.

By 1991, Felipe González and his socialist administration had been in power for almost a decade, and Spain was poised with eleven other European countries to close out the century as part of a remarkable confederation: the European Community. January 1, 1993, was the date set for the twelve EC countries to dismantle barriers to the free movement of goods, services, and people. This means no more trade barriers like tariffs or import quotas. It also means no more people barriers like questions from customs agents at the borders of the various countries. The schedule also calls for a single, pan-European currency by 1997.

By the end of the century, Europe is projected to be a confederation of nations that will more closely resemble the United States in structure than the Old World as we know it. While each country will remain a self-contained and sovereign entity, any European can live in any of them, free to work and do business.

Is each of the twelve EC countries really ready to unite economically and socially with the others? In a time when nationalism is the spark setting off bloody wars around the globe, this is a geopolitical experiment in the opposite direction: based on the idea that European interests are broader than national borders.

Spain had "gotten on the train," as Prime Minister González liked to put it. The country had been accepted into the European Community in 1986 and its economy had taken off, fueled by a large infusion of Euro-dollars. EC aid to Spain between 1986 and 1991 averaged over $3 billion a year. In 1986, foreign investment in Spain was under $7 billion, but by 1991 that figure was more than $15 billion, and fully half of the industry in Spain is foreign-owned. Life has changed rapidly for many of Spain's approximately forty million citizens, especially those in urban and industrialized areas.

Polls show that a substantial majority of Spaniards support the idea of a unified Europe, but there are those who are concerned that traditional parts of the Spanish culture might be lost in the rush to conform with European standards. They worry that the cost of common market membership may be higher than it appears.

So do I. Membership at the table of Europe's powerful and prospering is sure to have its down side. What will the price be for Spain to join the First World, to become a full partner in consumer society with equal access to credit cards, computers, and the free market? How much of their culture will Spaniards be asked to give up, leave behind, or modify beyond recognition?

These questions are on my mind as I take delivery of the keys to my flat. Even a brief look at the headlines in the local newspapers tells me that Barcelonese are dealing with the same problems as North Americans: things like drugs, abortion, crime, pollution, debt, and a general breakdown of the old order of morality. What solutions are being applied? What is the city like, I wonder? How has it been altered by a decade free of dictatorship, ten years of socialist rule, by the EC, and by the pending Olympic Games?

Barcelona is the capital of that autonomous region of northeastern Spain called Catalunya by the Catalans, Cataluña by the rest of Spain, and Catalonia by the English. There has been a city at that indentation along Spain's Mediterranean coastline for two thousand years, and the Catalan language has been written there since the twelfth century, making it one of the oldest surviving European languages. Catalan was being spoken long before it was written, and is considered by some to be the oldest Latin-based language. It considerably predates Castilian, the language the rest of the world calls Spanish, and is a different tongue.

The Catalans have a deep, strong culture, full of living traditions that stretch back for centuries, and are thriving. There are, for instance, as many young Catalans as old ones who gather every Saturday afternoon and Sunday morning on the plaza in front of the city's cathedral to dance the *sardana*, a folk dance that has been danced for generations.

Catalans celebrate a number of holidays marking events in their history, and both young and old serve the traditional food at these times, and celebrate in the traditional manner. Catalan cuisine remains popular, both at home and in restaurants. There are daily newspapers, television channels, radio stations, books, records, and films in the Catalan language. The strong culture, and the living traditions bring many Catalans comfort and security. They also give rise to strong nationalist feelings, and contribute to the reputation Catalans have in the rest of Spain as a closed, unfriendly society.

Most Catalans are comfortable speaking either Castilian or Catalan. To one another they speak Catalan, both at home and in public. Speakers of Castilian are always understood, but Spaniards who come to Barcelona and Catalonia from other regions of the country never lose their sense of being foreigners. While a certain number of weekly hours of instruction in Castilian is mandatory in the schools, Catalan is the language in which everything is taught in the elementary grades, and children in Catalan-speaking homes might not really learn Castilian until they are out of grammar school.

There is a strong Catalan independence movement, and Catalonia—the wealthiest region in Spain, and one the federal government would never consider allowing to secede—has been struggling against the hegemony of Castile and Madrid practically since the day, January 2, 1492, when Isabella and Ferdinand conquered the last Muslim stronghold, Granada, and proclaimed Spain united. The centuries since then have been punctuated with Catalan separatist movements, often violent. The struggle continues in 1991, but rarely in the form of violent resistance. Some ten to fifteen percent of the Catalan population is generally thought to favor total independence from Spain accompanied by the establishment of the sovereign nation of Catalunya, and a majority of Catalans questioned in surveys favor greater autonomy.

Catalan separatism has not been marked by the kind of terrorism that characterizes the Basque independence movement. The Basque region of northern Spain, called Euskadi in the Basque language, spawned the armed separatist group Euskadi Ta Askatasuua (Euskadi and Freedom), known to the rest of the world by its initials, ETA, which has been wreaking terrorist havoc across Spain since 1968. Although Catalan *independentistas* almost never resort to violence, the issue excites strong emotions.

Catalans! Espanya ens roba (Catalans! Spain is robbing you) reads the yellow and red poster—the national colors of both Catalonia and Spain—pasted up on the wall of my building. Many of those who have no sympathy for the secessionist cause feel this financial sentiment is at the nub of the Catalan independence movement, not the thousand years of culture, language, music, poetry, and war that Catalan nationalists like to stress. Taxes, not honor, are at the heart of separatism they say, and resentment that the Spanish government taxes Catalans for money it spends elsewhere: things like social programs in Andalusia or Galicia, or national parks in Estremadura. If Catalans have to submit to taxes, they want the money spent in Catalonia.

Resentment of the government in Madrid is understandable—the Catalans had it hard under Franco's dictatorship, following the end of the civil war in 1939, a war in which more than a million people died. Franco despised the Catalans, and never forgave Barcelona for the way it held out against his forces during the war. He immediately made it illegal to speak Catalan. "Speak in a Christian language," his soldiers told the Catalans, at gunpoint, when they took Barcelona in January 1939.

There was no regional autonomy under Franco's government, and any reference to Catalan history or culture was ruthlessly repressed. That attitude did not change as the years passed. Some families continued speaking Catalan at home, among themselves, but no one spoke it in public for fear of being reported, just as people did not openly criticize the government during the Franco years, nor speculate out loud about political alternatives or labor unions. Informers were everywhere.

For almost forty years, Franco and Spain's Catholic church imposed social and political isolation on the country, locking it out of the Europe that was just across the border to the north. Life was lived in a totalitarian shadow as grey as that of any Eastern bloc nation. It was not just "speak Christian," but also "act Christian," which in Spain meant Roman Catholic. The church was able to legislate its moral precepts into law, and there was no sphere of public life that remained untouched. Private life, too, fell under the purview of the church. All forms of sex were illegal, except what went on between married couples without the use of contraceptives strictly for the purpose of procreation. A woman was a second-class citizen, legally subject to her husband in all things. Her roles in life were restricted to those of wife and mother.

By now, things have changed almost totally. Spain is the country that most symbolizes the "forward progress" of a united Europe. The nation has achieved an incredible modernization in the sixteen years following Franco's death. Freedom of speech, democratic elections, and a free press are public reflections of the liberty with which people live their own private lives. Spain has become thoroughly contemporary.

Barcelona, with the Olympics scheduled for sixteen days next summer is on a roll all its own. Over the centuries, the city has had a history of staying the same for decades, then sprucing itself up in the space of a few years, spurred on by some impending great event. In 1888, it was the Universal Exposition, which left behind the 150-acre Ciutadella Park near the port; and in 1929 it was the World's Fair that gave the city the spectacular Plaza España (Plaça d'Espanya in Catalan), with its National Palace and wonderful fountains, as well as the stadium where the Olympics' main events will be held on the hill above the plaza. In both these instances, the city ran up huge deficits with which it was saddled for years.

After three futile bids by its predecessors to secure the summer Olympics in this century—1924 (Paris); 1935 (Berlin); and 1972 (Munich)—the socialist administration of Mayor Pasqual Maragall was successful. On October 17, 1986, Maragall announced the good news, and people came into the streets to drink *cava* (the sparkling wine that is the Spanish equivalent of Champagne) cheering and celebrating.

The world will be watching Barcelona in 1992, and the city fathers are determined that the world will see the city at its most European, its most sophisticated, attractive, and artistic. Barcelona: Make Yourself More Beautiful has been the motto of the city for the six years leading up to the Olympics. More than $1.5 billion is being spent on buildings and infrastructure, changes that will remain in place long after the Games are over. 1992 is to be the year in which Barcelona realizes and celebrates its conjunction with the world's big-time cities.

There is another side to Spain's success, however, to the blossoming of Barcelona, and to the approaching events of 1992. Two anniversaries which testify to the dark side of the Spanish character, to the long Iberian history of wars with their hatred and blind aggression; of a people willing to be governed by greed and savage righteousness, to obey strong authorities in the form of church or state, and to commit atrocities for those authorities, or stand by passively while they are being committed, with scarcely a whimper of protest.

One is the five hundredth anniversary of Columbus's first voyage to the New World, and the commencement, under Isabella and Ferdinand, of Spain's age of conquest. Not everyone views this quincentenary as a date for celebration. While Europeans generally regard it as a high point of modern history, Native Americans tend to note it more as an occasion for sackcloth and ashes.

The other quincentenary falling in 1992 marks Isabella and Ferdinand's edict of Expulsion, decreeing that all of Spain's approximately 200,000 Jews had four months to either convert to Catholicism or leave the country. The Iberian peninsula is thought by many historians to have been the westernmost point of Jewish immigration after the destruction of the Second Temple at Jerusalem in 70 A.D. In four months during 1492, a people and culture that had been on the peninsula for more than a millenium was systematically and totally wiped out. This was, furthermore, the final, bitter end of the generally peaceful and fruitful coexistence of Islam, Judaism, and Catholicism that had produced so many wonders in both the arts and the sciences over six centuries. (Muslims outlasted the Jews only a little—in 1525 they were forced to convert or leave, and in 1609, the descendents of those who had accepted normal conversion were expelled from Spain.)

The coming together of Muslims and Jews in Al-Andalus, the southern half of Spain now known as Andalusia, seems particularly poignant given twentieth-century political realities. In the medieval centuries of Al-Andalus there was an amalgam of the two great semitic traditions of knowledge. While they had their struggles, the two desert monotheisms generally worked together and exchanged their best. Many learned Jews spoke Arabic during those centuries, and there were Muslim scholars who read Hebrew. Most of the important literature in one language was translated into the other, and the Muslims brought the works of the Greeks to the Jews and the Catholics.

Gone. Finished, in 1492. What an infamous year! Isabella and Ferdinand acted to wipe out ancient cultures in the Old and the New Worlds. At the same time as they converted, exiled, or killed every Jew living in Spain, they launched a national policy of colonization that would exterminate the millenia-old civilizations of the New World, while bankrupting Spain economically and morally for centuries. In both worlds, people were made to bend the knee before the church. Catholic Spain would impose its morality and judgment on both subjects and citizens for hundreds of years to come. Almost without respite, Spain would be under the dominion of the church until the late 1970s.

Columbus and his three caravels had to sail for the New World from the small port of Palos de la Frontera instead of the larger Cádiz, which would have been the normal point of departure, because Cádiz was clogged with thousands of Jews frantically searching for passage out of Spain. There were no Jews in Spain for the next four hundred years, but in the twentieth century they were once again making the Iberian peninsula their home, and their numbers were slowly growing.

There are a handful of observances scheduled for 1992 in memory of the Expulsion, but by and large, Jews, like other Spaniards, choose not to dwell on the mistakes of the past. What everyone wants is to bask in the glory of the year, to enjoy and to profit from their moment in the international spotlight. After all, Seville is to be the site of a world's fair, Expo '92; Madrid is designated 1992's cultural capital of Europe; and Barcelona is buzzing with activity in preparation for the Olympics.

CHAPTER ONE

The Ramblas

Friday, September 20

The first full moon of my stay in Barcelona, I find myself crossing the Ramblas on my way to the Plaza del Rey to hear some outdoor jazz. The moon is bright, high over the plane trees in a clear sky. The edges of the buildings, with their delicately wrought balcony railings, are sharply shadowed in the moon-lit air. On this particular Friday night, there is even more life than usual on the Ramblas because of the *Fiesta de La Merced* (Festa de La Mercè in Catalan), a week-long celebration and festival in honor of the Virgin of Mercy, Barcelona's patron.

The Ramblas is the best place to begin getting acquainted with Barcelona. It is a broad, mile-long pedestrian boulevard lined with plane trees, running like a wide concrete seam from the Plaza Cataluña down to the port. There it ends at a huge, bronze statue of a larger-than-life Christopher Columbus atop a tall pedestal with his arm raised level, finger pointing out to sea.

The two oldest parts of the city flank the Ramblas. On the left, going down to the port, is the *barrio gótico* (barri gòtic in Catalan), the gothic neighborhood. It is the city's oldest, a warren of clean, narrow streets and medieval buildings, incorporating, and often built on top of the walls left by the Romans, who founded Barcelona shortly before the birth of Jesus. The barrio's population ranges from prosperous old Barcelona families to newly arrived immigrants. The barrio gótico is second only to medieval Prague as the largest inhabited Middle Ages neighborhood left in Europe.

The area on the other side of the Ramblas is called the Raval. The city began to grow here as early as the fifteenth century, and by the end of the 1700s, its neighborhoods were full of winding, cobblestone streets. They are not so clean as those across the Ramblas in the barrio gótico. The Raval has long been home to some of the city's poorest people. It also incorporates what is called the *barrio chino*, despite the fact that the area has never had a Chinese population. This part of the old city has traditionally serviced the port with bars, cheap hotels, prostitution, and drugs.

The Ramblas was laid out in the late 1700s, along the course of a stream that flowed down from the hills to the sea. The stream bed was filled in, and the Ramblas built on top of it. The word comes from the Arabic, *ramla*, meaning watercourse. It is one of the great pedestrian avenues in the world. At the top of the Ramblas is the Plaza Cataluña with its classical sculptures, fountains, and grassy banks where students sit eating sandwiches, and flocks of pigeons clean up their crumbs. The plaza is dominated by a large, nine-floor department store, El Corte Ingles, along one side.

Just about any time, night or day, there are crowds on the Ramblas. It is never deserted. The nature of the people rambling there changes as the day waxes and wanes, but there is almost always something, or someone to catch the eye. Passers-by are a cross section of the population of Barcelona. Sooner or later just about everyone from every part of town crosses the Ramblas.

Commercial space along it is staked out by the elderly, bird sellers, flower vendors, cafes, street performers, and news kiosks in a tacit turf agreement. At the top of the Ramblas, any hour during the day, a knot of older men gathers and discusses something, anything, in animated tones—from politics to soccer to the weather. Just below where they stand around are rows of comfortable metal chairs. People can rent them for small change and sit as long as they want: a cheap seat in a remarkable grandstand. Sitting in the sun on the Ramblas, watching the people pass by, is real and enduring entertainment.

The Ramblas is lined along its length with huge news kiosks featuring daily newspapers and magazines from many countries, along with paperback books, postcards, maps, and an impressive collection of written, drawn, and videotaped pornography. For anyone who wants a copy of the *International Herald Tribune*, or *El País* at 11 P.M., the Ramblas is where they go. News vendors there are open around the clock, whereas the news kiosks in other parts of town keep shopkeeper's hours.

There are other large metal kiosks that change the nature of the products they offer for sale as the Ramblas descends toward the sea. The bird sellers occupy the top third of the boulevard, birds in stacks of cages, squawking, hollering, and singing: finches, parakeets, canaries, and parrots all for sale. The bird sellers on the Ramblas stay open until the last light of day. Pigeons gather on the pavement around the bottom of the stacks of noisy, birdsong cages, plucking up whatever seed falls through the bars. Barcelonese have a big affection for cage birds. Lots of folks put them out on their balconies during the days, or put the cages by open windows, and the air is frequently filled with the trilling of canaries or the squawking of parrots.

(The parrots apparently escape from time to time, because there are flocks of free-flying, small green ones living in palm trees in different parts of the city. There are very few really cold days in Barcelona, and the temperature never falls below freezing, so the parrots have obviously learned to survive. They join pigeons and seagulls for swooping exercises during the day, their raucous jungle squawks in harsh contrast to the cries of gulls and the throaty trills of pigeons.)

Farther down the Ramblas, the bird sellers' kiosks give way to those of flower vendors who are busy from early morning until long after dark. Plants and flowers are offered in profusion. Farther still toward the port, restaurants arrange tables and chairs outdoors, where the unwary tourist can enjoy some pricey food and drink.

There is street theater up and down the Ramblas, pretty much around the clock. The performances vary widely in both kind and quality, and include jugglers, flamenco dancers, musicians from the Peruvian Andes, mimes, and a host of other entertainers. Many are in residence there, duly licensed by the *ayuntamiento de Barcelona*, as city hall is called, and some have made their shows their lives' work, present and accounted for on the same place year in and year out. Others are just passing through, doing their thing for a day, a week, a month, then getting moved on by the flow of their own lives, or by the police.

As a rule, jazz is hard to find in Barcelona, and rarer still outdoors. The Fiesta de la Merced is the exception, with a week of outdoor performances. Many Barcelonese consider it to be the best fiesta of the year. In addition to music, one can enjoy theatre; a huge outdoor Mass celebrated on Sunday; giants on stilts parading through the streets in a Catalan tradition dating back to the Middle Ages; a dangerous night of fire when fireworks are set off amidst large crowds, resulting, some years, in serious burns, or blindness, or even death; and an auto parade on Sunday afternoon, which includes anyone who wants to decorate their cars and participate.

There are free concerts for every taste held around the city: traditional Catalan music is available in the square of the Plaza San Jaime (Plaça Sant Jaume in Catalan), in between the Ayuntamiento on one side, and Catalonia's seat of government, the Generalitat, on the other, both built in the 1400s; rock and roll in the 35,000-seat soccer stadium at Camp Nou, home to the city's much beloved professional soccer team, el Barça; and *salsa* in the Plaza Real. The majority of the free jazz concerts take place in the Plaza del Rey (Plaza of the King), a small, ancient square surrounded by the high stone walls of medieval Barcelona. The plaza was built on Roman walls, still visible at basement level. Legend has it that the large stone hall at one end of the Plaza del Rey, the Saló de

Tinell, was where Isabella and Ferdinand received Columbus when he returned from his first voyage to the New World.

"What is known for certain from Columbus's journals and letters is that he came to Barcelona to see them when he returned in 1493, although it is not recorded where that meeting took place, and we cannot know for sure," said Jaume Riera i Sans, a Catalan, who is the chief librarian at the archives of Aragon, which are housed in another fourteenth-century building overlooking the Plaza del Rey. These archives are *the* historical resource for the autonomies of Aragon and Catalonia, which were collectively known as the kingdom of Aragon. The archives encompass a collection that begins with documents from the ninth century.

"It is possible that the meeting was in the Saló de Tinell, because the monarchs did use it sometimes to receive visitors, but we cannot be sure," said Riera. "When Ferdinand and Isabella came to Barcelona they lodged in the homes of noble families, the king in one and the queen in another, each with their retinues, and the meeting with Columbus might also have taken place in one of these homes."

What we do know for sure is that the Plaza del Rey is where the Inquisition was headquartered in Barcelona, beginning in 1488. Its offices were, fittingly, around the corner from the cathedral. It was here that the church's Inquisitors judged whether a person's faith was strong and real, or whether that person was guilty of being a Catholic only in name. The Inquisitors had the job of rooting out sinners and nonbelievers, whether they were among those born Catholic or those who had converted. Reports from anonymous sources and torture were among the tools they used to do the job. Accusations against a person's faith were made in secret. The accused were arrested, taken to a secret prison, and tried by the Inquisitors without the right to confront their accusers. Those who confessed their guilt had the chance to repent their sins in public, pay heavy fines, and perform penance. Those who refused to confess and were found guilty were "relaxed," which is what the Inquisitors called being burned at the stake, taking their inspiration from the New Testament admonition in John 15:6: "If a man abide not in me, he is cast forth as a branch and is withered: and men gather them and cast them into the fire, and they are burned."

The *quemadero* (burning place) wasn't in the Plaza del Rey itself.

Relaxations were carried out at a site beyond the city's medieval walls, close to the sea (and, close to the site of the Olympic Village, the housing complex being built in 1991 to lodge ten thousand Olympic athletes).

The Sefarad, as the Spanish Jews called themselves, who continued to practice Judaism, were immune to the Inquisition. It only had jurisdiction over the *conversos* and their descendants, those Jews who had converted to Catholicism. The conversos, alone, were plentiful enough to keep the Inquisitors busy. For many Jews, conversion had been a way to escape the frequent outbreaks of antisemitism that erupted on the Iberian peninsula during the Middle Ages. Jews converted to protect, or save their lives, and numerous families continued to practice Judaism secretly.

Many of the Sefarad felt themselves to be more Catalan or Iberian than Jewish, and if the way to continue raising children and doing business here was to be washed in the Blood of the Lamb, then they chose to get sprinkled, and kept their fingers crossed. They simply could not imagine leaving Spain. Their families had been here too long to leave, many of them for more than twenty generations, partaking in one of the world's most vibrant centers of Jewish culture, where their forefathers had led total, fulfilled lives. They had lost any sense of the diaspora, of being outcast, wandering Jews.

Other medieval Sefarad were not so deeply attached to their homeland. They converted as a temporary measure, a means of keeping their neighbors' holy terror at bay long enough to sell everything and find a ship to take their families to some more hospitable shore. This type of conversion was not regarded in Jewish religious law as a transgression of the first commandment—Thou shalt have no other gods before me—but simply as a temporary expedient.

Even Moses ben Maimonides, the most famous of medieval Sefarad philosophers, advised that people convert for a short time so as to avoid becoming martyrs, then flee to wherever they would be free to practice their true religion. Maimonides, born in Cordoba, spent most of his life in Egypt. While still a child, a period of Muslim persecution forced his father to profess a conversion to Islam for a short time, and to flee Al-Andalus at the first opportunity.

Outbreaks of antisemitism in Christian Spain increased over the centuries, with a corresponding rise in the number of converts. Many Jewish communities suffered annually during Easter Week, when Catholic resentment of the Jews as Christ-killers was naturally at its highest. Mobs formed, and angry Christian warriors descended on the Jewish ghettos and raised hell, killing and burning. Worse, there were years in both Muslim and Christian Spain where attacks on Jews were more or less constant. In one town, then another, people were murdered, those who weren't murdered either converted or left town, expelled, driven from one place to another, from pillar to post. Conversion seemed one way of ending the exhausting and frightening cycle.

The mob attacks on the Jews were inspired by the idea of reward both in this world and the next. That the Jewish people were allowed to live, having killed Jesus, seemed blasphemous to many Christians and they saw merit in serving the Lord by ridding his flock of these pestilent unbelievers. In addition, many of them owed lots of money to particular Jews who they were glad to see get murdered, or run out of town.

A particularly large number of Jews joined the church after the riots of 1391, when Catholic mobs rampaged through Jewish quarters all around the country. There were outbreaks of violence against Jews during the spring and summer of that year in almost every one of the more than one hundred Jewish communities across Spain, but nowhere were they worse than in Barcelona—there the citizens anticipated the Expulsion by 101 years. The Barcelonese rapidly drove out or murdered every Jew who would not convert on the spot.

Jewish communities in other Catalan towns and cities recovered after 1391, and some of them had substantial Jewish populations, but the violence and hatred in Barcelona had been so ferocious that Jews did not come back. They were offered repeated inducements to do so from some Catalan officials who missed the revenues they had generated, but Barcelona's Jews had seen enough.

Many of the city's prominent Jewish families had converted as soon as the trouble broke out. For some, it proved a successful way to protect themselves and their families. Their descendants went to Mass on Sundays at the cathedral near the Plaza del Rey, and prospered. Others were not so fortunate. While their conversions gained them an additional century of being able to live and work in Barcelona, their descendants were undone by the Inquisition.

In July 1487, the director of the Inquisition, Tomás de Torquemada, sent his envoys to Barcelona for the first time. The Inquisition established a network of informers to uncover false Christians, and allowed some of the accused to ameliorate their own sentences by providing the Inquisitors with the names of others. Even those who had converted with all their hearts and true faith were not safe from the Inquisition. A neighbor, desperate to save his or her own skin, might give up the true believer just for a name to speak. The Inquisition was perfectly capable of making a mistake and finding the innocent guilty. There was no appeal from such a verdict.

Between the time the Inquisition arrived to set up its offices in the Plaza del Rey, and the following year, 1488, when it officially opened for business, some five hundred converso families fled the city. In its first year of operation, the Inquisition carried out a sentence of relaxation against four of Barcelona's Jews, two men and two women. Things would get worse. The Inquisition would be a fact of life for conversos and their descendants in Spain for over three hundred years.

The Inquisition was not enough to satisfy Torquemada, who was a vocal and powerful proponent of pure blood and "ethnic cleansing." It frustrated him that he could not touch Jews who continued to practice their faith. He set out to convince the people of Spain, and their monarchs, that the nation should be free of everything but Catholics. It took him quite a while to get his message across, but he did it.

He was bucking tradition. For centuries, rulers of the various regions across the Iberian peninsula had protected the Jews from the effects of demagogues in the pulpit, and the prejudice of the people. Barcelona's Jews, for instance, were the legal property of the ruler of Catalonia. This arrangement was included in Barcelona's first legal code, established in 1150. Jews frequently paid a large share of the taxes that filled royal coffers, and were under the direct jurisdiction of the monarchs. They were not subject to the whims of either municipal or ecclesiastical authorities.

While royal protection was not always enough to save the Jews from the wrath and zealotry of their Catholic neighbors, it was frequently what made the difference between survival and destruction. And, after the worst of the mob attacks, the rulers, be they in Castile, Aragon, Catalonia, or Al-Andalus made reparations to the Jews, and prosecuted those guilty of inciting the riots.

Isabella and Ferdinand, or the Catholic Monarchs as they liked to call themselves, were the first to unite the various kingdoms of the Iberian peninsula into the Spain we know today. In order to do so, they spent the initial years of their rule engaged in a war with the Muslims for Al-Andalus and Granada. While the war was going on, they were disposed to continue providing their Jewish subjects with the traditional rights and protections. They were, no doubt, influenced by the fact that Jews bore a disproportionately heavy burden in providing the revenues to finance the campaign against the Moors. On July 9, 1477, Isabella wrote: "All the Jews in my kingdom are mine and under my protection, and belong to me to defend and shelter and maintain in justice."

However, once the reconquest was complete and Spain was brought under their rule, on January 2, 1492, Ferdinand and Isabella began to listen more closely to Torquemada's constant insistence that the Jews had to go, his claims that they represented a persistent threat to the spiritual well-being of Spain. On March 31 of that year, fifteen years after Isabella signed her commitment to protect the Jews, the Catholic Monarchs issued a proclamation giving every Jew in the country four months to convert, or get their affairs in order and leave.

"The night of July 31, 1492, Torquemada slept peacefully," Jaume Riera told me one day in the archives of Aragon, seated in front of a tall window looking out on the Plaza del Rey. "Torquemada's concern was never to physically exterminate all the Jews in the world, he just did not want to see one in the street or ever have one in front of his eyes. He convinced the king and queen that the Jews represented an infection and a danger to the true faith, and that they should be expelled."

For Sefards in exile, the typical Jewish longing for Jerusalem and the holy land was replaced by a heartsickness and homesickness for Spain. Exiled Jewish families did not entirely give up their Spanishness over the centuries after they left. Food and language both survived, although they were dispersed to the four corners of the world.

At the beginning of this century there were still over 100,000 people in Turkey who spoke a medieval form of Spanish brought by their ancestors to the Ottoman empire when they fled from the Iberian peninsula. Travelers during the seventeenth century reported that there were Jews in the ghetto of Venice speaking that same language. Since the early days of the state of Israel there has been a weekly radio broadcast in the Spanish of the medieval Sefarad. In Buenos Aires, Jewish mothers teach their children to cook dishes whose recipes are unmistakably Catalan, handed down since the Spanish diaspora began. The exiled Sefarad carried Spain with them, it was something they could not leave beside the road to lighten their burdens. There had been too much mixing of the blood. Too many generations lived and died in Iberia to slough it off like an old skin. There were too many Jewish genes in the veins of Spain to easily abandon the country.

Spain passed more than four hundred years with no Jewish communities inside its borders. A few Jews came to Madrid and Barcelona during the 1860s as representatives of the French-based Rothschild banking empire, but it was not until the early twentieth century that communities reappeared. The first group of Jews to arrive came from Turkey, descended from Sefarad who fled to the Ottoman empire during the Middle Ages. Their families had been living there ever since. They were eventually joined by descendants of Sefarad who came from other European countries, as well as Jews displaced by one or another European upheaval who had no family ties to Spain.

During World War II, Franco, despite his fascist sympathies, provided refuge to a certain number of European Jews fleeing the Third Reich. There was always widespread apprehension among Spanish Jews during the war that Franco might open the country's borders to the Nazis, whom Spain supported. But he did not. Franco never encouraged Jews to come to Spain, nor did he grant their religion official recognition, but they were allowed to live there in relative peace and, eventually, to organize congregations.

After the Second World War, Jews continued to arrive in small numbers from all the pre-war points of origin. They were joined in the 1950s by thousands of Moroccan Jews, who chose to leave when that country gained independence from the French. There was another large wave of immigration during the late 1970s, when many Argentine Jews fled their repressive military dictatorship. Throughout those years, the Catholic church controlled life. It was the state religion, and there was no warm welcome waiting for those Jews who chose to settle in Spain. They faced stereotypes built up by Spaniards during more than four hundred years of having no practicing Jews in their midst.

When Mònica Adrian went to elementary school in Barcelona, in 1966, her nine-year-old classmates asked her, in all seriousness, why she drank the blood of Christian children at Easter. That is what their priests and their parents had told them Jews did.

"They also wanted to know why I didn't have horns if I was Jewish," said Adrian, the director of Barcelona's Baruch Spinoza Foundation, which was organized in the quincentennial year of the Expulsion to gather oral histories from the Jews who had come to Barcelona this century.

"It was all pure ignorance. They had never known a Jew and, to them, Jew was synonymous with bad. This was, of course, not the sort of thing that would make a nine-year-old girl very happy. What matters at that age is what the other kids think of you, and it was hard for me."

During the Franco years, religion was an obligatory class in school. In many classrooms, whenever Jews were mentioned during the lessons, the children were taught to spit on the floor. Textbooks of Spanish history during the Franco years portrayed the Jews as traitors to Catholic Spain, and as people who ritually tortured and murdered Christian children. What would never, ever be mentioned was the substantial amount of Jewish blood flowing in the veins of Spaniards, nor the role that medieval Jews played in making Spain what it is today.

As the quincentenary approached, there was a spate of television shows to mark the date. Most of them featured interviews with contemporary Spanish Jews, and for many viewers it was the first time that they had seen someone they knew was a Jew, according to Jaume Riera. "Even these days, many, many Catalans have never consciously seen an example of what a Jew might be. There is not one single thing to mark the Jews among them. When a Jew passes them on the street, or does business with them, they have no way of knowing that person is a Jew.

"When you talk to older people they all have the same idea of a

Jew—old, greedy, counting his money at night, and with a beautiful daughter. This is the typical image of the centuries. Why they should all be thought to have beautiful daughters I don't know, but don't forget that the Blessed Mother, the Virgin, was herself a Jew, and is considered the most beautiful of all women."

Another explanation occurs to me while I am sitting in the Plaza del Rey, listening to some amazing flamenco/jazz work by guitarist Pedro Javier Gonzalez and his two percussionists. As I look at the female occupants of the seats around me, I think that the Catalans applied that particular stereotype to Jews because it was so true of themselves. Catalans certainly have a reputation as the most enterprising, and thrifty of all Spaniards. And, their raven-haired daughters are exceptionally lovely, with Mediterranean, olive-dark skin that looks as soft as suede.

The metro has stopped running by the time the jazz ends at 2 A.M., and I have to take the twenty-minute walk home. The Barcelona metro is clean, made up of almost entirely new cars and generally efficient. The stations are often decorated with art, and they are well lit. There is always music coming over the public address system, and it is of a wider variety and higher quality than most public background sound. Everything from John Coltrane to Emmylou Harris to Johann Pachelbel. The worst thing about the metro is that, inexplicably in a city known for nightlife, it closes early. There are infrequent buses running nighttime routes, and taxis are plentiful and fairly cheap, but the metro closes at 11 P.M. during the week. On weekends and fiestas, it stays open to 1 A.M., which is just about the time people are going out for their first drink of the evening.

When I leave the Plaza del Rey, the moon is still up and the Ramblas is crowded with people. At 2 A.M. on a warm, fall, fiesta night, it is a varied crowd: people pushing baby carriages; families with small children eating ice-cream cones; innumerable couples of all ages strolling arm in arm or kissing passionately in the shadows under the branches of the plane trees; crowds of teenagers making noise, singing, clapping in rhythm, drawing self-conscious attention to their brashness; shell-game

hustlers with their collapsible cardboard stands, three thimbles and a gar-
banzo bean; a mime; a group of Andean musicians singing the lilting
songs of the Peruvian mountains—short, dark-skinned Indians wearing
colorful ponchos and black bowler hats, accompanying themselves on
Pan pipes and stringed instruments made with tortoise-shell sound
boxes; a man seated in a straight-backed wooden chair playing a harp;
and a wide range of other talent.

Some of the flower vendors are still open, mostly for the passing
pairs of lovers who stop to buy a rose, but the bird sellers have been
closed since sunset. When the sun goes down so do the metal shutters
over the fronts of the bird kiosks. Walking by them you can hear the rus-
tle of warm, feathered bodies shifting, muffled half-squawks in sleep, an
anxious avian tossing and turning on the roost.

There are, however, a fair number of human night-hawks and
night-owls about, looking as if they had stayed on their roosts most of
the day, before darkness brought them out to prey on the crowd. There
is a liberal scattering of the battered, the drunken, and the sinister, min-
gled among the strollers, the lovers, and the families. As the hour grows
later, the Ramblas, and the surrounding streets of the old city, become
increasingly unsafe places to carry a purse that is easily snatched, or to
keep a wallet in a pocket that is easily picked.

In addition to the birds of prey, there is the occasional bird of paradise, a much done-up and done-over transvestite sweeping down the
Ramblas, brilliant plumage turning heads as he swirls by in a rush of
color, cutting a swath through the less fortunate, dowdy, inelegant peons
in his path. One such person passes me by in a flaming dress of red lace,
wearing a wig of upswept raven hair covered by a mantilla, heavily
rouged, clicking castanets in the air with two thick, square, middle-aged
hands. He gives me a disdainful glance and lifts a haughty shoulder as he
passes. Everyone turns to look as he goes by, but there are no tsk-tsks or
disapproving clucks, and older Catalan couples, arm-in-arm, smile be-
nignly in his wake.

Barcelona is known as a city with a tolerance for transvestites, as
well as most of the other forms of sexual self-expression in the human
catalogue. While Franco and the church reigned this was not, of course,
how it was. During those years, Spain was an extremely puritanical

country. All films were censored before they were shown, pornography was outlawed, there was no divorce, and homosexuals were put in prison. Public displays of affection were not simply frowned on, they were against the law, as was any deviation from heterosexuality within the bounds of marriage. A deep kiss between a man and a woman outside the privacy of their own home was considered a misdemeanor under the law, and the offending parties could be fined under the criminal code statute regarding "public scandal."

When Franco died, the Spanish followed the lead of most of the other European countries, and demanded that both the state and the church had to stay out of the bedroom. While most of Spain seems comfortable with the new sexual freedom, Barcelona tends to flaunt it. Its reputation puts it among the top cities on the map of erotic Europe.

"When Franco died, it was as if someone had pulled the cork out of the bottle, there was a lot of sexual energy released," a Barcelona journalist told me. "There was an incredible explosion of sexuality that had been repressed and hidden all those years."

Things have settled down some since those first years of freedom, but there is still a lot of sexual exuberance, a lot of pornography, and a notable absence of the Puritan spirit. It is evident everywhere, from the housewives and grandmothers who sunbathe topless on local beaches to the state-licensed sex shops, offering X-rated equipment and entertainment, in various neighborhoods around the city. When it comes to nightlife there is an offering for just about every taste.

In order to enjoy partying in Barcelona, North Americans have to stay up later than they are used to. In clubs with live music, for instance, the first set does not begin until about midnight, and things do not get rolling until 2 A.M. After that, people head to whatever entertainment suits their fancy in the way of bars, nightclubs or discotheques. There are discos that do not open until 5 A.M. The younger set that frequents these places will leave only in time to go home, shower, change their clothes, and go to work.

How people in Barcelona or Madrid can keep the hours they do and still get any work done at all is often a mystery to foreigners, particularly those weaned on a capitalist work ethic. There are those who have lived in Barcelona for years and never grown accustomed to the schedule. Even the Japanese, well-known for their late nights, are cowed. Kiyoshoi Sekiguchi is the director general of Nissan Motor Iberica, Catalonia's fourth largest company, with annual revenues of about $1.5 billion. Sekiguchi has come to Barcelona from Tokyo, and two years later is still having trouble with the schedule. He is frequently obligated to go out to dinner with Spanish businessmen, and to accompany them somewhere for entertainment after the meal.

"This means we'll start out with a drink at 9 P.M., then the food will get to the table at 10 P.M. and we'll be there for two or three more hours eating and drinking," he told me. "I come into my office every single workday at 8 A.M., so it has not been easy for me to become accustomed to the way in which people in Barcelona do their entertaining."

The Spanish schedule, in general, is one of the outstanding questions concerning how Spaniards will remodel their lives in the European Community mold. Executives in Berlin, Paris, or London go to lunch for an hour at noon and return to an afternoon of work. It is an endless annoyance to them that it is nearly impossible to find a Spaniard in the office between 2 and 5 P.M. Nor is it always possible to catch them in the mornings, because at 9:30 A.M. they are likely to be out having a little something, and they are gone again at midday for a second breakfast. They are generally reachable in their offices from 5 to 8 P.M., but by then other Europeans have already dragged their weary selves home. The Spanish sense of time is bred deeply in the bone, and it seems likely to be a point of contention with the rest of the EC for some years to come. Presumably, if the EC thrives, Spaniards will eventually have to give in and learn to eat on the run.

Yet, one of the things that makes living in Spain so enjoyable is the pleasure that most people still take in life's basic routines. They like to eat, drink, and enjoy themselves, and this is what makes Barcelona's social life so varied and interesting. Day or night, there are always lots of places to go for a little something. At night, the choices range from elegant bars and discotheques, created by the city's leading designers, to dance halls that have been open for fifty years with a decor of gilded columns and plush red velvet draperies, and a large polished dance floor where old and young couples came to waltz.

When the sun is up, there are the small neighborhood bars, at least one on almost every block, where someone is always sitting, sipping, and talking. There are customers in these bars for breakfast, lunch, dinner, and at all hours in between. Spain has about as many bars as the other eleven Common Market countries combined, according to a 1991 EC study, and Barcelona certainly does its part in contributing to that statistic.

Another ingredient in the potent mix of Barcelona's nightlife is love. Like Paris, Barcelona thrives on romance. Couples are everywhere. Park benches are filled with people locked in embraces that would earn them a trip to jail in some parts of the States. Groping and squeezing with unabashed ardor goes on everywhere. Even elderly couples walk down the street with their arms around each other or holding hands. Barcelonese like their love and love their lust, and they are tolerant of the many ways people find to enjoy each other.

Given the city's relaxed attitude toward the varieties of physical pleasure, it's hardly a surprise that sex for sale is big business. There is a thriving pornography trade, and plenty of working prostitutes. The classified ads in *El País*, *La Vanguardia*, and *El Periódico*, the three largest, most respected, daily newspapers, offer everything from standard sex to transvestite sado-masochism, accompanied by addresses, phone numbers, and a list of acceptable credit cards. There are clubs where couples come to exchange partners for the evening, and these places have bedrooms on the premises. Things have clearly come a long way from the Franco years.

CHAPTER TWO

Emigrants & Immigrants

Sunday, October 6

Close by the Plaza del Rey, and around a couple of
corners from the Cathedral of Barcelona in the barrio gótico, is the lovely little Plaza San Felipe Neri,
named for an Italian saint. In the center of the cobblestone square, two large and leafy acacia trees flank
a small fountain. The noise of the fountain's gently
falling water, muted by the thick branches over-
hanging it, imparts a tranquil air to the open space.

On one side of the plaza is the small Museum
of the History of Shoes, featuring footwear from
Roman times to the present. Another side is dominated by the church of San Felipe Neri, and the
grammar school attached to it. There are pockmarks
around the doors of the church, and along its wall
gouges up to about the height of a man's head. More
than one person told me that these are bullet marks
from executions of Republicans who were lined up
against the wall and shot when Franco's forces captured the city in 1938. This legend is not true. The
walls were pocked when the neighborhood was

bombed by Franco's forces in 1938, according to neighbors who had been there. Entire buildings around the plaza were flattened by bombs. Many Republicans were executed, but not here.

I wander back to the plaza in search of a small dose of peace and quiet. The shoe museum is closed on Sunday, and there is a middle-aged man sitting on its front step. He wears shiny black trousers and a tattered sweater. He is playing flamenco music on a nylon-stringed guitar, and singing. He is obviously not a Catalan, since flamenco is the music of Andalusia, far to the south, and few Catalans appreciate it with the fervor of other Spaniards. The ringing tones of the man's voice fill the air of the plaza with shimmering laments.

The music reminds me of the first time I realized something distinctive about the Spanish character. It had not happened in Spain, but in the south of France twenty years before. I was sitting in the back of a bus, grieving, coming back to the mean-spirited, little French town of Saint Hippolyte-du-Fort where we were living in the hill country. I was traveling from the small, grey city of Nîmes, where my son had died being born prematurely in a cold, reproachful Catholic hospital staffed by French sisters with no sympathy for an unmarried couple out of money.

It was fall, in the season of the grape harvest, and there was a group of Spaniards on the bus with me, who had come up to France to pick grapes and make some money. One of the men had a guitar, and they were singing songs of Andalusia, clapping to the flamenco rhythms, passing a wineskin around the back of the bus. The front half was occupied by the local French going from one town to another. They sat erect, backs straight, necks stiff, never once turning around to look at the Spaniards. But each and every upright Gallic soul among them radiated waves of contempt, surrounding them with an aura of disapproval. The Spaniards continued to while away the journey through the French countryside by warming up the back of the bus—and, incidentally, my heavy heart—with their music and vitality.

In those days, immigrant workers were often the first Spaniards with whom a European came in contact because, while Franco was alive, Spain was a nation of migrants. Men went north to perform the jobs northern Europeans did not want to do: stoop labor in the fields;

low-paying factory work; non-union construction labor; and street sweeping, for instance. They were glad to do anything and everything they could find, and most of them sent the lion's share of their wages back home. In much of Spain there was no work for unskilled labor, nor any help for strapped farmers. Many men could earn enough to keep their families afloat only if they looked for work far from home. In 1972, for instance, about 184,000 Spanish workers went to West Germany on temporary labor contracts. Remittance monies from outside Spain were one of the primary sources of income for Spaniards during the Franco years.

In those same years, many people gave up their land in the south of Spain, and moved to Madrid or Barcelona looking for work. Urban areas were flooded with people tired of living in rural Spain under conditions of direst poverty, often without enough food to eat. For many of them, the move to the cities eventually paid off, and they succeeded in bettering their lots by dint of sheer persistence and hard work. But there was plenty of poverty in the cities, too, and sometimes newcomers could not find work. Sometimes, what little they found did not last long. There were not enough steady jobs in Barcelona to go around, and the Catalans themselves were often part of the emigrant labor force that went to northern Europe.

By the late 1970s, the tide had begun to turn. Spain became a country to which people immigrated in search of work. By 1991, there were some 500,000 legally registered, first-generation immigrants in Spain, and an estimated 250,000 on top of that who were undocumented. Although no one can say with certainty how many immigrants, legal and illegal, live in the greater metropolitan area of Barcelona with its 3.5 million inhabitants, most observers agree there are more than 200,000 of them from around the world.

A study in 1987 concluded that forty-two percent of the immigrant workers in Catalonia made under $400 a month, twenty-six percent earned between $400–$500 a month, and another fourteen percent were between $500–$600. The current median salary for nonimmigrant Catalans is about $1,500. A Spaniard makes more than immigrant wages staying at home and drawing unemployment, but for someone from

North Africa, or Latin America, or the Indian subcontinent, or the former Spanish possession of Equatorial Guinea on the west coast of Africa, it could seem like a lot of money.

Many of the immigrants found work in the country, in the fields, doing farm work that was yet to be mechanized, but that was too menial for Spaniards. Planting, weeding, and harvesting—the things that put food on a businessman's table. In the cities, too, the immigrants did the work that needed doing but that Spaniards did not want to do. Women frequently had an easier time than men finding work in the urban areas, because there was a demand for domestics, for cooks, for someone to be at home caring for children or an elderly parent during the day, while a couple went to their jobs. The housewife's lament—good domestic help is hard to find—was repeated frequently, and a woman from the Dominican Republic living in Barcelona who was willing to do a good job of cleaning a home for low wages was a godsend.

One of the few jobs that exist for immigrant men in Barcelona is keeping people warm in the winter. Much of the city's housing stock consists of roomy, high-ceilinged flats, large apartments built around the turn of the century, which are hard to heat. Although the temperature in Barcelona virtually never falls below freezing, these flats are often draughty and cold. Almost none of the buildings have any kind of furnace or central heating, and there are still a substantial number of them that are not even hooked up to a source of natural gas.

Although increasing numbers of Barcelonese use electric space heaters, electricity is expensive, and most people continue to spend November through March wheeling butane space heaters from one room to another, just as they have every winter for the past thirty years. The butane, which also fuels gas stoves in the older apartments with no gas lines, comes in stubby, bright orange iron tanks, each of which weighs about twenty-five pounds. The orange tanks are a ubiquitous sight on the balconies of Barcelona. People buy two for each appliance, one to keep in reserve on the balcony and one to have in the space heater, or stove. The tanks are filled and sold by a state-owned gas and petroleum monopoly called Repsol, which does more than a half billion dollars of business annually.

Once a week during the summer, and every two or three days during the fall and winter, a man in an ill-fitting orange and grey jumpsuit pushes a dolly down the street in each neighborhood, with six or seven orange tanks stacked on it. He beats on the tanks with a stick or calls out, *"Butano, butano"* (pronounced boot-ahno), to herald his presence. People lean out over the wrought-iron railings of their balconies and call down to him what floor they're living on, and how many butanos they want.

The man pushing that 150 pounds of butane down the street is not likely to be a Catalan. It is immigrants' work, and no wonder. Few of those older buildings have elevators, but they do have five or six floors. It is common to pass men on the stairs delivering a tank—dark-skinned men, not always young, trudging upstairs, stooped over, balancing a twenty-five-pound, orange iron cylinder on their shoulders with one hand. They are paid for the full tank they deliver, and pick up an empty in exchange. The price is about $9 a tank. The delivery men do not get paid a wage, but make their living from tips. Tip or no tip, they carry the much lighter empty downstairs and continue pushing the dolly as quickly down the block as possible.

"You don't stop during the winter. There's someone on every balcony calling you, and you can make a hundred thousand pesetas [$1,000] a month. But during the other seasons when the only butano people buy is for the kitchen stove, you make much less," said Geraldo Rojas, a twenty-four-year-old from the Guayaquil coast of Ecuador. "This may sound strange, but I'd rather deliver to a building without an elevator, and the reason is people are going to give you a hundred pesetas [about $1] if you climb the stairs, but only twenty-five if you come up in the elevator."

Rojas was short, lean, and muscular, with skin the color of *café con leche*, jet-black hair, a round face, and brown eyes that laughed a lot. When I first saw him on the streets of the Raval, wheeling a dolly loaded with butano tanks down the narrow sidewalk, he was smiling. He is an exception in his trade, and not just because he sometimes smiles. There are very few South Americans who deliver butano; it is mostly done by North Africans, Pakistanis, or Bangladeshi.

It isn't hard to observe that delivering butano is labor reserved for Barcelona's undocumented workers. Everyone knows it, but while the immigrants are working in their orange and grey jump suits, pushing their dollies, they are free from worry about having to produce papers. Police turn a blind eye to them, because everyone also knows that someone has to deliver the gas, and these guys are the only ones willing to do it.

"My brother lived here, so I came. But I couldn't find a job here before my three months of being legal ran out. Without a work contract I couldn't get working papers," Rojas told me over a beer one evening in the two-bedroom apartment, far out on a metro line, which he rented for $650 a month with four other people.

"It's a vicious circle—you need a work contract to get papers, and you need papers for a work contract. All I wanted to do was work. I didn't come here for fun, and I spent four months looking for a job, anything. But no one would hire me without papers.

"I didn't know about butano. My brother knew, but didn't tell me because he didn't want to see me doing this kind of work. Finally, a Spanish woman told me to go see about butano, that they didn't ask for papers. It was hard work at first, I didn't have the rhythm and I didn't sell many tanks, but I stayed with it. I'm here to work."

Those butano delivery men in Spain illegally are not covered by any worker's benefits, have no access to the national health-care system, as every Spanish citizen does, and are not eligible for unemployment if they get injured and cannot work, another right of every Spanish citizen. Repsol does not take responsibility for the workers, because they do not directly employ them. Repsol employs salaried truck drivers to deliver the butano. It's the drivers who, in turn, hire the men to carry the tanks. Each truck is assigned a certain zone, and the driver hires two deliverymen to walk this beat. While they work a zone, the driver waits for them in the truck.

Not all the poor immigrants who come to Barcelona looking to better their lives wind up delivering butano. There are greater success stories. Atiqullah Sarder, or Tony as he introduced himself to Europeans, left Bangladesh to come to Europe in 1976. "I did not have a family, but I knew I would have one in the future. I wanted to raise my family in European society, in European culture, because it's better and more advanced than in Bangladesh."

His English was heavily accented and strange to my ears, but eminently understandable. Along with it, he spoke German, Spanish, and his native Bengali. One morning, while I had a café con leche and a croissant at his dark, small, shabby bar in the Raval district's barrio chino, he told me how his search for a place to live in Europe had gone. First, he went to Germany where he met his wife, who had also recently arrived from Bangladesh in search of a better future. They had a daughter and stayed in Germany five years, but it was too hard for an immigrant to get ahead there. Tony decided to look for somewhere with less administrative obstacles to his ambition.

He settled on Catalonia, and arrived in Gerona, sixty miles north of Barcelona, in 1981. There, he joined other immigrants selling jewelry in the public market for three years, and saved his money. In 1984, he was able to move to Barcelona, where he stayed for some time in a cheap hotel while he "looked around." By the time I met him, he owned the apartment where his family lived, and also another three-bedroom place, which he rented to seven or eight men at a time (usually other immigrants from Bangladesh) for $150 apiece per month. He bought a bar in the Raval, on the edge of the barrio chino, in the same area where his apartments were located.

The bar was three blocks from the port, in a dirt-poor part of the city, but it was a big step up from selling jewelry in the market at Gerona. The clientele in the bar was seedy, but Tony's prices were cheap. There were hand-written notices on sheets of lined notebook paper posted on the wall by the door and by each of the three tables in the bar to remind people that they were not welcome unless they bought something. These were written in both Spanish and Bengali.

"Look at those two focking old Spanish men," he told me, gesturing toward the door where two elderly, practically toothless, shabby senior citizens, unshaven, sallow skinned, one leaning on a cane, were slowly making their way toward the nearest edge of the bar. They each ordered a glass of wine, which they tossed off with trembling hands as soon as Tony put them down. Then, they each put a few coins on the bar beside an empty glass, turned, and shambled out.

"They get 60,000 pesetas [$600] in pensions every month, and they spend it in about two weeks, going around here and there, and drinking wine," said Tony, contemptuously. Then they spend the rest of the month begging in the streets and making about 2,000 pesetas [$20] a day. They've been coming in here since I opened the place. These focking Spanish just don't like to work the way people do in my country. These people like to sleep, and eat, and drink."

Tony, thirty-two, led anything but a life of leisure. He opened the bar at 9 A.M. and closed it at 1 A.M. Business was good, he said, but he had no intention of resting on his laurels. There was a laundry for sale down the street, and he was thinking about buying it, he told me, his round face beaming beneath a head of dark, thinning curls. He was short and stout. The fingers and palms of his brown hands were cross-hatched with hundreds of little lines. Each looked like a thin razor-blade cut. They were the hands of someone who has done a lot of work. He had not seen the village in Bangladesh where his extended family still lived for fifteen years, although he had brought his mother and siblings to Barcelona for a visit.

"If you struggle in your life, you can shine, but otherwise you do nothing. If you keep struggling, and you are honest, people respect you and you can slowly shine in your life. That's what I want to do.

"Spain has been good to me," Tony said. "Here, if you have some money, the government will let you do things. I'm a Muslim, but I respect all religions, and that's how people have also treated me. The Spanish people have treated me well. My children have Spanish passports."

Prudencio Mdomio is not so happy with his treatment. He is a Spanish citizen from the ex-Spanish territory of Equatorial Guinea on Africa's west coast. He, too, spent his life's savings on a bar in Barcelona. At the age of forty, he wanted to establish his future. Mdomio's choice was a place for sale in a working-class barrio, away from the center of the city. Prudencio is an easygoing man, with a slow, laid-back, African rhythm behind the bar, serving up plenty of conversation and laughter while he works. One of the primary reasons he was attracted to the place was because, when he saw it, there was a feeling of peaceful sociability inside. He bought it from a white Catalan who wanted to retire.

He was puzzled when some of his customers advised him to keep a weapon behind the bar. But it did not take him long to understand why. There was a bar just down the block where a lot of young Catalan men gathered in the evenings. Most of them wore combat boots and had shaved heads. They tended to stand around together outside the place and yell insults down the block at Mdomio's customers. Flyers began appearing under his door, waiting for him when he opened in the mornings. They carried messages like, *Una Europa imperial, limpia de negros y judiós* [One imperial Europe, clean of blacks and jews]. He found similar messages scrawled on the wall outside.

"It came to a crisis on a Thursday night," he told me one morning, shortly thereafter, in his bar. "My wife was closing. I was already at home, and she called me to say I should come back quickly. She was terrified.

"The skinheads were shouting and swearing at her when she closed, then kicking the locked door and urinating on it. We called the police. They came and arrested one down the street, but the others got away. Since then, it has been quiet, but I keep a machete under the bar now. I'm ready for them if they want to cause more trouble."

Mdomio's experience is not an isolated incident. Although neo-Nazis are neither as numerous nor as well organized in Spain as in France and Germany—each of which has far greater numbers of immigrants—racism and xenophobia are present in Barcelona and seem to be growing. With communism no longer the unifying threat that it was in Franco's time, the ultra-right has returned its focus to its traditional enemies: non-whites, homosexuals, and Jews. They found an audience waiting for their message and a willing legion of shock troops in the gangs of skinheads, modeled after those that grew up in England a decade earlier around soccer clubs. Barcelona's skins started out as a bunch of bad boys who liked to get violent and rowdy after home games of the widely adored pro soccer team, the Football Club of Barcelona, better known as el Barça. From those early rampages of football hooliganism, they grew into something more hateful and focused.

Barcelona's police estimate that the city is home to about seven hundred skinheads, and, of these, a third was deeply committed to a violent, Nazi ideology. They acknowledge that the groups have spread over the past few years. Now there are skinheads in all of Spain's largest cities, including Madrid, Bilbao, Seville, and Valencia. Barcelona's skinheads have been photographed on a number of occasions at rallies as far away as Dresden, Germany. To what extent they are being funded by ultra-right groups like Blas Piñar's National Front—allied with the party of the same name in France, headed by Jean Le Pen—is a matter of debate.

"At the moment we have no actual evidence that the skinheads are being financed by political parties, but there are probably some common points of interest between these groups," Paco Castro, a spokesman for Barcelona's police department, told me. "If those parties were able to organize and use these groups of violent youths it would be dangerous, but right now we know who the skinheads are and we feel we have them under control."

Nevertheless, he also told me that hardly a week went by without a complaint of aggression by skinheads. People are beaten on the metro, or on the street, or the skins pick a fight with long-haired neo-hippie students in the district of Gracia, where the two groups of ideologically opposed young people each have their favorite weekend hangouts.

Skinheads and neo-Nazis are not the only Spaniards to harass immigrants. Foreigners labor for low wages, so they tend to live as cheaply as they can. Groups of men pack into a rented flat or house, sleeping three or four to a room, exactly as the Spaniards did less than thirty years ago in France or Germany.

"It's getting harder and harder to find a decent place to rent anymore," a Spaniard who had come to the city from Andalusia, many years before, complained. "The immigrants rent these places and stuff ten people in a small apartment, and each of them is paying, and the rents have just gone too high for a working Spaniard to afford. There's nothing left for us after the immigrants are done. I'm not racist, but that's how I see it."

That is how a lot of Spaniards see it. A house down the block full of Africans or Asians provides a focal point for Spanish resentment, particularly in poor neighborhoods where a lot of people are out of work. Spain has the second highest rate of unemployment in the EC, right behind Ireland's, with between fifteen to twenty percent of the working population unable to find a job in many parts of the country. These are fertile seedbeds for racism and xenophobia to prosper. A 1991 study by the respected, Madrid-based Center for Sociological Investigation concluded that eleven percent of Spanish voters would consider voting for a party that espoused "racist principles."

Across the country, in neighborhoods where crime and drug use are on the rise (and there are many of them) these things are often blamed on immigrants, sometimes justifiably, sometimes not. There have been occasional incidents where Spaniards get liquored up and outraged, then go out to attack immigrants. Stores have graffiti scrawled on their walls. Homes have been firebombed and burned. Dark-skinned people get jumped and beaten in the streets at night. It is not common, but it happens.

The 1992 Olympics are being billed as the first time in thirty-two years when politics will be taking a back seat to sport. For the first time since the 1960 summer Games in Rome, no nations are boycotting or being boycotted, and South Africa is being allowed to compete again.

Now, seemingly out of nowhere, Olympic committee officials have been ambushed by a racial controversy centered around the small Catalan town of Banyoles, about seventy miles northeast of Barcelona. Lake Banyoles, at one end of the town, will be the site of the Olympic rowing competition. The problem is a stuffed African warrior, poised erect in a glass case inside Banyoles's Darder Museum of Natural History. He has stood there, a spear and shield in his hands, since 1916.

A Haitian-born Spanish physician, Alfonso Arcelin, living and practicing in Banyoles, has taken exception to the exhibit, calling it racist. He has begun talking about an Olympic boycott by African nations, applying political pressure on the Banyoles town hall to have the diminutive dried corpse shipped back to its homeland in southern Africa and given a decent burial. Banyoles is one of the places in Catalonia where African immigrants have settled in substantial numbers, and the doctor says the dried warrior is an insult to the town's black citizens.

The Catalans in Banyoles are proud of the museum, which houses a wonderful naturalist's collection assembled by a noted Barcelona physician, Francisco Darder i Llimona, around the turn of the century. The museum also contains the dry, parchment-like skins of two white

Brazilian people, spread out on the wall opposite the warrior's case, as well as Darder's vast collection of stuffed birds and animals and other exotica, like a two-headed calf. His specialty was embalming, and Barcelonese paid high prices to Darder to protect their bodies from corruption after death. In one display case are human fetuses at varying stages of growth, pickled in formaldehyde, the object of much wide-eyed attention by children tramping through the museum. Darder left the whole collection to Banyoles in gratitude for the use of Lake Banyoles for his fish-farming experiments.

The city council has voted to leave the warrior on display, and Arcelin is talking about a boycott of African nations. The more pressure that the Olympic committee applies to the municipal authorities of Banyoles, the more entrenched they become in their refusal to consider even taking the stuffed man off exhibit during the Games.

Saturday, October 19

Six hundred years ago on this date, Rabbi Hasday bar-Abraham bar-Hasday bar-Yehuda Cresques wrote a letter from Zaragoza in Aragon to the Jewish community of Avignon, France, describing the destruction of Barcelona's Jewish community between August 5 to 8, 1391. It is a poignant letter, full of mourning for all the slaughtered Jews, and for one in particular—Yehuda Cresques' own son, who was in Barcelona to be married, while his father, an adviser to the royal court, had stayed with King John I in the castle in Zaragoza.

Nowadays, Barcelona's estimated four thousand Jews have an advantage over other, darker-skinned immigrants, in that they look just like native Catalans, and are not likely to be singled out and beaten up by skinheads. Nevertheless, they are extremely sensitive to the swastikas that regularly appear on the walls of the city. They worry that xenophobia will increase in Spain if times get tough, and they know Jews can always count on being included among the targets of hate.

There is a book fair each year in Barcelona, and each year a group of skinhead neo-Nazis rent a booth, where they sell racist printed matter from the National Front and other groups. At the 1990 book fair, they were selling soap bearing a label saying it was made from Jews. That was too much for some.

"Two young men from the Jewish community went there to object, and they got into a fight with the skinheads," said David Grebler, a Barcelona businessman who is president of Barcelona's only Jewish congregation. "Then, the police arrested the Jews for disturbing the peace.

"They should have already had the Nazis under arrest. Racism and the dissemination of Nazi propaganda are against the law in every other European country but Spain. They need this kind of law here, or this relatively small number of skinheads could escalate into something more serious. There needs to be a law to deal with this."

For many immigrants, the law that most affects their lives is the *ley de extranjería*, or foreigner's law, passed in 1985. It enumerates the ways in which a foreigner's rights differ from those of a Spanish citizen. Foreigners can be held for seventy-two hours without being charged with a crime. While in custody, they may be required to prove their identity, establish their legality, and document the amount of money they have at their disposal. If a decision is made to expel them from Spain, they can be held by judge's order for an additional forty days while the expulsion procedure is carried out.

The foreigner's law was sponsored by the socialist government in response to pressure from other EC members. France and Germany, in particular, were demanding that Spain take measures to tighten its southern borders. There were hundreds of thousands of North Africans in northern Europe who got there by crossing through Spain.

The foreigner's law has provisions for an immigrant to appeal an expulsion decision, but they are not much help, according to Jordi Oliveras, an attorney, who has served as chairman of the human rights committee of Barcelona's bar association. "The problem is not so much with the law in theory, which contains a number of recourses for someone threatened with expulsion from the country, but with the law in actuality. If a person is expelled, they have thirty days to appeal it, but they must have assigned the power to do so to an attorney before they left.

"For a poor person who is here to work at anything, who hardly speaks the language, and doesn't have any means, all the theoretical guarantees in this law are good for nothing. These are all things that are of use to a person who has a lawyer, and knows something about the law. But by the time most people find out about what they could have done, they are already back in Morocco or wherever they came from."

Moroccans make up the largest number, by far, of the immigrants who have come to Spain looking for work. Of the more than one hundred thirty thousand people who applied for documentation under an amnesty program in 1991, about half were Moroccans, according to the Department of the Interior. The next numerous groups were about eight thousand each from Argentina and the Dominican Republic.

Spain's southern coast is only a little over eight miles across the Strait of Gibraltar from the coast of Morocco. Eight miles in which the economy changes from Third World to First. In Morocco, the primary means of transportation is still the burro. A large number of working-age men have nothing to do during the day. The unemployed are everywhere. They spend their days simply sitting on the ground, staring off into the middle distance. Those who are lucky have something alive to watch—a few sheep or goats. Others sit under a tree by the highway with a basket of cactus apples, offering them for pennies to passing motorists. Most of them want to work, but there is nothing to do, nowhere in the economy where they can earn anything at all. It is no wonder that they are willing to accept the risks and loneliness that often accompany emigrating to Europe in search of work.

"In Morocco, there are seven million Moroccans living below the poverty line, according to figures from the United Nations, and there is no significant development going on in most of the country," said Abdel Aziz, an associate of the Averroes Center in Barcelona, which is a support organization for North African immigrants in Catalonia. A round-faced, dark-haired man with dark skin and a moustache, he was from Marrakech. He had been in Barcelona for five years and spoke good

Spanish, which he said was the result of "breaking my head to read three or four newspapers a day."

I went to visit Aziz one afternoon in the Averroes Center, located in an apartment in the Ensanche district. "Ten percent of Morocco owns ninety percent of the nation's wealth," he told me. "The situation in the country is getting worse all the time, people are poorer and poorer. This is what needs to change, and then there will be no need to emigrate looking for work."

Thousands of immigrants cross the Strait of Gibralter each year. The most desperate of them do not have the resources to come as tourists in planes, or on passenger ships, but in tiny, wooden boats called *pateras*. They come packed in the pateras, twenty or twenty-five people to a boat during the height of the summer. They are charged steep prices by the boat's owner. If they are lucky, they will be dumped on a Spanish beach. Often, they are forced to climb out of the boat a hundred yards out to sea, and make their own way ashore. It is not unusual for tourists and vacationers sunbathing on the beaches to encounter wet, scared Moroccans clutching soaked bundles of belongings, looking up the beach in bewilderment, wondering where to go next. The Spanish press estimates that more than three hundred people have drowned during the last decade in the Strait of Gibralter.

When Moroccans began crossing the strait to look for work, in the 1950s and '60s, they only stayed in Spain long enough to reach, and cross, its northern border. In those years, there was a saying that North Africa began at the Pyrennees. No one stopped to look for work in Spain, because there was no work there even for Spaniards. The Moroccans kept going until they reached northern Europe, where they competed with Spaniards for leftover work in France and Germany. In the 1960s, however, Franco allowed a group of young, middle-class university graduates who were known as technocrats to shape the country's economy, and things began to improve. The occasional Moroccan began to stay in Spain rather than continuing northward.

"There are still two basic groups of people who come to Spain from Morocco," said Aziz. "There are people who come with no information and expect to find paradise here, and there are others, from the north, closer to Spain, who have watched a lot of Spanish television and know what they'll find here. For most of them, Spain is just a station from which they can go somewhere else like France, Holland, or Belgium, where there is the possibility of a life with some stability. They know Spain is not a solution to their problems.

"Spain used to be better. There was a time when it could be a solution for some. But since they passed the foreigner's law it is much harder to live here. Many more have been marginalized. Now, there are many people sleeping in the streets of Barcelona who say, 'If I had known what was waiting here for me, I would have stayed in my home.'"

Most of the Moroccans who manage to find a job and shelter in Barcelona want to work hard, send money to their families, and go back to Morocco as soon as they can. Moroccans, particularly those who labor for a living, do not find life in Barcelona particularly congenial. For professionals, like scientists or academics, there is often more incentive to stay, things like higher pay and better research conditions. But for most, even those who bring their families and try to settle down, Spain remains a foreign country.

"Here, there is not enough stability to the community for there to be a large second generation," said Aziz. "For those who are here there has been no attempt by the Spaniards at integration, no effort to understand the other culture, or to understand the other religion and try to integrate it into society. The North African child here is going to have a lot of difficulties.

"They encounter a complete difference between school and home, and either they fail entirely at school or they speak Catalan and Castilian and practically forget their North African culture."

In Barcelona, the majority of Moroccan workers live in the old city—in the Raval, and around the Ciutadella Park. There are an estimated seventy thousand Moroccan immigrants in metropolitan Barcelona, Aziz said, but there is an almost complete absence of institutional culture. There are two small mosques, a few Islamic butcher shops, and a handful of restaurants featuring *couscous*, but there are no libraries, no films, and no Moroccan newspapers.

Immigrants generally agree that Barcelona and Catalonia are particularly difficult parts of Spain in which to be a foreigner. "Catalan society is very closed in the sense that Catalans tend to keep to themselves more than other Spaniards and, while they will tolerate foreigners, they do not really accept them," said Aziz.

"In my judgment, however, the Catalans are more open than other Europeans like the French or the Germans. And I don't believe it's basically a racist society, although there are certainly racists here, and racist attitudes, and discrimination."

Many immigrants from Latin and South America have as much trouble as North Africans adjusting to Barcelona, even though they have the advantage of speaking Spanish, according to Ana María Ojeda Jaksic, a Chilean attorney. She came to Spain as a refugee after Pinochet took power in Chile, and she has spent twenty years in Barcelona, "fighting for immigrants from Latin America," as she likes to put it.

Many of the estimated sixty thousand immigrants from the Americas living in Barcelona, not only have to overcome the numerous obstacles placed in their path by the Spanish government, like all other immigrants, but also must adjust to being marginalized on a social level despite the shared language. There is a racist stereotype applied by many Spaniards to people from South America. The hate word to describe this stereotype is *sudaca*. It implies a dumb, poor, and dishonest dark-skinned person who speaks a strangely accented Spanish and is not to be trusted. South Americans frequently have to cope with a tremendous loneliness in Barcelona.

"There is the big thing here about Catalan individualism, and how they don't want you touching anything that is theirs," said Ojeda, a square-bodied fighter, whose father was from Chile and mother from Yugoslavia. "Catalans don't have the warmth and tenderness that Latin Americans are used to. They don't even have it among themselves in their own homes, much less towards others. This can be a tremendous shock to people from Latin and South America.

"Here, people live in the same building, and when they see each other outside on the street they don't even say hello. Barcelona is impenetrable. It is very hard for a Latin to learn that he or she has to call a friend a week in advance to make an appointment to have a coffee. They're used to just dropping by. For single men who are here looking for work, they go week to week with never a kind word from anyone, no one asking how they're feeling, or what they did on their day off. They have no human contact, and their only pleasure comes when they get a letter from home. If they are finally able to leave and go back, they do not want to remember what happened during the time they lived in Barcelona, even if it was for years. It's extremely sad."

While life among Catalans has always lacked the warmth to which South Americans were accustomed, it was easier in many respects to live here under the Franco regime than under the socialists, according to Ojeda. South Americans could come and go at will during the dictatorship, and if they found work, they could take it.

People from the Spanish-speaking Caribbean, Central, or South America do not need a visa to enter Spain. However, on arrival at the airport in Madrid or Barcelona, if requested, they have to show enough money to provide them with $50 a day during the length of their proposed stay, or they can be turned around and sent home. This year it looks like more than three thousand people will be sent back to the southern half of the American continent, denied entrance into Spain.

"Over eight million Spaniards have come to Latin and South America to live since Spain's civil war, as both economic and political refugees, and they were always welcomed with open arms, but Spain has not done the same for people who wanted to come here from South America," said Ojeda. "And, don't forget that in many cases we just want to come here and live in the place that our families came from, where our grandparents or great-grandparents lived. But, the government has not made that easy."

Jews did not begin to immigrate to Spain in any numbers until the second decade of this century, and they did not begin to gather in Barcelona until the 1920s. Most of the first arrivals were from Turkey and they came from families whose daily language, in their homes in Istanbul or Smyrna, was what scholars called Judeo-Español, a medieval Spanish that only continued to live in the mouths of Jews whose ancestors had been expelled or exiled. Many people erroneously call this language Ladino, which was the name of the liturgical Spanish used in religious services by the medieval Jews and which they also carried away with them, but which subsequently died out.

In December 1924, the government of military dictator Miguel Primo de Rivera passed a law that allowed Jews descended from Sefarad to claim Spanish citizenship at the nearest Spanish consulate. Alberto Arditti from Smyrna, took advantage of this opportunity and arrived in Barcelona that same year. He was ninety-one years old when I went to see him at his daughter's flat.

"When I first got here, there were not many other Jews and everyone was struggling, one person working selling clothes, another a peddler, another with a little factory. There was no synagogue. We got together in different houses to celebrate the important holidays."

Arditti was a short man who sat sunk back in the sofa, and his polished black shoes barely touched the living-room floor. He was wearing grey flannel slacks, a white shirt and a blue cardigan sweater. He had a rounded face, a fringe of white hair and white eyebrows, alert blue eyes, and a good memory. He laughed easily at his recollections.

"These days, with the synagogue and the religious life that we have here, it's hard to imagine how few of us there were, and how little we had. After a while, we formed a group and we made a small community. We rented a place for 200 pesetas a month. There were eight of us, and that was the beginning of things. Each Saturday we had a service there. It was nothing official, but we were tolerated," Arditti shrugged.

That was in 1931—and it was the first synagogue in Barcelona since 1391. It was located at the corner of Balmes and Provença streets, in the Ensanche district. That same year, Primo de Rivera's government was replaced by an elected Republican government. It was staunchly and idealistically left-wing, and despite its anti-clerical tendencies, the Republican constitution guaranteed religious freedom for all. What it also did was draw sharp lines of separation between church and state, and left the Catholic hierarchy without secular political power.

The Jewish community continued to grow during the 1930s. The

Nazis came to power in Germany in 1933 and the number of Jews coming to Spain increased. It was estimated that by early 1936, and the beginning of the civil war, there were some seven thousand Jews living in Barcelona.

"We carried on until the spring of 1936 when the civil war came," said Arditti. "Then the Catholic church came under attack from the Republicans. Churches were burned, monks were killed, nuns were violated. It was terrible. On the other side, it soon became clear that Franco was a fascist, and an antisemite. He was always talking about the Jewish-Masonic-Communist conspiracy. We closed down the synagogue because we were scared, and we began meeting in houses again."

He put the tips of his thumb and forefinger together and drew them across his closed lips. "That's how we were. Quiet. We didn't make any noise. Those were hard times and we stayed as hidden as possible, away from anyone's notice. People asked, 'What are you?' and you answered, told them a Frenchman, or a Turk, or a German, or whatever, and you kept your mouth closed.

"These days, there's liberty for everyone. These days are golden. To me, they're pure gold."

The world of the medieval Sefarad would have been both familiar and strange to Alberto Arditti and the other Jews living in Barcelona today. In the Middle Ages, as today, Barcelona's Jews were generally a law-abiding people: they were tax payers, good citizens, orderly and well-behaved. The medieval worship services, the prayers, the kosher diet, the Hebrew, the holy and sacred texts of the Sefarad would all be familiar.

Contemporary Catalan Jews, on the other hand, might be surprised by the medieval belief in astrology, shared by Jews, Catholics, and Muslims; or the custom among wealthier Jews of owning Christian or Muslim slaves. Jews who lived in Christian Spain owned Muslim slaves, as did their neighbors. Those who lived in Mohammedan Spain owned Christians, as did their neighbors. A Jewish man was allowed to contract "semi-marriage" with a female slave by liberating her from bondage and converting her to Judaism.

These days, numerous interfaith marriages take place between young Jews and Catholics from the same social classes, but such a thing was unheard of in the Middle Ages. Sexual relations between Christians and Jews were prohibited by both religions under pain of terrible punishments. The Christians specified death by fire for a Jew and a Christian who engaged in sex, although wealthy Jews were occasionally able to buy, at high cost, a pardon, according to Abraham Neuman in his book *The Jews in Spain*.

The Jews were no more tolerant than the Gentiles. Each Jewish community appointed vice officers who were delegated to investigate sexual transgressions, particularly those involving Christians. In one case for which records are extant, a Jewish woman publicly admitted her affair with a Christian when she became pregnant. The rabbi ruled that "her nose be cut off so that the beauty of the face which she adorned for her adulterous wooer be disfigured. . . ."

The amount of concern evidenced by both Jewish and Christian authorities regarding relationships of men and women of different faiths indicates that if such affairs were not common, they certainly existed. Officials in some Jewish communities recommended tolerance toward Jewish prostitutes, and the houses where they worked, so that men would not be tempted to patronize Christian brothels.

Monday, October 28

It is a cold, drizzling midnight when I meet the transvestite prostitute who asks me to call him Margarita. He is working his usual beat: the streets around the Ciutadella Park. The streets that run outside the walls of the park are one of the three best-known locations to find a transvestite prostitute in the city. The other two are behind Camp Nou, the soccer stadium that is the home field for el Barça, and on the lower end of the Ramblas.

It isn't the kind of evening one wants to be working outdoors, but Margarita usually works seven nights a week, rain or shine. He is wearing a stylish thin blouse under a brown leather jacket, and a black leather skirt that comes to mid-thigh, black stockings on his long legs. His make-up is heavy, but not garish, and with his long brown hair in a ponytail he makes a tall, attractive figure. He sells sexual pleasure to men who drive by and pick him up in their cars, and who pay him about $20 for the use of sundry parts of his body.

When the sun goes down, the blocks around the Ciutadella fill with hookers, both real women and those men who admire the women's style so much that they imitate it, transforming themselves with a heady mix of art and artifice. They stand or walk back and forth under the wide circles of streetlight brightness along the dark, nearly deserted streets. Police cars drive lazily by, passing at a snail's pace, checking out customers, offering protection to the hookers, and keeping an eye on them at the same time.

"The work is theater," Margarita told me. "You get in the car with them, and they expect you to give them sex and love too, for 2,000 pesetas. They want this, they want that, and they're always complaining about money.

"Last night started off well. Right away, a customer came by and I made 2,000 pesetas. Then a second guy stopped and we drove to some little street somewhere. He was a big, fat guy. He parked and rolled up the windows—to keep the heat in, he said—then he took out a knife and robbed me of the 2,000 pesetas and kicked me out of his car. Look where he cut me," he cocked his head back under the streetlight and I could make out a crusted nick there under his jawbone, which he touched ever so lightly with a long, scarlet fingernail.

On this particular night, he says, business has been so bad that he might as well not have come out at all. When his working night is over, Margarita will go sleep in an abandoned car with his boyfriend. They both have heroin habits, and have been recently evicted from their last apartment. They are looking for another place to live, but the money for a month's rent, plus a another month's deposit, is not easy to get together and keep until they find one.

He does not think business will get better during the Olympics, despite the huge numbers of people who will be coming to town. "The mayor and the police will do something to ruin it for us, you'll see. They want to pretend that this is a city with no beggars, no prostitutes, and I think they'll make it tough for us."

When Margarita first went on the street, he was sixteen, living at home with his Catalan parents and four siblings just outside of Barcelona. He found out from an older friend in the neighborhood that he could sell himself on weekend nights down by the park, and make a lot of money. "It was fun then. Not the misery that it is now. We were all really friendly and used to have a good time. There was not the same kind of sinister feeling on the streets as there is now. I used to look forward to coming to work. But not anymore. Now, I just do it because there's nothing else I can do. Business is way off, there are nights when I don't make more than 2,000 pesetas."

Shortly before I met Maragarita, a transvestite known as Sonia was sleeping in the Ciutadella Park after work one night, and was beaten to death. A homeless man sleeping near Sonia was also severely beaten, but he got a good look at his assailants before they stomped him into unconsciousness with their heavy boots. He saw a group of young men with shaved heads. There is a growing fear that the city's skinheads are being allowed to run wild without having to worry about police interference. Death threat graffiti addressed to the transvestites from the skinheads appears with regularity on the walls of the park.

Margarita knew the murdered Sonia, and he takes the threats seriously. "The skins are one reason I don't enjoy coming to work anymore, because they really scare me. In addition, there's a lot more heroin than there ever was, and a lot more strung-out people. You can't trust anyone anymore. No one is really your friend. Drugs have really gotten between people. Another thing is that everyone is worried about AIDS. That's why business is off," said Margarita, who, despite being at double risk as a homosexual and an intravenous drug user, has never had a test to see if he is HIV-positive.

Despite all the hassles, hustling is still his favorite thing to be doing when everything is going smoothly. "It's great to be able to get paid for being what I want to be and bringing someone pleasure. For me, though, it's not the money that makes me want to dress up and look pretty, it's the aesthetic more than anything else. That's why I won't be like so many of these guys and have a straight job during the week and just come out on the streets on weekends. I want people to accept me for who I am."

The aesthetic, however, is being compromised by a problem with his feet: they swell up each night as he stands on the sidewalk, or leans against a parked car and waits for someone to stop. His feet are so swollen and painful that a pair of unlaced tennis shoes has replaced the high heels he normally wears, and the Nike knock-offs clash absurdly with his leather skirt and black hose. He does not want to go to a doctor about his feet, because he isn't covered by health insurance. In order to get coverage, he would have to fill out a lot of forms, be asked about his employment status, and be required to have a permanent address. His parents and four siblings have disowned him, and will not even let him pick up his mail at their homes.

CHAPTER THREE

Within These Walls

Saturday, November 2

I am sitting at an outdoor cafe on the Rambla Cataluña, enjoying the soft evening air and drinking a café con leche, when I realize how I am beginning to settle into this city. I look across the street at the front of a building that has beautiful, high-ceilinged, glassed-in sun rooms on every floor, with tall leaded windows jutting out into space from the wall of the building for the light to pour in through. On almost any street in Barcelona there is at least one edifice that demands attention. All I have to do is look up to see a building that makes me catch my breath and look again.

The Rambla Cataluña is not the Ramblas that runs down to the port, but rather the continuation of it above the Plaza Cataluña, running uphill to the Avenida Diagonal. The Rambla Cataluña is lined with fancy, expensive shops and the broad stretch of walkway that divides its lanes of traffic offers an un-broken row of comfortable sidewalk cafes for block after block. The buildings along the street are prime examples of the highly liveable, carefully designed eye-pleasers that make up much of the Ensanche district.

The pace of life creates time for sitting in cafes with friends, sipping good coffee, and regarding lovely buildings. I am beginning to believe Barcelona is much kinder to its residents than the North American cities I know. I have already sloughed off lots of layers of my calloused stateside skin. Here, most citizens are surrounded by a much more comfortable, less fearful life than that allowed in Yankee cities.

This, despite the fact that Barcelona is the most densely populated city in Europe, wedged between the Collserola hills and the sea. It is thrown in on itself, compressed into one of the most-crowded-per-square-foot urban areas in the world. Even so, there is a sense of space within the city that is reassuring. The apartments are usually tall and ample, and there are many public places that relieve the urban pressure.

The Library of Catalunya, where I spent a fall afternoon reading, is an example. It is just what the name says: a library whose books all pertain in some way to the region of Catalonia. And what a library! It is in the Raval on the Calle del Carmen (Carrer del Carme in Catalan), a few blocks off the Ramblas, part of a complex of buildings that went up in the late 1400s as the Hospital of the Holy Cross. It was one of the largest hospitals for the poor in Europe in its day, and had been the city's first school of medicine for Catholic students. Before that, the only medical university belonged to the Jews, and Catalonia's physicians had all been Jewish.

The library's two reading rooms have cut stone walls, with vaulted beamed ceilings that arch thirty feet above the tiled floor. Fifteen feet up one wall are tall, leaded, stained-glass windows. When I was there, they were opened to the autumn air, even though it was growing late in the afternoon. Outside there was a falling, crepuscular light, grey clouds rushed across a delicately tinged blue sky, blown across the city in front of a cleansing wind off the Mediterranean.

The library users sit at sturdy, dark, oak reading tables, with three comfortable chairs to a side. Each reader's place is numbered, and has its own reading lamp. Up and down the great stone hall, people sit in their individual pools of light, heads down, reading in pockets of brightness surrounded by shadows under the vaulted ceiling.

The setting is superb, but service is slow. Readers write their requests and the number of their places at the tables on slips of paper, which they give to a librarian. The book is delivered by a man pushing a cart stacked with books. The wait can be half an hour while the volume of requests builds up enough to make a trip into the stacks worthwhile for the cart pusher. He did not seem to be snowed under with things to do, judging by the time he spent sitting at the librarian's desk, watching the requests pile up.

Outside the library is a lovely, quiet, open patio, with a statue of Saint Peter in the middle of it. There are stone benches under arches, built against the tiled walls around the patio's perimeter. This is a courtyard designed for reflection and meditation, and it works. Despite being not more than thirty yards from the Raval's busy and crowded Calle del Carmen, it is quiet and tranquil in the courtyard, a refuge from the city on the other side of the wall. Seagulls cross the open sky above the patio, calling raucously to each other. I sat there and watched the light fade out of the air.

The city has many such surprising spaces and quiet corners, and they are sorely needed. In addition to its chronic high-density population with too many people living in too little space, the noise level has kept pace with the city's growth. In 1991, a Japanese study of decibel levels in European and Asian cities ranked Barcelona as the third noisiest, behind Tokyo and Madrid. Since it is by far the smallest of the three, Barcelona has to produce an inordinate amount of noise to achieve such a dubious distinction.

Among the major contributors to the general level of noise pollution is, of course, traffic, with the city's 125,000 registered motor bikes, motor scooters, and motorcycles deserving special mention. There are a tremendous number of motorized, two-wheeled vehicles in the streets and they are used by a broad cross-section of the population. It is not at all unusual to see a businessman in a suit and tie riding a Vespa scooter, with his attache case strapped on behind him. Secretaries dressed in skirts and blouses, heels and stockings on little Hondas are a common sight, and I saw more than one grandmother wearing a fur coat and a motorcycle helmet, zipping through the streets.

These adults are not, however, responsible for the motorcycle noise pollution, because they usually ride newer, quieter models. The worst offenders are young men whose ear-splitters fill the streets with the racket such a machine can make when its muffler has been removed or bypassed. These guys love to sit on their unmuffled bikes at stoplights, in neutral, with the throttle twisted up as far as it will go, producing a loud, high r.p.m. engine roar.

Another audio offender mentioned in the decibel-level study was the electronic slot machine. These are in every bar and cafe in the city, and they are programmed to burst into a loud, short electronic melody every few minutes to attract drinkers at the bar with a few coins in their pockets. Barcelonese are feeding more than $200 million into these machines annually, according to figures kept by the regional government of Catalonia. Catalans love to gamble. Daily lotteries are run by the state and by ONCE, the country's society for the blind and handicapped. ONCE is selling $490 millions' worth of tickets annually in Catalonia now. In addition, people are spending more than $700 million playing bingo in one of Barcelona's ninety parlors.

(North Americans out to play bingo in Barcelona are surprised at first: the bingo *salas* have elegant facades and ornately decorated lobbies with chandeliers and wide reception desks. Before being allowed into the sala to play, people check in at the front desk, where their names are entered in a computer to see if they are among the city's approximately three thousand registered gambling addicts—signed up by themselves or by their families—and therefore barred from playing. Once cleared, bingo players are admitted through a set of double doors into the sala itself, and here North Americans feel right at home. They find a familiar crowded room, full of cigarette smoke, with people at tables hunched over bingo cards and anxiously marking off numbers.)

In addition to public sorts of noise pollution like the roar of traffic or electronic slot machines, Barcelona also suffers from private noise. The outside world often intrudes in people's private lives and homes. Residents not only have to make the best of standard urban sounds like sirens screaming in the street, planes passing over, jackhammers and construction equipment pounding, horns honking, and brakes squealing, but they also have to support the noises of their neighbors' lives. Barcelona is a city of old, not-so-thick walls, and people in most apartments and flats can hear every neighbor's grunt and cough. It is a city where other people's lives impinge at every turn, where the smells of what's cooking next door signal what day of the week it is: white beans and *botifarra* sausage, it's Monday, if fish are frying, it is probably Friday. The lives next door are so audible that people know the names of their neighbor's children, the illnesses they suffer from and problems they have, although they may not see the actual kids from one year to the next, except to pass them briefly on the stairs or share an elevator with them.

The price of those not-so-thick Barcelona walls rose astronomically after Spain joined the EC in 1986. In the years that followed, Spain received over $8 billion in "structural funds" from EC headquarters in Brussels, along with a flood of foreign investment, nearly $19 billion in 1990. Hundreds of Spanish-owned companies were bought by multinational corporations, and a lot of money was pumped into the economy. In Barcelona, this combined with the prospect of the upcoming Olympic Games to drive real estate prices through the roof. A lot of people found themselves suddenly flush, with investment capital on their hands. The price of living space began to climb rapidly. A real estate "boom" struck a city that was already close to fully occupied.

A typical family flat, a *piso* in Spanish, in an older building in the Ensanche district, for instance, is likely to have high ceilings, tiled floors, two bedrooms, a study, a kitchen, a bathroom, and a dining/living room, with a hallway connecting all the rooms, and a narrow balcony in front looking out over the street. The door to the front balcony will remain closed even in hot weather, because there is too much noise and dirt from traffic below to live with it open. At the back of the flat is often another balcony, or a terrace, with a view of an inner courtyard (frequently used as a parking lot), surrounded by the back terraces of other buildings. These back windows are frequently left open. The apartments are roomy and substantial enough to raise a family in, but they are also cold in the winter, and often have antiquated plumbing and low water pressure. In 1985, such a piso might have rented for $300 a month.

That same place is now commanding about $900 a month. And even at that price landlords are still not responsible for the cost of repairs. If there is a problem with the plumbing, the tenant pays the plumber. While there are a few furnished places for rent, most tenants in Barcelona initially rent an empty piso, one that does not even come with a stove or refrigerator. They have to furnish everything, and while they are living there they have to pay for everything, including all the necessary work to keep it habitable.

For tenants, the threefold increase in rent prices was a disaster. Salaries did not keep pace, and lots of people are paying a higher percentage of their wages for shelter than they ever have before, up to fifty percent of their paycheck in many cases. The only saving grace for renters as prices skyrocketed was Spain's rent control law, which prohibits landlords from raising rents more than an annual cost-of-living increase for people who had been in a flat before 1985, or from raising the rent for any of their descendants who live there.

This, explained Javier Moreno Chaparro, my short, balding landlord, was why the flat I rented in Ensanche, with its narrow hallway and small rooms rented for $900 a month, while another nearby flat he owned, twice as big as mine, rented for $80 a month. There was absolutely nothing he could do about it, because the family in that apartment had been renting at just about that price for twenty-five years.

The landlords are not absolutely powerless. If the tenants make any improvements to a place, the rent can be raised by a substantial amount. This leads to the common and paradoxical practice of tenants making secret repairs, improvements, and renovations on their apartments, without letting the owners know about it. Almost every residential building has a portera, a concierge as the French call them—a woman who looks after the place all day, who keeps the lobby mopped, and monitors the comings and goings of residents and guests. In exchange, she is usually given a cheap or free place to live. She is the eyes and ears of law, order, and the landlord. Tenants often have to wait until summer, when their porteras go on vacation, to retile their bathrooms, or put new cabinets in their kitchens. Because, if the landlord finds out work is being done on the apartment, he will raise the rent.

"Under the current law, the tenant cannot make renovations, and we landlords, who frequently have people paying virtually the same rent they were forty-five years ago, have taken advantage of this sole resort to tell tenants they may renovate, but if they are only paying 2,000 pesetas [$20] a month in rent, the rent will go up to 3,000," said Moreno, a man in his forties who originally came to Barcelona from Huelva in the south of Spain as a policeman, a Guardia Civil.

"There are many people who are making decent wages, have a second house somewhere on the coast for weekends and summers, and don't have a bathroom in their home in Barcelona. They have a water-closet for the commode and a sink in the kitchen, and they will never accept that I could charge them an extra thousand pesetas a month if they renovate the piso and put in a bathroom. I have a pair of sisters in one of my places that have been renting it since the 1940s. One is a widow, the other a spinster, and they have a modest but sufficient amount of monthly income. They don't have a bathroom. They pay 1,500 pesetas [$15] a month, and they know that if they put in a bathroom I'll raise the rent by a thousand pesetas, so they won't do it."

Another thing the landlords can do is join together in an association and lobby hard for the repeal of the renter's law. They were partially successful in 1991, when it was announced that the socialist government had decided to revise the laws governing rental housing. There was an outcry from renters and, eventually, despite concerted pressure from landlords, the pre-1985 rent control was left in place. One change the landlords lobbied for and won was that children were only allowed to live in inherited rent-controlled apartments until they reached the age of twenty-five, at which point they would be subject to drastic rent increases by the landlord.

After 1986, the price of buying a flat made the same kind of jump as that of renting one. The notion of owning an apartment in Barcelona is not something new that has sprung up recently under a name like condominium. People have been owning pisos for centuries. In Barcelona, when people imagine owning their own home, they envision owning a flat, not a house. In 1985, the price of one of those typical family pisos in the Ensanche was around $30,000. Five years later it might well have gone on the market for $200,000. That was a lot of money, particularly considering that Barcelona banks often require a borrower to make a twenty percent down-payment.

A lot of people made a lot of money in the Barcelona real estate market after 1986, but the news was mixed for people who owned the apartment where they lived. Their pisos were worth more, but the rising cost of shelter affected them negatively as well, particularly if they had grown children. For young adults in Barcelona during the late 1980s and now the '90s, it is often too expensive to move out of their parents' home. They hang around until they are married, and sometimes after that— often less than comfortable for older parents who might prefer a little more space and privacy, and extremely inhibiting for younger couples.

Another social side-effect of the high cost of housing is that many women marry men who have always lived at home. Men are accustomed to having their mothers cook all their meals, and do all their washing and ironing, as Spanish mothers have traditionally done for their sons. These days, in order for a young couple to have the basic tokens of middle-class membership in the EC economy—like a car, a flat, a nice television, sound system, video camera, and foreign vacation— both of them have to work. A woman who has a full-time job often needs more help maintaining a home than a man used to a lifetime of mothering is inclined to give.

University students occasionally leave their parents' homes by getting together with other students, renting a flat, and dividing it two to a room, but this is something more frequently done by those who come to Barcelona from other parts of Spain, and are already far from their parents' homes. The university is free for those whose grades and test scores qualify them, but students can't earn much money and are often poor. Those at the University of Barcelona, who have family in the city are likely to continue living at home, and spend what money they have on a motorcycle, or a car.

Living space, and how it is filled, has long been a prime concern for Barcelonese. They are obsessed with architecture, fascinated by facade, and have been that way for centuries. Their history has often been delineated in terms of space, a chronology that began with the Roman walls around the city through the thirteenth century, followed by a set of expanded walls whose construction was not finished until the mid-1400s. After the Bourbons conquered Barcelona and the Catalans in 1714, they constructed yet another expanded series of walls. By 1865, those walls were being demolished, and the city was opening up toward the hills, away from the sea. This was when construction of the Ensanche district started, just above the old city and the Ramblas.

The modernist school of architecture flowered in Barcelona at the end of the nineteenth century, leaving a legacy of beautiful and bizarre buildings all over the city, and particularly in the Ensanche. The best-known modernist is Antoni Gaudí i Cornet, whose unfinished cathedral, La Sagrada Familia (The Holy Family), has become the symbol of the city, with its eight phantasmagorical towers visible from much of Barcelona. Then, as now, close attention was paid to what was being built. Architects in Barcelona get used to working under close public scrutiny, according to David McKay, who moved from England in 1962, and became a partner in one of the city's most influential architectural firms.

"Informed opinion, that is to say among the intellectual and political classes here, is very sensitive to what is being built in Barcelona," McKay told me. "That has been true for a long time. When the Eixample [Catalan for Ensanche] was being built, you had an extraordinary moment when artistic trends and middle-class culture coincided. This allowed the modernist movement to flourish and produce for forty years.

"A lot of people in Barcelona are aware of their surroundings. When I got here thirty years ago, the cab drivers knew where all of Gaudí's buildings were. A lot of thought is put into things, even when it is nothing more than the owner of a business who is doing a front for his shop."

Barcelona has been created in explosions of architectural and civic energy, and when I arrived this year, it was clear to even the most casual observer that the city was in the middle of one of its periodic eruptions. The headlong rush to prepare Barcelona for the 1992 Summer Olympics was going full steam, and there was a lot of demolition, construction, and renovation underway. It was impossible not to notice the fact that a lot of money was being spent, and that the city was being permanently altered.

Once Mayor Pasquall Maragall announced that the city would be the site of the '92 Olympics, the face of the city began changing. Maragall comes from a family with deep Barcelona roots, and his grandfather was the city's best known poet at the turn of the century. He had been in office since 1982 (when his predecessor Narcis Serra left to become vice president under Felipe González in Madrid), and he was ready to put his stamp on the city. He knew what had to be done. City planners, architects, and designers had been elaborating projects to renovate Barcelona for twenty years, but there had never been enough money to pay for more than a plan. Projects that had been proposed, discussed, and postponed, again and again, suddenly leapt up off the drawing boards and began to get public and private funding, and take shape. The prospect of the Olympic Games provided a reason to get done in half a dozen years what would otherwise have taken decades.

The largest changes the city will get for the $1.5 billion it is investing are drastic alterations to three densely populated districts—the old city, Vall dHebron, and the Barceloneta/Poble Nou neighborhoods—and a ring road, a perimeter highway that will encircle and feed into the city. It is designed to pull traffic out of the interior streets, particularly the peak-hour commuters. Engineers also hope the ring road will relieve the habitual congestion of traffic leaving and returning on weekends and holidays. On Sunday evenings, five-mile-long lines of frozen traffic returning to Barcelona from the mountains in the winter, or beaches in the summer, are not uncommon. It can take people three or four hours to cover those last ten miles home.

The first of the neighborhoods to be permanently changed was the old city, particularly the Raval district. This encompasses two square miles of narrow shadowy streets that run down to the port, abandoned by the middle class when they began moving out to the Ensanche over a hundred years before. Since then, many of the old city's neighborhoods had deteriorated badly. The buildings were aged and dilapidated, inhabited mostly by the poor, the elderly, and those newly arrived from underdeveloped countries. There was a lot of crime and drug abuse.

The city has spent more than $300 million trying to reclaim the old city. More than 3,300 households have been relocated, and whole blocks razed to create open spaces of light and air. The budget for social services there has been increased by more than four hundred percent. More than 150 blocks were repaved. Flophouses and whore houses were closed, and a branch of the university opened. There is even a trickle of private investment in the old city. Now it is only a trickle, but it is the first in a long time.

The Vall d'Hebron, a working-class neighborhood on a hillside near the Collserola along the upper limits of the city, also received a heavy pre-Olympic facelift. A five-block-wide stretch of land was cleared by demolishing numerous small businesses, warehouses, and apartment buildings to make room for the four-lane ring road to pass through, and for a sporting complex and community center to be constructed for Olympic competition. After the Games, this will be made available to the public. A modern apartment complex of 489 units has been built to house some twenty-five hundred journalists during the Games, which will afterwards be sold to private owners. They are nice flats in well-designed buildings with balconies, and a good view of the city below. A one-bedroom piso in the complex sells for about $100,000, and they are going briskly, even though buyers will not be able to move in until after the Games are finished.

The third area to undergo drastic, pre-Olympic changes, and the most controversial of them all, is the two and a half miles of coastline beginning at the port, just below the statue of Columbus, and running north. Most of it had been nothing more than a strip of dirty sand, bordered by railroad tracks and warehouses. No one objected when that was all removed. What people complained about was the destruction of many tiny restaurants along the beach in the Barceloneta neighborhood, which had been serving fresh fish and seafood around the clock for a hundred years. Down they came, bulldozed into oblivion in a few hours, replaced by clean, open public beach with only an occasional palm tree interrupting the flat expanse of sand.

The fifteen square blocks of Barceloneta, densely packed, narrow streets, full of small buildings with tiny pisos inside, has housed the city's fishermen since it was built in the 1750s, and has been left virtually untouched. Even without the kiosks and restaurants along the beach, the barrio is one of the best in Europe for fresh seafood restaurants.

The beach ends further north, beyond Barceloneta, in front of the twin towers of the Olympic Village. One will house offices when the Games are done, and the other a five-star hotel. At forty-four floors each, these squared-off glass-and-steel towers are the two tallest buildings in Barcelona.

Nearby is the residential complex being built to house the athletes, coaches, trainers, and officials of the Olympic delegations from 172 countries. There will be 2,012 apartments constructed and, like those at Vall d'Hebron, they are being offered for sale as private pisos. They are more expensive than those up on the hill, starting at about $117,000, and most of them, even those looking seaward, do not have balconies. They are selling slowly.

For all the work and renovation that is going on—and it sometimes seems as if every block in the city has some sort of work being done on its sidewalks, or buildings, or streets, or subterranean pipes—Barcelona remains a visual delight. The city presents constant surprises to my North American eyes, accustomed to the drab bulk of squat buildings with sharp-edged corners. The fact is that in just about any part of Barcelona, certainly any part that has existed more than fifty years, all I have to do is look around and I am likely to spot an amazing balcony thrusting its curved, wrought-iron railing out into space; or a remarkable gable; or beautiful, decorative tilework; or a turret at the corner of a rooftop, put there solely for the joy of its spiral in the air.

Catalans do have a reputation in the rest of the country as industrious, hard-working people, often excessively concerned with making money. But there is another side to the Catalan character, evident just about any time I look up at the buildings around me: the whimsy, the humor, and the appreciation of pleasure and beauty for their own sakes.

Of course, I have to remember to return my gaze every so often to the sidewalk ahead, or else the solid cement will suddenly squish beneath my shoe sole. There are a lot of dog turds on the sidewalks of Barcelona. Lots of people keep a dog or two at home, not so much for protection as for company. Small-dog owners seem to go in for Pekinese and terriers, while among big-dog fanciers, German shepherds are a clear favorite. The Barcelonese like dogs, but most of them refuse to clean up after their pets and carry the turds to a big green garbage dumpster, which are at either end of every block. There is no law requiring them to do so. Every block has piles of turds left by German shepherds that are as big as the feces of adult human beings, and there are sundry small piles of Pekinese, terrier, and poodle droppings.

"One of the worst things about Spaniards is their attitude of, 'Me first, me last, me always,'" a friend told me one day, as I stood cursing and trying to scrape dog shit off the sole of my shoe on the curb. "It has a bad effect on almost everything from the way they drive to the fact that they don't recycle. "And when you go to a national park or out into the country, the ground is littered with empty food packages and Coca Cola cans. That's why the city is so dirty.

"It's a matter of pride. Spaniards are taught from the cradle to do whatever is the most convenient for them without considering the people around them. It's true about Catalans, Aragonese, Andalusians, people from all over the country."

Barcelona has never been known for its cleanliness. The watercourse that was filled in by the Ramblas, which used to run beside the walls of the medieval city down to the sea, was said to have more closely resembled a slowly moving cesspool of sludge and sewage than a stream. Municipal services were almost nonexistent in the Middle Ages, and people lived in the crowded streets of the old city with little light and no running water, even more densely packed in than they are today.

Aljama is the Spanish word for a Jewish ghetto. The Catalan word is *call*. Jews are thought to have been living in Barcelona's call as early as 200 A.D., and the first medieval synagogue was founded there as early as the tenth century. By 1200, there were about ten thousand Jews in Catalonia as a whole, an estimated four thousand of whom were living in Barcelona's aljama. The spoken language of Catalonia's Jews was Catalan, and their written language was Hebrew. Residence in the aljamas was not mandatory for Jews until the last half of the thirteenth century, when the ruler of Catalonia and Aragon, Jaume I, ordered them all to live in the same neighborhood, and also decreed that they were to wear a circular red and yellow badge sewn on their clothing.

Even before it became obligatory, many Jews chose to live in the aljama. Outside the ghetto's walls, they were not full and free people but an odd cross between human being and property, possessions of the king. Inside the walls they were able to live fully, both as people and Jews. It was here that Jews carried on their daily lives, and many of them did not leave the aljama from one month to the next.

Each aljama was a community unto itself, and included all the services a Jew might need from birth and circumcision to the rites of death. Only the cemetery was outside the walls. In Barcelona, the grave-yard was on the high hill outside of town that came to be called Montjuich, hill of the Jews. (And where the main events of the 1992 Olympics were scheduled to take place in a stadium originally built in 1929 for the World's Fair.) With its view of the city and the sea, Mont-juich was later taken over by the city's Catholic cemetery. When Jews started to come back to Barcelona in the twentieth century, they had to find other quarters for their dead. The medieval headstones, with their Hebrew inscriptions, were used as stones in buildings, and some of them were said to have been used in the ongoing work of the Sagrada Familia cathedral.

The aljama occupied approximately fifteen square blocks in the barrio gótico behind the cathedral, but the area is as archeologically bereft as the cemetery. On the Calle de Marlet by the Arco de San Ramon, there is a stone with a Hebrew inscription extolling a rabbi, dated 1314. There is a church on the Carrer Ferran (Calle Ferdinand, in Spanish) that used to be a synagogue until the end of the fourteenth cen-tury. That's about it. Unlike the Muslims whose vast legacy to Spain in-cluded the nation's greatest architectural wonders, the Jews left behind no lasting signs of their centuries of residence. However, they did leave a lot of genes in the cells of Spaniards (including, perhaps, in the blood of King Ferdinand, co-signer of the Expulsion order, thought by many to have had a Jewish ancestor).

There are also surviving written records that tell of Sefarad lives lived in the embrace of a large and thriving aljama. The streets of these neighborhoods, in Barcelona and throughout Spain, were densely popu-lated and busy. There were public baths, kosher butchers, bankers, bak-ers, printers, wine shops, inns, rabbis, synagogues, houses of prostitution, and a great variety of shops and artisans' studios owned by Jews. Each al-jama was autonomous, with its own municipal government, its own laws, and its own courts. The sentences handed down by the Jewish judges were honored by the municipal government, and the police force of the civil authority was bound to execute any punishment called for by them.

These were certainly ghettos, but the streets were no smaller or meaner than those in the Christian part of town. A separate-but-equal segregation. Access to the aljamas was by two gates, which were often shut after a certain time of night, both to prohibit Jews from coming or going at late hours and to protect those inside from nighttime incursions by their Christian neighbors. The streets, like those of other neighborhoods, were narrow, and medieval living conditions were far below anything to be found in Barcelona's worst neighborhoods today, according to José Ramon Magdalena Nom de Deu, a professor of Hebrew and Aramaic at the University of Barcelona, who has written about daily life in the medieval aljamas.

"The norm in a city like Barcelona was four small rooms, with poor ventilation and little light," Magdalena told me. "In one room slept the mother and father, in the next all the children, and in the third were the domestic servants with the grandmother. Everyone slept on straw mattresses on the floor, and their household goods consisted of a pot, four plates, four basins, one cabinet for clothes, and nothing more.

"There was constantly smoke from the fire, and in the winter there was never sufficient heat to be comfortable. There was the smell of animals and people, and these places were often infested with lice and other insects. The life was poorer than anything people know today."

The richest homes, while presenting plain exteriors so as not to arouse envy and hostility, were sumptuous inside, with lovely inner courtyards open to the sky, which made them light and airy. A beautiful, renovated example of such an upper-class Jewish home from the twelfth century survives in Gerona, about fifty miles north of Barcelona, which has been incorporated into a museum and library open to the public.

Gerona was a city with a thriving Jewish community before the Expulsion. It was a world center for the study of the Cabala, a system of Jewish mystical practice. After the Expulsion, the entrances to Gerona's aljama were bricked up, and for almost five hundred years the streets were out of sight and forgotten. When they were uncovered in 1975, it was as if a time capsule had been opened. Light and air returned to Gerona's Jewish quarter.

Barcelona's aljama, in contrast to Gerona's, was known for being home to more earthbound types. There were two great rivers of Jewish thought during the Middle Ages. One was Cabalism, whose followers believed that study and practice would bring them to union with God. The other was a rational philosophy, based on interpretation of the Torah and the Talmud. Maimonides was a leading light of this school. Barcelona's medieval Jews were mostly rationalists who shunned the mysticism of the Cabalists.

The Barcelona aljama produced its share of scholars and poets, but the city's Jews were principally renowned for their material and professional accomplishments. There were a number of bankers among them, some of whom dealt with the court. Scholars believe that at least half the Jewish men in Barcelona worked as artisans or shopkeepers, while many others worked for them, one or two employees to a shop. There were lawyers and numerous physicians.

In the second half of the thirteenth century, Barcelona became known as a center of Jewish jurisprudence, primarily due to the presence of one man, Solomon ben Abraham ibn Adret, who died at age seventy-five in 1310. Rabbi ben Adret was born in Barcelona, and by the age of twenty was already known across Catalonia and Aragon as one whose understanding of Jewish law was extraordinarily deep. As he grew older, his fame spread. Rabbis and communities from across the Iberian peninsula and, later, around the world wrote to him, asking his opinion on a wide variety of scriptural, legal, and social questions regarding everything from erudite points of talmudic law to the punishment for sodomy. His was considered the final word in a case.

Over three thousand of Solomon ben Adret's opinions, known as *responsa*, have been collected and published, and they form one of our primary sources for an understanding of daily Jewish life in medieval Spain. Life in the aljamas was far from harmonious. The mundane world was filled with deals gone sour, broken contracts, cheated heirs, theological disputes, and marital disagreements. There were crimes of passion, quarrels, revenge, murders, assaults, temptations of the flesh and meddling in-laws. A world like any other. All grist for the mill of Rabbi ben Adret's wisdom.

As Jews began to reappear in Barcelona during this century, they did not choose to live in the old aljama neighborhood behind the cathedral, but tended to reside in middle-class districts, most notably the Ensanche. This is where the community began to regroup after the Spanish civil war.

During the war, Jews had served on both sides. Those from Morocco generally supported Franco. In fact, a number of Moroccan Jews were thought to have provided financial assistance to Franco during the early days of his military coup, which had begun among Spanish troops stationed in North Africa. On the other side were thousands of European and North American Jews who served with the Republicans, along with a handful of left-wing Spanish Jews. When Franco won the war in 1939, those who had fought for the losing Republican side either fled the country, or were executed.

More numerous than those Jews who actively took part in the war on one side or the other were those who laid low, who tried to find enough bread to put on the table to keep their families alive, and waited to see who would come out a winner. It was not an easy wait. In the years when the Republicans controlled Barcelona, there were regular appearances at the door by Republican soldiers who came in and grabbed anything they could sell or eat.

Things were no better after Franco's troops took Barcelona in January 1939, following devastating fighting. One of the first things the Nationalist troops did when they came into the city was to sack the former synagogue at Balmes and Provença. Even those Jews who had shown fascist sympathies during the civil war, or had been truly neutral, could not relax after Franco's victory. His troops were given a list of Jews to be apprehended, accused of forming part of a Masonic-Jewish-Communist conspiracy against holy Catholic Spain. They were subjected to late-night visits from the police, and arrest. In many of these cases, formal charges were never presented against the arrested individuals, but they were forced to stay in jail for months and, sometimes, years. In fact, some were not released until the mid-1940s, when they were finally let out of prison only on condition that they board the first ship to Palestine and never return.

Those Jews who were not subjected to arrest faced an apparently grim future following the civil war. Food and work were scarce, and the news from the rest of Europe was enough to keep anxiety high. In addition to the problems they shared with their Catalan compatriots, the

Jews lived with the fear that they might be turned over to the Third Reich at any moment. German planes and pilots had come to Spain to help win the civil war for Franco, and he was openly sympathetic to the Axis powers, endorsing Hitler and Mussolini, but, finally, declining to commit Spanish funds or forces to the war.

"What a scare we had," said ninety-one-year-old Alberto Arditti, sitting on his sofa and panting to illustrate how scary it had been, raising his white eyebrows to ask me if he was making himself clear. "There was a time when Hitler asked Franco for permission to march through Spain, on the way to Morocco to fight the French and English there.

"Luckily, Franco didn't agree. That was later in the war, and we knew there were camps in Poland and Germany. Franco saved us, but what a scare we had when we thought the Germans were coming. If they had come through Spain, I am certain we would have been sent to the camps."

As it turned out, despite Franco's oft-repeated warnings against the Masons, Jews, and Communists in league to subvert and conquer Spain, his diplomats in Europe saved the lives of numerous Jews. While historians agree that as an official, non-combatant nation, Spain might have rescued many more people than it did, there is no denying that Spanish embassies in a number of European cities were able, with the knowledge if not the encouragement of officials in Madrid, to save many Jews from death in the concentration camps. This happened in Rome, Bucharest, Budapest, Paris, Salonika, and other cities where Jews were provided passes of safe conduct from local Spanish consulates.

One person who was rescued from probable death in a concentration camp was Jaime Vandor, now a colleague of Ramon Magdalena's in the department of Hebrew and Aramaic Studies at the University of Barcelona. He had been a child in Budapest, Hungary, during the Second World War. "My life was saved by one of those safe conducts," said Vandor, shaking his balding, grey fringed head. "My family had documents of protection that we could show during the constant raids and arrests carried out by German Nazis and Hungarian Nazis. Those who did not have such papers were deported to Auschwitz.

"Those who did have papers were held in a house under the protection of the consulate. In our five-floor building there were more than twelve hundred people, and we were among fifty-two people living in a two-and-a-half bedroom apartment."

Vandor was born in Vienna, Austria, in 1933, and shortly thereafter moved with his family to Budapest. His father had suffered greatly during World War I, spending four years in a Siberian prison camp, and was determined that if war came again, he would be in a country where fighting was not taking place. After the civil war in Spain, he guessed correctly that the country was too beaten and exhausted to fight again, so he decided to move to Barcelona. He left Budapest in 1939, expecting to send for his family in six months.

"In order to get documents from the Spanish government you had to have a connection to Spain, and because we were on a waiting list to join my father, our lives were saved," Vandor told me in slightly accented Castilian, digging his hands deep into the pockets of his comfortable, old cardigan sweater.

"The Spanish consul in Budapest treated us well. Every week a truck was sent with food for everyone in the building. And every time that the SS or the gestapo showed up to look for hidden people or demand to see papers, someone would immediately come from the consulate and send them away."

Even now, the reason why Franco behaved with relative tolerance toward Jews during the Second World War is one of many questions about the dictator that remain unresolved, because Franco's heirs still will not allow anyone to have access to his papers. Neither scholars nor journalists have been permitted to read them. A few people I asked about Franco's surprising tolerance attributed it to the financial help he received from Moroccan Jews early in the civil war. Most believed he was simply being pragmatic—something for which he was famous—and hedging his bets in case of an Axis loss.

Whatever the reason for Franco's tolerance toward the Jews, his attitude was out of character, because in other respects the dictator was determined to create a Spain that was pure and ultra-traditional, uncontaminated by the tide of moral and religious laxity sweeping across western Europe. No challenges to the status quo of that state as it was perceived by Franco and the Catholic church were allowed.

During the brief years of the Republic, 1931–36, women had been given equal rights with men. Divorce and abortion had been legalized. Although the laws against homosexuality had not been repealed, a wide variety of lifestyles was tolerated by the government. Boys and girls were in the same classes in school, and free to associate with each other.

When Franco came to power, everything changed. Boys and girls were completely segregated. They had their own classrooms, and were strictly prohibited from any interaction. In fact, in 1939 a law was passed that prohibited coeducation as something "openly contrary" to the principles of Spain.

Girls were taught early that boys were to be feared, that every male was a potential corrupter, that each was in the grip of a sexual heat that would blind him to right and wrong at any moment. A girl's most important task was to bring herself intact to her wedding day. Boys were not expected to be virgins when they married, but their sexual experiences were tacitly expected to be limited to prostitutes.

All forms of sexual behavior, aside from that performed purely for the purposes of procreation between a married couple in the privacy of their home, were illegal. Anything that deviated from monogamous marriage was strictly forbidden. It was no joke for a girl to be caught talking to a boy in the open street after school, her reputation could suffer. Holding hands with a young man in public was enough to have her brought up on charges of improper behavior, and such cases were occasionally published in the newspapers to reprimand the impetuous couples. There was a vast and elaborate web of social mechanisms designed to instill in girls a sense of submission and second-class citizenship so strong that it would endure all their lives.

Everything was censored. All books and magazines had to pass the approval of censors, as did films and theater. Hollywood was considered one of the worst violators of public decency. The state board of film censorship, La Junta Superior de Orientación Cinematográfica, was composed primarily of clergy. A kiss between unmarried people was enough to earn a clip of the editing shears.

In this kind of cultural atmosphere, cabaret nightclubs flourished in

Barcelona. There was a row of them along the Avenida Paralelo, or the Parallel, a broad avenue that runs between the port and the Plaza España. They rivaled the cabarets of Paris's Place Pigalle, or pre-war Berlin. In the drabness of fascist Spain, the shows in the cabarets were pure pleasure, with dancers dressed in elaborate, colorful, scanty costumes performing suggestive choreography, interspersed with stand-up comic relief rooted in sexual innuendo. Many of these places predated Franco, places like El Molino, which is still there almost ninety years after it opened, with its windmill facade out front and its dancers of dubious gender performing inside.

The Parallel was a demi-monde of cabarets and nightclubs during the Franco years, populated by the sort of local criminal milieu that characterized the Broadway of Damon Runyon's tales of the New York underworld during Prohibition. The Parallel was headquarters for grifters and petty hustlers of all stripes. It was also a place for a middle-class couple to come for an evening, and to get a titillating whiff of a headier life than their own. The cabarets, music halls, and nightspots along the Parallel prospered for many years, and even in the 1990s their names evoked a strong nostalgia in many older Barcelonese.

The Parallel was also home to most of the city's transvestites during the dictatorship, because a cabaret show was the only place where cross-dressing would not earn someone a quick trip to prison. The most notorious of these cabarets was the Barcelona de Noche, where the floor shows evolved to a point that they were often thin excuses to allow men to dress and perform as women. Each week, the Minister of Culture sent a representative, a species of mind-cop, to the cabarets along the Parallel who picked up copies of the scripts for upcoming shows, and took them back to the censors at the Ministry of Culture. In order to win approval, the scripts had to put the male actors in a plausible predicament where they would have to dress as women. In this way, cross-dressing was justified as acting.

"In those years, the Barcelona de Noche was the best place for a transvestite to work," said Antonio Barranco, when I talked to him at the piso in the barrio chino, where he rented a room. "Sometimes you could dress up a little like a woman in a show at El Molino, but Barcelona de Noche was the best, and it was where you were generally allowed to get away with a little more. Barcelona was always a little freer under Franco than anywhere else in Spain, although not much."

Barranco worked at the Barcelona de Noche from 1960 to 1964 as a dancer. When I met him, he was tall, with thinning, short, brown hair and, although fifty-seven, still had a male dancer's lean, muscled frame. He also had remarkably smooth skin, and lovely, rounded, women's breasts, a modest but attractive bust. In the late 1960s, he had moved to Italy to escape the constant harassment from the authorities, and there he began the process of a sex change. He returned to Spain after Franco died and continued his feminization, although he has never been able to save enough money to complete the process.

"You could never get confident or comfortable during those years under Franco," he told me. "You never knew when the police would take you, and what would happen to you when they did. There was a lot of tension between the police and those of us who worked in cabarets.

"I remember one night at the Barcelona de Noche I had made a breast of cloth, and I took it out of my dress and a plainclothesman got up from a table down front, came up, and arrested me right there. Just for taking my breast out. That was before I got these," he said, unbuttoning the white cotton shirt he was wearing, and cupping one of his breasts in his hand.

"I remember another night, in the summer of 1962, when I decided to go into the street with a little makeup on. Very little. Just some eye shadow and mascara. Sometimes, after a show, I just felt like leaving a little on. A German grabbed me by the arm and started yelling for the police, claiming I'd robbed him, which I had not. When the police asked me where I worked and found out it was at Barcelona de Noche, they beat me up, and took me to jail. I did six months for that one."

CHAPTER FOUR

Life Inside the Law

Monday, December 2

The weather has changed to cold to greet December, and last night there was thunder and lightning, but no rain. The clouds raced and broke across a three-quarter moon high above the buildings, pushing the weather ahead of them. Today, first workday of the month, the air is clean, clear, washed, and good to breathe.

It is also the first time I am accosted by the police.

At 9 A.M. I'm dressed in jeans and a sweatshirt, feeling good with a breakfast of café con leche and a croissant in my gut, heading home to pick up the threads of the day. I am walking down one of the two broad pedestrian boulevards lined with plane trees and benches that border the Gran Via de les Corts Catalanes with its five lanes of whiz-by traffic, cars and motorcycles hurling themselves down from the Plaza España, five blocks away, trying to make every light as they cross the Eixample.

A police car pulls up to the curb in front of me,

and two uniformed Guardia Nacional get out, a man from behind the wheel and a woman from the passenger's side. Both are wearing side arms. The man pauses as he straightens up, leans back into the car and takes something out from under the driver's seat. A billy club. Yowser! He's expecting trouble, something's going on. I look around to see what danger he has spotted.

Much to my surprise, I'm the threat. They walk up, plant themselves in front of me, and ask for my documents. They have decided it would be worth their while to stop this dark-complected man, who looks, perhaps, a little shabby, and poor, and out of place.

I do not like the way the man cradles that club up across his chest while he goes through my papers. He frowns at the personal data typed in my passport. It looks like it would take him only an instant to drop the papers on the ground and bring that club down on my head. At the same time, the woman takes the role of nice cop and asks me in a friendly voice how long I have been in the country, what I do, and where I live. I give her the old bourgeois soft-shoe, the member-of-the-middle-class shuffle, a fast one-two, white-freelance-journalist-from-the-USA routine. After the man finishes turning the pages of my passport with a quick, practiced hand and eye, they wish me good day and get back in their car.

Under Franco, the forces of order operated with almost complete impunity, whether they were the Policía Armada in the cities or the Guardia Civil in the towns. It was extremely ill advised to question anything a police officer said or did. Best to just nod your head up and down, repeatedly, preferably while saying, *Si, señor.* No one was under any illusions about the police being public servants. They were there to support the dictatorship and the policeman was not a friend. Just one look at a guardia in those days was enough to get the point across to most people: their starched green uniforms, with hard, black, shiny, patent-leather tricorn hats. Nor did people easily forget the menacing presence of the police in the cities, weapons always at the ready. A wrong look could have repercussions far more serious than just being stopped and asked for your documents. It could get you pushed around on the spot, *then* arrested for whatever crime with which they decided to charge you.

Street theatre masquerading as revolution was going on in Paris in the spring of 1968, while real revolutionary courage was being displayed by university students in Barcelona, willing to come into the streets with banners and signs even though they knew the police would charge them, looking to rough people up. If a person was badly beaten and died, so be it. The police were secure that no word of it would appear in the papers the next day, nor would any charges be brought against an officer who killed a student under such circumstances.

For a time after the socialists came to power in 1982, it appeared that Spanish police were going to have to learn what it meant to work in a democracy. The guardia had their uniforms redesigned, and the black tricorns were replaced by a cap more like that of a North American police officer. Now the tricorns only appear on official occasions like parades and ceremonies. The rest of the time, no doubt, the old guard keep them at home in a special drawer, carefully wrapped in tissue paper.

More important than the change of uniform was that the socialists moved quickly to put strict limits on police powers, and to expand the personal freedom of citizens. It was no longer permissible to stop someone on the street and search them when there was no reason to believe they had committed a crime. People were not required to carry identification with them. Possession of a "personal use" quantity of hashish or marijuana was no longer illegal. And a person had to be detained on a specific charge before being taken into police custody.

Even while the police were operating under the new regulations of Felipe González's administration, there were not many people who resisted when they were stopped and asked for their documents, or told, without reason, to empty their pockets. When a cop asked for papers, automatic weapon slung on a strap across his chest, most Barcelonese produced their identity cards without question.

"People here went through forty years of *Franquismo*, with the concept of police and authority they had under Franco, and many are still intimidated," said Barcelona attorney Jordi Oliveras. "On the other hand, there are a lot of people here who are very sensitive to this issue, and put a lot of pressure on the state."

However, the socialist government has become increasingly conservative over the years, and nowhere more so than on issues of law and order—although the police have never regained the absolute immunity they enjoyed under Franco. The foreigners' law was sponsored and passed by the socialists. New drug laws ended the brief experiment with decriminalization, making possession of even a personal-use quantity a civil offense subject to fines. Then, just this year, the government successfully sponsored legislation that gives police the right to stop anyone on the street and demand identification. If a person cannot produce documentation, the police have the right to detain that person until he or she can produce proof of identity.

The most disturbing feature of the law, according to Oliveras, is that it also allows local police to refuse permission for a protest or a march if they believe it will be prejudicial to public order. "This is something that should not be allowed to happen. To subordinate one of the fundamental rights of the people to the opinion of a police officer is not right. This is obviously something that is going to be a very subjective decision on the part of that police officer, and it is going to be very easy to confuse what that police officer or his boss might want with something that is so-called 'prejudicial to public order.'"

The Citizen's Security Law—as, with an Orwellian touch, the new legislation was named by its socialist sponsors—generated a great deal of controversy while it was being debated and discussed in the Cortes. There were marches in Madrid and Barcelona against it, and letters in the press from groups of concerned lawyers and jurists opposed to its passage.

At the same time, however, there was a rash of vigilante actions in various neighborhoods of Barcelona and Madrid. Neighbors, claiming they were fed up with drugs and crime, formed posses at night, and went through the streets of their barrios. Anyone they believed to be selling or buying drugs was beaten, and told to leave and not come back. The vigilante actions in the barrios always focused on the small fish: dealers on the streets selling a little heroin, and the junkies coming to buy it. In many cases, the big fish were well known to the vigilantes, but the groups did not go knocking on their doors, because they knew the traffickers were powerful, wealthy people who would certainly retaliate if disturbed. Nevertheless, these barrio posses were given headlines across the country, and the government claimed that the proposed Citizen's Security Law would make it easier to address their concerns.

The original version of the law stipulated that anyone on the street without proper documentation was liable to a 25,000 peseta [$250] fine. The version that eventually passed the Cortes did not contain that clause, but did require people to produce identification if asked for it by the police. It also gave police the right to enter homes without a search warrant if they had reason to believe a crime was being committed or planned there, and that the delay involved in obtaining a warrant would be prejudicial to impeding the aforementioned crime. The law was touted by the government as something that would give police another weapon in combating Spain's two most serious security problems: drugs and terrorism.

"This law has absolutely nothing to do with combating or preventing terrorism, and not much to do with drugs, but it does represent an important erosion of the rights of Spanish citizens," said Oliveras.

Over the years, the drug problem has been treated from both the legalize-it and outlaw-it perspective. Not so ETA's demands that the Madrid government recognize its organization, and negotiate the independence of the Basque provinces. Successive governments from Franco's to González's consistently have refused to negotiate with representatives of the independence movement, so long as terrorism continues. Since 1968, ETA's bombings and shootings have accounted for the deaths of 702 people across the country, 269 of them civilians, including 115 people under the age of eighteen.

The three provinces of the Basque region comprise the second richest area of Spain, after Catalonia. The Basques enjoy the same linguistic, cultural and administrative autonomy as the Catalans, with their own television station in the Basque language, and the right to speak the language in the schools. Like Catalonia, there is absolutely no chance that the central government will ever consider allowing the region to secede from Spain.

ETA did, initially, have a claim of sorts on the government. While its role in bringing democracy to Spain was never officially recognized, most Spaniards were well aware that in 1973 it was an ETA bomb that blew up the car containing Franco's designated heir, Admiral Luis

Carrero Blanco, the deputy prime minister preparing to take over the dictatorship. It is generally agreed that democracy would have been a lot longer coming to Spain without Carrero's timely dispatch.

However, any credit ETA might have had with either the democratic government or the citizens was used up long ago by those 702 deaths. Most Spaniards are ready to hear the last of ETA, and have been for a long time. The worst attack in Barcelona was in 1987, when a car bomb exploded in a parking lot beneath a Hipercor supermarket in a crowded working-class neighborhood. Twenty-one people were killed.

People in Madrid and Barcelona, or the Basque cities of Bilbao and San Sebastian, have grown used to coexisting with the fear that comes from living where terrorist attacks, although relatively rare, can and do happen. Even under non–Olympic circumstances, life in Barcelona is not free of the threat of terrorist attack. People cross the street rather than walk in front of a police station (frequent targets of bombings), and they are hypersensitive about things like unattended packages and abandoned cars.

ETA shootings are often aimed randomly at anyone in a uniform. The car bombings have been even more indiscriminate in claiming victims. In May 1990, for example, in the Catalan town of Vic, about thirty miles north of Barcelona, nine people were killed one afternoon when ETA terrorists rolled a car packed with explosives down a ramp into the courtyard of a building that housed national police and their families. Five of the victims were children who were playing in the courtyard.

"It was just horrible," a doctor told me who had been on duty at the hospital in Vic that afternoon. "There was an avalanche of people who came to the hospital. Some were seriously wounded, some were cut from shattered windows, and others were in a state of shock. We did what we could.

"It was chaos," she said. "We set aside a room for families. It was afternoon, the kids were home from school and out playing, and no one knew whose children had been killed. They came in asking, 'Is my child here?' One little girl of four was so badly burned that her father had to identify her body by the watch she was wearing."

Spaniards outside of Basque country are ready for an end to ETA's mad-dog attacks. How the Basques feel is more difficult to assess. If a march is held in Bilbao one Sunday denouncing ETA violence, it may be attended by a huge crowd of fifty thousand marchers. The following Sunday, there could be a Basque march organized by the political arm of the independence movement, Herri Batasuna, closely aligned with ETA, and fifty thousand people would also show up for that. While many Basques are uncomfortable with the violence, they are drawn to the idea of Basque independence, and resent the massive numbers of Spanish police deployed in their region.

Monday, December 16

It's early evening when the police stop me this time. Their car pulls up to the curb behind me, as I'm walking. One officer stands outside on the sidewalk with me, while his partner sits behind the wheel in the patrol car, and radios in my name and passport number. We wait in silence for a couple of minutes.

The radio crackles. *"Es blanco,"* a dispatcher's voice says, loudly enough to be heard clearly by all.

"White?" I raise my eyebrows, as my guard reaches in the window for my passport and hands it back to me.

He shrugs off my question with a deprecatory laugh. He is young, and seems faintly embarrassed. "We do it by color, it's our code," he tells me as he gets back in the car, leaving me free to go on my way.

"If he had said you were black you would have been in here with us."

When I'm not being stopped by the police, it is a pleasure to be out on the darkening streets. There are Christmas lights strung across all of the broader avenues and many of the narrow, cobblestone streets. It was cold today. The temperatures are hovering between forty and forty-five, with grey, drizzly skies and a brisk wind. People are walking around in overcoats and scarves—never hats, Barcelonese do not wear hats—grumbling about what a cold early December it has been. Butane gas space heaters are on all day; blankets and comforters are out of storage and on the beds.

There is a silver lining in the cloud of cold weather, however, and that is the deep snowfall in the Pyrenees mountains, a two-hour drive northward. Everyone is amazed. This is one of the earliest beginnings to the ski season in memory, and that's exceptionally good news. The day's snowfall and the condition of the slopes open the nightly news on television, and the newspapers publish special ski sections, stuffed with ads from ski resorts and stores selling equipment.

Barcelonese love to ski. It is unquestionably the city's favorite winter sport. Suddenly it seems like there are more cars with ski racks on their roofs than without them. The first long weekend of the ski season began with Constitution Day, which fell on Friday, December 6, and the slopes were covered immediately with people. By Saturday morning, there were ten-mile-long traffic jams leading into some resorts, and many shops in the small mountain villages sold their wares right down to the bare shelves, then closed for lack of inventory.

There were long lines for the lifts, and the crowds on the slopes meant many more chances to have an accident, and no chance to ski full-out downhill. Service at the hotels and restaurants was overwhelmed, and far from adequate. On Sunday, it took seven hours to make a two-hour drive back to Barcelona. The only thing most people stuck in traffic could think about was doing the same thing the following weekend.

That proved even more difficult, because on Friday the thirteenth, early in the afternoon, ETA announced its intention to be a player in the upcoming drama of the Olympic Games, and they did it in grisly fashion. Two policía nacional were standing in a garage in the Les Corts neighborhood, investigating an abandoned car report, when two ETA gunmen appeared in the doorway and opened fire with semi-automatic weapons, killing the two policemen on the spot.

Police closed the city down. There were only two primary highways leading out of Barcelona, one at either end, each five lanes wide, and both were blockaded. Police reduced the five lanes to one at each end, and stopped every car, ski rack or not, to check the documents of its passengers. Cars driven by young men were searched, as was each truck. Traffic immediately began to back up all over the city and within an hour Barcelona's streets had come to a frozen halt. A normal, twenty-minute trip across town took four or five hours. Horns blared everywhere as traffic lights went from green to red to green again. Day finally faded to night with absolutely no forward motion. The logjam of cars did not break up until around midnight, and those who were lucky enough to get home stayed there, and did not leave for the mountains until the next day. Not surprisingly, the terrorists did not choose to try and leave town when the police closed it down, so only innocent citizens paid the price of having their plans entirely disrupted.

Despite these difficulties, the early arrival of the ski season has boosted lots of spirits and, combined with the lights and the display windows, seems to have put people in a shopping mood. It does not take much to put Barcelonese in a shopping mood—it is another of their favorite pastimes—and they are in a feeding frenzy as the Christmas holidays approach.

Most Spaniards, including Catalans, do their serious gift-giving on January 6, the Day of the Kings, in celebration of the arrival of the three wise men who journeyed to the manger bearing gifts. In recent years, more and more people, especially kids, have also received something on December 25 to keep up with the televised images of how it is done elsewhere in the First World. There is a lot of buying that needs to be done in preparation for the holidays. It gets dark early as Christmas approaches, and by 5:30 P.M. the lights are on in the streets. Each shop is also brightly lit within, their interiors glitter and are full of people looking, fingering, buying, laden down with packages, and still forging ahead.

Spaniards get paid fourteen months of wages for every twelve they work, with an extra month's pay before Christmas and, again, in July. The two months of *sueldo extraordinario*, extra salary, are a tradition that began during the Franco years. During his rule, the summer payment was issued on July 18, to commemorate the beginning of the Falangist uprising against the Republic in 1936, and it is still called the *sueldo de 18 de Julio,* even though it is no longer given out precisely on that date. It is, though, always given out before August 1, which is the beginning of a month's vacation for most of Spain.

The majority of working Spaniards get paid vacations for a week at Christmas, a week at Easter, and a month in the summer. While many people are allowed to choose between taking July or August in the summer, they are not free to take their month's vacation any other time. August is the most popular choice, and during that month, normal business virtually stops functioning in Spain. Tourist destinations are flooded with people spending their extra month's pay. Of course, employers simply divide annual salaries into fourteen instead of twelve so that, in reality, it is not two extra months' pay. But it does provide people with a little more liquidity just when they need it most.

The Corte Ingles department store (the name means the English Cut) is packed with shoppers. There are two of these immense emporiums in Barcelona, the original one on the Plaza Cataluña, which opened in 1962, and another nine-floor giant built on an expensive stretch of the Avenida Diagonal, just below the posh neighborhood of Pedralbes.

Many of the Christmas shoppers pay for their purchases with credit cards. The first credit cards in Spain were introduced in 1954, and came from Diner's Club. Twenty-five years or so later, the Spaniards have some 31 million bank cards. Maybe not many when compared to the approximately 850 million in the States in 1991, but enough to rank Spain the third highest in the EC, and credit card use is continuing to grow rapidly.

The citizens' fondness for credit spending is mirrored by the government's, and Spain's trade deficit has tripled since 1986. Now it stands at 3.4 trillion pesetas ($34 billion). In addition, the country has the largest gap between imports and exports in the EC. This situation is bad enough, but economists predict it will dramatically worsen as trade barriers are dismantled and the eleven other EC countries gain full access to Spain's consumers after 1992. Many goods sell cheaper in other places than in Spain, particularly big-ticket items such as automobiles or domestic consumer products such as televisions or dishwashers.

It did not take long for the values that had informed life under Franco to be undermined and eradicated. What had gone around came around, and Spain was colonized by multinational free market consumerism about as rapidly as the indigenous population of the New World had been colonized five hundred years before by Spaniards. The acquisitive force hidden in credit cards and televisions was proving every bit as strong as the viruses that Columbus's men had transported hidden in their penises and lungs. Like those viruses, consumerism could wipe out a way of life in a brief time. The Catholic, conservative culture that

Franco exalted, rooted in a nation of small landholders, is rapidly disintegrating, and some observers predict it will eventually disappear as completely as that of the Taino Indians in the Caribbean, or of the Aztecs in Mexico.

The shift to the values of a consumer economy came more easily to the Catalans than to people in other parts of Spain. Catalans were already accustomed to budgeting their resources, and working hard for their money. They had been excluded from the age of exploration, prohibited by Madrid from investing in the colonies or doing business with them for almost three hundred years, until 1770. Catalans had been forced to make their money at home. By the time they got a shot at the New World, all the best fruits had long been picked by others.

People from the rest of Spain had their ideas about making money shaped by colonization, and it proved an unmitigated disaster in preparing them for the twentieth century. Their ideal was, quite simply, to have so much New World money coming in that there was no need to have anything to do with it on a daily basis other than spend it. During the initial phases of Spanish colonialism there were such large fortunes made from pillaging the Americas that numerous Spanish aristocrats never did a day's work in their lives. Many of them bought huge expanses of land in Andalusia and hired peasants to clear it and grow olive trees. Generations of peasants worked with those trees, while the owners of the land lived comfortably in Madrid or Seville. Regardless of where it was lived, a life of leisure was the mark of distinction to which all aspired. That, and a title.

Both the disinclination to work and the title were handed down from father to son, and by the time the twentieth century arrived there were plenty of poor noblemen whose fortunes had been used up long before, but whose pride kept them from taking a job. The most admired and respected man in many a Spanish town or village is the aristocrat whose daily routine is to read or putter around at home during the morning, then go to town for a midday walk and apertif at a cafe, then home again in the afternoon—even though his family fortunes might have been so reduced that he lives on less money each month than a peasant. Sometimes these aristocrats have so little that they cannot afford to marry, have children, or even repair their crumbling homes. Nevertheless, they prefer to extinguish their genetic line rather than join the consumer society and work hard all day at a meaningless task to keep payments current on credit cards.

The Catholic church also plays a role in the ambivalence that many Spaniards feel toward work, and the accumulation of wealth. While the church as an institution may have spent centuries putting up riches, its doctrine has always discouraged congregants from doing so. Everyone needs a certain amount of money, granted—but its pursuit can only lead to perdition.

Since the church's beginnings, moneylending had been prohibited in theory, but during the early Middle Ages this canon was usually ignored in practice. Then, in the twelfth century, a wave of conservatism saw it widely enforced. That was when the Sefarad came in handy, and it was thanks to the church that moneylending became a Jewish profession. Moneylenders were a necessary evil to keep the wheels of commerce turning, and since Jewish souls were already lost for eternity, Jews could be moneylenders without worry. The actual dirty lucre could pass through their hands. This gave medieval Jews an important role to play.

Jews frequently collected taxes for the king, and often served other wealthy Catholics as debt collectors. Somehow, Jews were always more effective at getting money out of people than Christians, probably because they had no fear that doing so would send them to hell. The number of Jews engaged in this kind of business was minimal, but they were often members of the upper class of the Jewish community with connections at the royal court. Members of these families served on the councils that administered the aljamas, and had a high profile among the Gentiles.

Barcelona's Jews were prohibited from investing in the city's two most profitable industries: marine commerce and textiles. From the middle of the twelfth century, they were also increasingly restricted by law from competing with Catholics in other fields. Strict rules were implemented concerning the ownership of land in Catalonia by Jews, for instance, and Jewish farmers were often required to sell their land at a loss. Even so, there were a number of ways to get rich as a Jew in Barcelona during the Middle Ages. Many Jews amassed fortunes serving at court. There, over the centuries, Jews grew wealthy as tax collectors, treasurers, physicians, counselors, astrologers, astronomers, and diplomats.

An excellent education was provided for the sons of the Jewish middle and upper classes, those fortunate enough not to have to go to work as soon as they were able to help put bread on the family table. In addition to a thorough and constant education in Jewish law and thought, they studied Hebrew and Arabic, read the Greek philosophers, and received instruction in logic, mathematics, music, astronomy, physics, and medicine.

Of course, most of the sons of the aljama did not get that kind of education. What they got to learn were their letters well enough to read the Torah, and the rudimentary arithmetic necessary for keeping simple accounts. Modest as that education might have been, it was far superior to that of the Gentiles, most of whom were totally illiterate. Once the Jewish boys possessed a basic level of learning, they would turn their time to an apprenticeship in preparation for earning their livelihoods in the aljama. They became potters, or book binders, or bakers, or cobblers, or any of the myriad trades needed to keep a community of four thousand people functioning.

There were many people living in the aljamas in poverty who were barely surviving, according to Ramon Magdalena. Conflict between rich and poor was always present, and it increased as the centuries passed. "There were numerous poor Jews in every aljama, and each community had organizations to aid and protect them, organizations to feed the poor and protect orphans and widows," he told me one morning in his office at the university.

"There were places of hospitality where poor people who came as strangers would have a place to sleep. Unlike in the Christian community, where the city or the church might feed the hungry once or twice a week, the Jews had a systematic organization to take care of the poor. It worked better in some places than in others, but it was always there."

In the thirteenth century, Barcelona's lower- and middle-class Jews increased their demands for a share of the decision making in the community. They demanded representation on the Council of Thirty, which administered their aljama, and did everything from appoint judges to set taxes. It was a reduced reflection of Barcelona's medieval city council, the Council of One Hundred. The Council of Thirty was traditionally made up of upper-class Jewish men who had connections at court.

"As in countries and cultures all over the world, it was not the richest in the aljama who had to bear the greatest load of the taxes, but those beneath them," said Magdalena. "The richest of the Jews were people with powerful connections in the Christian world, and they sometimes treated the middle and lower classes as the Catholic kings treated them. The lower classes eventually mounted a fierce fight to resist this."

After years of conflict and debate, the composition of the Council of Thirty was made more equal, with ten men from each strata of the community on it. However, the rich continued to have more power because of their connections at the king's court, according to Magdalena: "There was some smoothing out of the inequities in raising taxes and administering the finances of the aljama in the thirteenth century, although the administration always showed a bias toward the more powerful and richest residents."

Now sixty-five, Victor Papo arrived in Barcelona after fleeing Paris with his parents and siblings in 1941. The effects of the civil war were still greatly in evidence. Everyone was poor, Gentile and Jew alike. Much of the city was in rubble, food was scarce, and jobs were scarcer.

Papo's grandfather had lived in Turkey, descended from Sefarad who fled to the Ottoman Empire when expelled by Isabella and Ferdinand. His father had moved to France, where he took advantage of the law passed by Primo de Rivera's government in 1924 to obtain Spanish passports for his family, although he had no intention of ever leaving Paris. It saved his family's life. Because they were under the protection of the Spanish consul, they were able to continue living in Paris for almost two years after the Nazi occupation.

"When the Nazis came into Paris, the Spanish consul was protecting the Jews," said Papo, when I interviewed him in his large, comfortable piso. "That consul's name was Bernardo Rolland and he was an unsung hero. He told us, 'Don't go to the French police to get a J stamped on your identification papers, as the French Jews are required to do. You are Spanish citizens and you don't have to do it.'

"He also told us that there would come a day when he would no longer be able to help us. 'When that day comes,' he said, 'take your passports and go to Spain.' Some people waited too long. There were Jews with Spanish passports who were picked up, interned, and sent to concentration camps in Poland."

Barcelona was not only poor, it was under the control of a government friendly toward the Nazis, and a rigorous, anti-semitic Catholicism was the state religion. Nevertheless, to be out from under the direct daily observation of the Nazis was a big relief.

"Just to be on equal footing with everyone else in the streets was wonderful," said Papo, his gaze direct under a furrowed brow, a fringe of grey hair. "There wasn't much food, and work was hard to find, but with our passports we were treated like Spaniards, and had the same opportunities they did. We did not tell anyone we were Jewish, and they didn't ask. Everyone was assumed to be a Catholic.

"My father brought us to Barcelona because we had relatives here who had come from Paris six months earlier. My native language was French, but both my grandmothers spoke the Judeo-Spanish that their families had always spoken in Turkey, so Spanish was familiar to me."

Many Jews were arriving in Spain from all over Europe, and Barcelona was the first stop for a lot of them. In addition to those who came with Spanish passports intending to settle down, many came on tourist visas that would allow them to stay in the country until they could find passage to North or South America.

"When they got to Barcelona, the Jewish refugees stayed pretty close together," said Papo, who has now retired from his career in import and export. "People were arriving every day, and the main topic of interest was who was coming tomorrow. When someone left a city, say Paris, they would tell friends, 'I'm going to Barcelona,' and the news would often precede their arrival.

"There were two or three cafes where the men would gather to exchange news. One was the Oro del Rin on the corner of the Gran Via and the Rambla Cataluña. There was a big cafe in the old style, the Casa Libre where the Hotel Avenida Palace is now on the Gran Via, and then there was the Bavaria at the corner of Paseo de Gracia and Calle Caspé. The Jewish men would sit at one in the mornings, one in the afternoons, and one in the evenings. They would talk for hours over coffee. Everyone was sure to be home at night for the most important hour of the day—listening to the BBC news broadcast on the radio."

In addition to the Jews with legitimate passports and visas, Jews without any papers at all also made their way to Spain. For many, it was the closest point of refuge not under Nazi dominion. People came across the Pyrenees mountains on foot. Guides were available for high prices to lead them through the rugged mountain passes to Spanish soil.

"My father-in-law came in over the mountains," said Papo. "He walked into Spain. He had come from Poland. He was headed for Barcelona, but the Spaniards arrested him before he got here. At first, they brought him here and kept him in jail, then they sent him to a detention camp near Zaragoza.

"After two or three months, the American Joint Distribution Committee delegate in Barcelona went to that camp and talked to everyone there. He found a job for my father-in-law, and within another two or three months he was released to come to Barcelona. He wanted to go to the United States, but at that time the American government was ignoring the Holocaust and giving out very few visas."

Saturday, December 21

A winter solstice weekend, and the Sants train station is mobbed with holiday travelers. Normally, the city has two large train stations, Sants for travel inside Spain, and the Estacío de França, close to Barceloneta and the port, for international travel. However, the França Station has been closed for renovations since 1988, and Sants is serving as the terminus for both national and international trains. The goal is to get a remodeled Estacío de França open in time for the Olympic summer. In the meantime, Sants has to carry the burden.

In addition to the normal compliment of suitcases and shoulder bags, travelers are loaded down with gifts. Many carry big shopping bags full of wrapped packages, others an elaborate pastry wrapped in tissue paper and carefully held by the string tied around it. There is a constant movement of people across the station's marble floors, the public address system stays busy announcing arrivals and departures, children wander around, and their parents sweat under their loads on the cool winter's day as they struggle behind the kids, calling to them to wait, stop running, slow down.

In all this flow of people there are some who are as still as stones in a river: the old, the pensioners who come to sit in the heated station each day during the winter, holiday season or otherwise. On any given day there are a lot of them warming the metal benches in the station, men and women; decent, respectable, retired, living on small pensions after a lifetime of hard work. They speak in quiet voices, or read, or just sit watching the world move through the station. They are exceptionally keen-eyed for any magazine or newspaper left behind by a traveler. These are quickly appropriated, read, and passed along to one of their colleagues. The police regularly roust out the homeless or the intoxicated who come to ground in Sants, but the elderly are left alone.

A squat man, dressed as a woman in a black wig, long dress, and heavy makeup, walks across the marble floor carrying a suitcase in one hand, and a garment bag over his other shoulder, listening to a tall, dark-haired, pale woman walking beside him. She also carries a suitcase, and looks down slightly on her companion's bewigged head as she speaks. The old man sitting on a bench next to me nudges the old man sitting on his other side. He looks up briefly from the few pages of *El Mundo Deportivo (The Sporting World)* that he has salvaged somewhere. He focuses on the odd couple for a moment, shakes his head slightly, smiles, and returns to reading the soccer news.

"I can't say why this is true, but I think Catalans have always tended to mind their own business and be a little more tolerant than people in other parts of Spain, at least those Catalans who live in Barcelona," said

Javier Fernàndez, a bartender at the Marsella, who spent his early adult years living in France, until Franco died.

"Under Franco it didn't make much difference. A man could not go out in public dressed like a woman, and that was that."

The Marsella is an odd, inexpensive bar about six blocks deep in the barrio chino, on the Calle San Pablo. For three generations, it has been run by the same family, and its decor was new in the 1920s. Although it has lost some of its original shine, the large mirrors and dark wood still have their charm.

The bar has a large clientele of young foreigners, many of them English speakers who come to Barcelona, rent a place to live, and teach English to Catalans and their children. The going rate for English teachers is about 2,000 pesetas ($20) an hour. Many Catalans have decided that in order to prepare for the new Europe, they, or their children, need to learn English. They take an hour or two a week, or send their children to do the same, even though the kids might already be studying it in school. Hardly anyone learns enough English this way to be of use in any real-world situation, but between the numerous language schools, and regular private lessons, English teachers can make pretty good money in Barcelona.

The Marsella also has its core group of neighborhood regulars. One of these is a tiny, wizened woman who looks old enough to be a great-great-grandmother. When she needs to go to the bathroom, she walks slowly and stoops. Otherwise, she passes each night seated at a small table with a beer in front of her, which she drinks over the course of three or four hours. She is often joined by another regular: a pudgy, balding man with gapped teeth and an insane, high-pitched cackling laugh that explodes out of his mouth every few minutes for no apparent reason. The other regulars call him *el gallo* (the rooster), but his laugh has less the sound of a rooster crowing than the eerie nighttime call of a loon across a lake under a star-filled sky. Newcomers to the bar always give a start, jerking their heads around when el gallo's laugh goes off.

There is a small stage in one corner of the club, and occasionally an acoustic band will come in, and play a couple of sets. Every Thursday and Sunday night, Javier performs dressed—very dressed—as a woman, lip-synching and dancing to taped torch songs. He is a *transformista*, he told me, not a transvestite, nor a transsexual. A transformista, he explained, is a cross-dresser who can be heterosexual or homosexual, but who likes to dress as a woman. A transvestite is a man who dresses up like a woman because he feels like a woman trapped in a man's body. And then, there are transsexuals, people who have actually undergone a sex-change operation to release their true selves. Transformistas generally work in the job world as men, and transsexuals as women, but dedicated transvestites have difficulty finding a regular job. Even post-Franco, their only options may be whore or dancer—walking the streets or working in a cabaret, of which there are fewer and fewer.

Although he does not depend on them for a livelihood, Javier takes his Thursday and Sunday night performances very seriously. For him, this is the time to be creative, and he approaches his work as an artist. He has been doing this for a long time. The process of transforming his dark-haired, overweight, short self into an ample, blonde bundle of feminine fun is not easy. "It takes me over an hour to get ready, to put on everything inside and out that I use, the pads for my hips, the makeup, the wig; everything just right," he said.

Javier is a Catalan, from Barcelona. At the age of fifteen he discovered the pleasure he got from dressing up as a woman, but in those days he could do so only as long as he was dancing in a club like the Barcelona de Noche, where he worked briefly. His parents disapproved strongly, and he wanted to be somewhere he could dress in public as a woman without spending time in jail, or hassling with his father.

He left Barcelona for Paris, determined to escape the censure of parents and government, and did not come back until Franco was dead. "Things had changed a whole lot when I came back. When I left, a woman had to have her husband's permission before she could work. Homosexuality was against the law. And, men certainly did not dress up as women outside of a theater.

"Now, it's as different as night from day. Last Sunday I picked up a friend of mine in my car and we went out driving. I was dressed as a woman. I stopped to get a newspaper and left my friend and the keys in the car. He got out to come get a paper, too, and locked the door when he got out, so the keys were locked inside. Well, I went and found a policeman, and he managed to open the door and get us back in the car.

"He treated me with perfect respect the whole time he was helping us out. That's the kind of change I'm talking about."

CHAPTER FIVE

Riches of the Table

Saturday, January 4, 1992

The last shopping day before the Day of the Kings, January 6, the biggest holiday in the Christmas season, when people spend the day with their families, visiting relatives, eating, and exchanging gifts. People are out stocking up on food. Barcelona is a big city full of small food shops, and they are all doing a brisk business. Most people go to a number of small stores for the different components of their meals. These include the butcher's, the baker's, the vegetable and fruit stores, a *lechería* for milk and butter, and a *bodega* for wine, whiskey, beer, bottled water, and vinegar. Neighborhood bodegas have huge casks of local wines from which they fill up their customers' empty bottles. Meat is even more specialized: there is the *pollería* for chicken and eggs, one *carnicería* for veal or beef, another for pork products, and the *pescadería* for fish and seafood.

Large supermarkets—the sorts of places North Americans are accustomed to—do exist in Barcelona, bringing together all the components of a daily diet under one roof in a variety of departments, each item in shrink wrap. Their prices are generally a few cents lower. Many people buy the most expensive things they regularly need at the supermarket to save money, and continue to do the bulk of their shopping in more traditional venues where they are served by the shopowner and known by name. Catalans have a long tradition of small business ownership, and they like to patronize neighborhood stores.

The rhythm of buying food is entirely different from that in the States, where the whole industry of buying and selling food has been studied, analyzed, shaped, reshaped and ergonomicized. Yet, despite the speed and efficiency with which most North Americans generally buy their food, they are still prone to grumble if a grandmother throws off the pace of the check-out line by fumbling with her change. In Barcelona, on the other hand, people think nothing of waiting fifteen minutes to buy meat for the next meal, then going down the block and waiting another ten minutes to buy vegetables. The shopkeepers serve each customer in turn, and are never too busy to have a bit of conversation with a customer (sometimes more than a bit). None of the people waiting gets annoyed. At least, none of the Catalans. North Americans and Japanese find it difficult.

"I had a lot of trouble getting accustomed to standing in line ten or fifteen minutes to buy a pound of ham, while the butcher took his time and chatted with each customer," said a Japanese housewife, who asked me not to put her name in print. "For me, buying food was one of the hardest things to get used to when we came here."

The woman's husband was transferred here three years ago to manage a Japanese construction firm in Barcelona as part of the pre-Olympic boom. The couple brought two children with them. The husband goes to work early each day, and gets back late, just like in Japan. She is home all day, caring for the children when they return from their private Japanese school. She has a lovely, oval face, and her jet black hair is fashionably styled. Her clothes are well tailored. The family lives in a large, rented flat in the wealthy district of Pedralbes, on the city's western slopes, where many of Barcelona's estimated fifteen hundred Japanese residents stay.

"After you finally buy your meat, you need to go to another little store for vegetables, and you will probably have to wait there too," she said, shaking her head with a tiny grimace of amusement and irritation. "For me, it is difficult always to be waiting. In Japan, things are very efficient and practical, but Spaniards are not at all like that. Their sense of time is completely different from ours."

I know full well that my neighborhood pork carnicería is going to be crowded with people provisioning for the Three Kings holiday. But lunch is on my mind, and I have a strong hankering to cook up a couple of the exceptionally good *morcillas de cebolla* that they sell, blood sausages made with pine nuts and onions, stuffed into stubby, black casings. They have a rich, thick flavor, and a smooth texture. Warmed in a bit of olive oil in a pan and served with a chunk of bread, they are superb.

The carnicería is just as busy as I anticipated, the two young guys behind the long, white, refrigerated display case working steadily, cutting, slicing, weighing, totaling, and making change. There are over a hundred hams hanging around the walls, a loop of rope around each trotter, and the other end slung over a steel hook. Above each ham is a sign indicating the region it comes from and what it costs. Prices range from plain, locally grown ham at about $6 a pound, to the ham with a black trotter grown around the Aragonese city of Teruel, generally considered one of Spain's most flavorful, and selling for about $40 a pound. There are over twenty different kinds of sausages strung up over the display case, and five different leannesses of bacon.

Welcome to pork country. There are no greater connoisseurs of the pig than the Spaniards, Catalans and non-Catalans alike, and they have recipes using every part of the porker, from tail to snout. It is as if the expulsion of the two religions that forbid their followers to eat pork had compelled Spanish Catholics to eat swine at every opportunity.

There are a half-dozen housewives waiting to be served in the carnicería, and a couple of men, and everyone is spread out along the length of the display case, getting hungrier, and mentally adding items to the list of things to ask for when the time comes to give their orders. I sing out as I come through the door, "Who is last?" A middle-aged woman down at one end of the counter answers, "Me," and now I know who I follow. People do not line up to wait their turn, they form a line of the communal mind without actually having to fall in behind one another.

There is no confusion. Woe betide the person who contravenes the order, because it will not pass unnoticed, as I can testify from embarrassing experience.

Another piece of food shopper's etiquette that I learned the hard way was not to pick out my own produce. The lesson came on the first day I went shopping in my neighborhood vegetable store, and reached down into a box of big, sweet red peppers for the size I wanted. I did not need to be told I had transgressed: the look on the face of the woman who owned the shop was enough to let me know. After that, I told her what I wanted, along with an approximate size, and let her pick it out. When she saw I was going to be around a while, and after I had remonstrated with her a couple of times about the quality or size of her choice—too-ripe bananas, less-than-crisp lettuce—we reached the balance that most customers maintain with their shops. She generally let me inspect whatever she chose for me and I could reject it with no hard feelings between us.

The most enjoyable, but also the most time-consuming of all the forms of food shopping in Barcelona is at one of the city's numerous, big, covered markets, vaulted buildings with huge iron arches inside. They were built at the turn of the twentieth century on sites where open-air markets had traditionally stood. The oldest of these is called La Boqueria. It faces the Ramblas and the Liceo metro station, built on the site where there was once a huge open-air market just outside the medieval walls of the city.

Each market has a cement floor beneath the vaulted ceiling and is filled with stalls. Produce gets off-loaded in the wee hours, when refrigerated tractor-trailer trucks with license plates from all over Europe disgorge their cargoes, as do farmers' vans from rural Catalonia. There is lots of shouting, hollering, lifting and grunting, lots of hubbub and truck gears shifting, muscular short men in full-length blue cloth aprons wheeling dollies through the aisles, and women in white aprons building up the displays on the counters of the stalls, working easily, but quickly, with the energy of a new day.

Soon the aisles will be full of shoppers. While waits can be ten or fifteen minutes in front of the most popular stalls, the food is extremely fresh and a little cheaper than in the stores. Older women with well-worn shawls, black shiny pocketbooks, and plain shoes chat amongst themselves while they wait. They all pull behind them the two-wheeled wire carts that people bring shopping. Purchase after purchase goes into the zippered sack on the cart, and by the time a shopper wheels it home, the day's meals are contained inside. Young women are there also, housewives who have just dropped their children off at school, or new mothers with one hand pulling a shopping cart, the other pushing a baby carriage or with an infant riding on a hip.

Each market also has its own bars, of course, where tasty food is available at reasonable prices, in addition to liquid refreshment. Not all the older women filling the aisles are widows. Many have husbands, and some of them have husbands waiting for them at one of the tiny, four-stooled cafes in the market. Each place also has its regulars from the market community—men who sit in front of coffees, or glasses of wine, cigarettes dangling from their mouths, heads wreathed in smoke, talking in gravelly voices to the man in an apron behind the bar. I like to start my market mornings there because they are excellent places for a typical Catalan breakfast of coffee and *pan con tomate* (*pa amb tomàquet*, in Catalan), toast rubbed with a clove of raw garlic and the open half of a cut tomato, then served with olive oil poured over it.

The profusion and variety of food offered for sale in these markets is astounding. The counters of the vegetable stalls are piled high with the reds, greens, and whites of fresh tomatoes, lettuce, and garlic. There are stalls that sell only olives, thirty or forty different varieties ranging in size from cherry pits to ping pong balls, each with its own unique taste. Butchers have their own sections in the markets, rows of brightly lit display cases. They offer a wide variety of meats. The rabbits, skinned, but with their heads still attached, are a particularly startling sight. Some people cook the whole animal, others have the butcher chop off the skinned head. The rabbits are stretched out on a bed of crushed ice with the tendons and muscles of their raw, skinned meat shining, their dead, glazed eyes like dark berries gleaming on their heads.

There are stalls where people sell nothing but dried cod, called *bacalao*. In another section are the fresh fish and shellfish vendors, with their wares displayed on mountains of ice. Even though there are a number of stalls with more or less the same inventories of vegetables, or meat, or seafood, each has slightly different prices and quality, and shoppers have their favorites. The markets of Barcelona are testimony to the good fortune of Catalans, who have a fertile soil and a well-populated sea at their disposal.

Such an embarrassment of agricultural and marine riches was not always the case. During the 1930s, and early '40s, well within living memory, hunger sat at many a table in Barcelona. People who grew up during those years still eat everything on their plates, because wasting food remains unthinkable. Food shortages during the civil war were so acute that there were people in Barcelona who died of malnutrition. Things were a little less desperate after the war ended, but food remained scarce for the next decade. People had ration cards for all kinds of provisions and, as a sacrifice for the general welfare, they were asked to forego dessert one day a week, and to do without meat on another.

Now, Juan Torres and his mother will not eat rabbit, because they remember the years when rabbits did *not* come with their heads on them, and what was sold under that name was often cat. "You ate it, and you didn't think about it, but it's not nice to remember now.

"We ate very basic food, things like potatoes, chick peas, and lentils, and everything was strictly rationed," Juan Torres told me one afternoon in the Joan Miró Park, where he was sitting with his elderly mother on a bench beside me.

The Miró park is a strange and lovely place. Strange because it is a large, six-square-block park of hard-packed dirt without grass; lovely because its walkways are lined with date palms and banana trees, giving it a lush and rich, tropical geometry. It is located between the Plaza de España and the Sants train station, and until the 1980s was the site of a large slaughterhouse.

Torres is a solidly-built, sixty-year-old man with a jowly face, bushy moustache, and iron-grey hair. His eighty-five-year-old mother is a small woman, white haired and blind. In front of us were some elderly men playing *petanca*, tossing, rolling, and cajoling their small steel cannonballs through the air and along the dirt. This same game is called *boules* in France and *bocce* in Italy, and is played everywhere around the Mediterranean by old men in parks. Our conversation was punctuated by the pleasing click that the balls made when they struck each other, or the thud as they came to earth out of the high tosses preferred by some players.

"You had a ration card for each thing, for vegetables, for potatoes, for bread. Each time you bought something they punched the card," Torres said. "Things got a little better after the civil war. Until then, you didn't even talk about meat. We didn't see meat from one week to the next. I don't think bread rationing stopped until 1951. You could go in and get a loaf a day, about two fingers wide and a hand long. In those days you ate what you could. Right, mother?"

There was nothing wrong with her hearing. She nodded her head in profile to me, sightlessly gazing toward the petanca players. Behind us loomed the twenty-four-foot-high colorful cement and mosaic sculpture, "Woman and Bird," done by Joan Miró, who was, along with surrealist Salvador Dalí, one of Catalonia's best-known artists. Miró created the immense, flowing sculpture for the spot on which it stood, overlooking the park of palms which bore his name.

The days of food shortages seem like ancient history when you stand in the middle of the Boqueria, and to Barcelonese born after 1960, food shortages *are* ancient history. Nowhere is the current abundance of food so evident as at the seafood stalls in the markets. There is no country in Europe where the taste for seafood equals that of Spain's, none that even comes close. Each Spaniard is estimated to eat over ninety pounds of fish and shellfish a year, compared to Britons, who each manage only about twenty pounds a year. The numbers are still lower for the United States, where each person eats a measly sixteen pounds annually.

"Stick with beef when you visit the United States, that's what I tell people," said Juan Martín Torrell, who owns and operates my neighborhood bodega with his wife. Last August they took a standard, three-week plane and bus tour with a group of other Catalans: New York, Chicago, San Francisco, Las Vegas, Los Angeles, Miami, back to New York and Barcelona.

"We were shocked at the poor quality of the seafood," he told me. "Both the kinds of seafood they eat and how they fix it are bad. Other than that, the food was fine. I couldn't believe how cheaply you could eat in the United States. I'll never forget being in Las Vegas and eating a delicious steak for two dollars. I just couldn't believe it. I'll never forget that. We stuck with beef, and ate very well."

The cost of living is so high in Spain that a lot of people who want a cheap vacation go to the United States, for the same reasons that North Americans used to vacation in Spain: food, hotels, shopping, and travel are all much cheaper than at home. Barcelonese who spend August in the States usually have only a couple of complaints: one is the ever-present threat of sudden violence, and the other is the quality of the seafood.

The Mediterranean still supports a remarkable variety of marine life and what it does not have, the Atlantic provides for Barcelona's markets from the coast of Galicia, or Basque waters. In the city, there are auctions down at the fish docks of Barceloneta twice each day, in the early morning and again in the evening, when fishermen come in with their catches. Each of Barcelona's covered markets has a dozen or more seafood stalls, and the variety displayed on the ice piled on each is astonishing: oysters; clams of different sizes; scallops; mussels; a profusion of shrimp and prawns; all manner and shape of fish ranging from sardines to mackerel with their toothy grins to tuna fish with heads the size of a human being's; a half-dozen different sizes of squishy squid; eels; and octopus. Each stall has a hanging scale, usually with a woman working behind it. Many are no longer young nor light on their feet;. yet, they stand for hours behind a heavy round chopping block at waist level, fileting, peeling, eviscerating, and scaling each customer's choices, able to make conversation while wielding a razor-sharp cleaver with amazing dexterity and speed.

There is almost nothing sold from fresh water, it all comes from the sea. An exception, oddly enough, is the Louisiana crayfish (called *Procamburus clarkii* by biologists and crawfish by Cajuns), which is usually offered for sale at one or two stalls as *cangrejo del rio*, or river crab, at a rock-bottom price. This is the same fierce, red crawfish that Cajuns like to eat by the pound, and that they boil up so flavorsomely with some ears of corn and whole potatoes.

Unfortunately, the crawfish have just about finished the job that pollution began of wiping out the native Catalan species. These white-clawed crayfish (*Austropotamobius pallipes*) could only survive in cool, fast-running mountain streams to begin with, and land development in Catalonia has drastically degraded their habitat. Even before the arrival of the Louisiana crawfish, there were fewer and fewer of the native species. Unfortunately, they were also vulnerable to a bacterial disease that did not affect their Cajun cousins, but that traveled with them to Spain, and decimated what small stocks remained.

The original batches of swamp crawfish were brought from the Atchafalaya basin in southern Louisiana to the southwestern province of Estremadura in 1974. It was an aquacultural experiment to see if poor farmers in a rural area could raise the crawfish and sell them on the Spanish seafood market. It seemed like a good plan: the Louisiana crawfish did not need clean water, nor attention, to thrive.

The idea was strongly pushed by aquaculturists at Louisiana State University and by the state's agricultural department, both of whom promoted aggressive campaigns during the 1960s and '70s. They worked hard to develop markets for the mudbugs, as Cajuns lovingly call their crawfish. The animal has been sent around the world, to places as disparate as Sweden and China. James Avault, a professor at LSU and an aquaculture specialist, helped sell the idea to the Spanish Ministry of Agriculture.

In fact, for a number of years, Louisiana practiced a policy of crawfish imperialism, according to Raul Escosa Serrano, a young, bearded biologist who worked for the Catalan government. "For a long time, Americans have been interested in spreading the Louisiana crayfish around the world. They have represented it as a source of abundant protein that grows rapidly and cheaply, but wherever they have introduced them there have been unforeseen consequences."

Crawfish being the way they are, the original stock brought to Spain in 1974 began to proliferate and left the confines of the ponds where they had been planted in southwestern Estremadura. Soon, they were moving northeastward through Andalusia, and their descendants reached Catalonia in about 1983. Their relatively rapid diffusion over more than a thousand miles of Spain will surprise no one who has ever seen a group of determined crawfish crossing a highway in southern Louisiana to get to a ditch on the other side.

When the mudbugs reached Catalonia, they settled in the Ebro River delta, the region's prime rice-growing area, about ninety miles south of Barcelona. A substantial amount of the Ebro delta is set aside as a national park, but there are also about fifty thousand acres broken up into small rice farms where each farmer cultivates ten to twenty underwater acres. By the late 1980s, these farmers were increasingly plagued by crawfish. The area has just about the same weather and environment as southern Louisiana, and the mudbugs settled in easily. They made their homes, which for crawfish are burrows, in the rice fields, and proceeded to undermine the delicate infrastructure of the fields, destroying their ability to hold water when flooded in the spring. Suddenly, rice farmers had a brand-new pest, and they could not find a way to exterminate it.

The mudbugs continue to thrive despite the fact that the Catalan parliament has designated them a public enemy, and called for their extermination. It has appropriated a little money and told the Department of Agriculture to employ whatever means are necessary to exterminate it. Biologist Raul Escosa was given the job of developing and implementing a means of confining and controlling the population, but he tells me he has still not found a way to do so.

"There was an open, ready-made ecological niche waiting here for *Procamburus clarkii*," said Escosa, when I talked to him in his laboratory near the small Ebro delta town of Deltebre. "Normally a species has a very difficult time adapting to a new environment, but the crawfish have found an ample supply of everything they need: food, spaces and habitat.

"They have a high reproductive level and there are no predators here that can keep their numbers down. The waterfowl eat them, but the birds hunt during the day and crawfish are most active in the evenings. They are becoming a serious problem."

Escosa and his colleagues have tried a number of weapons in an effort to dislodge the mudbugs, including injecting lethal gas down the burrows, but, so far, nothing has proven feasible. "I can't see how we're going to elminate this crawfish. It's a remarkably hardy species, and it spreads too rapidly. All we can hope is to control the population, and we haven't started doing that yet."

It would have been some consolation if James Avault's original, optimistic predictions about the market value of crawfish in Spain had been correct, but they were not. Neither Catalans nor people from the rest of Spain were drawn to a crustacean harvested from the standing, turbid, muddy, knee-high water of a rice field. If they are going to be peeling the shell off of something to eat, they prefer one of the astonishing variety of fresh shrimp and prawns heaped in high mounds on their beds of ice at the markets.

Monday, January 20

Every morning on my way to buy provisions at the covered San Antonio market, a few blocks from my piso, I pass a half-dozen big, scarlet, Wanted posters pasted on walls. They are all over the city, in metro stations and reproduced daily in newspapers. The posters display two unsmiling, intense faces of men in their mid-thirties: the two ETA members who police allege are behind the recent wave of terrorist killings in Barcelona, which began with those of the two policemen on December 13. Each morning I feel a little tingle of fear that we innocent shoppers in the crowded aisles of the Mercado San Antonio would make a good terrorist target.

Within these first three weeks of the new year, the duo has been accused in the killings of four more people, three in Barcelona and one in Valencia. Among them are an Air Force commander and his assistant, whose car was raked by gunfire in broad daylight in the middle of a street at the foot of Montjuich, the hill that is crowned with the Olympic stadium. Those killings took place in what will be the heart of the Games, the maximum security zone. Almost as if the terrorists wanted to let the world know they can strike there now, and may do so again.

"ETA was not in any way directing these recent attacks against the Olympic Games," said Eladeo Jareño, a spokesperson for the Department of the Interior, which was reponsible for overseeing security arrangements for the Games. "These were unsophisticated attacks, quickly and casually executed against anyone in uniform, with very little advance preparation or planning. They could not have been carried out under the security arrangements that will be in place during the Games.

"I don't mean to say that ETA would not like very much to have a little of the international echo that would come from an action against the Olympics, but at this time we do not have any indication of a direct connection between the recent murders and the Games."

Until now, residents of the city have willed themselves to believe the authorities' reassurances that the Games will not create security problems. Now people are getting nervous, jumpy, security-conscious, worried that the city might be in for a long string of terrorist acts right up to the Games. Seven months of ETA shootings and car bombings would be a high price to pay for being the Olympic city.

"There is no need for people to be concerned," Jareño told me when I went to see him in his office, shortly after the Wanted posters went up on the walls. "Security leading to, and during, the sixteen days of the Olympics will be unprecedented. An extra one thousand police have been in the city since New Year's, and they are only the first wave of fifteen thousand who will be brought from other places by the time the Games began on July 25. These, added to the fifteen thousand representatives of law and order normally in Barcelona, including municipal, regional, and national police, will create an immense and highly visible force.

"I am positive that there will be no terrorist attacks against the Games, and that as we move closer and closer to them, acts of terrorism will diminish and disappear. This is because we have elaborated a security plan that has grown out of many meetings and consultations with international experts, and it will be completely effective. We are maintaining a constant contact at high levels with countries like France and the United States, and both residents and visitors can feel perfectly secure in Barcelona."

This has translated into a noticeably increased police presence in the streets. Already there are cops in every metro station, wearing bulky, bullet-proof vests over their uniform shirts, with automatic weapons slung across their chests. The sound of helicopters flying low above my building, the whump-whump roar of rotor blades shaking the walls, has become a daily annoyance. Every hundred yards along the Ramblas, a pair of police stroll, and the back streets of the Raval are full of them, night and day, stopping anyone they deem suspicious and asking for their documents. More and more police seem to be arriving with nothing to do except make their presence felt. Anyone with a dark skin wearing anything less respectable than a sportcoat is liable to be stopped. I'm used to the nuisance and carry ample identification.

Last week, I was accosted by a couple of strolling Guardia Nacional, while I was standing, waiting to meet a friend, under the Arc de Triomfe. Much like the one in Paris, the Arc is at the top of a lovely two-block pedestrian esplanade lined with palm trees that runs down to the Ciutadella Park. It is an easy, prominent place to meet someone. The cops were wearing bullet-proof vests and loosely holding big shotguns, painted black, down by their sides. What, one asked me, was I doing standing here?

He kept eyeing me suspiciously, while the other filled out something called a Foreigner's Information Form, taking down my passport number, asking me for my mother's and father's names. Something about calling out the parents' names to a couple of cops who could not even pronounce them annoyed me.

"I can wait here for someone, can't I? It's a public park, right?" I asked. They just looked at me balefully, returned my passport, and walked away.

A walk through the Boqueria around 10 A.M. on any weekday is enough to convince even the most casual observer that Catalans, at least those in the capital city, spend a lot of time and money on their food. All that time and money notwithstanding, bad food has killed thousands more Spaniards in the past twenty-five years than terrorists. Enforcement of standards by the public agencies charged with overseeing food production and food handling was notoriously lax under Franco, and has improved only slowly since the dictator died. Over the years, this has had some predictably tragic results.

Now, 233 people have been hospitalized in Barcelona and seventeen other Catalan cities and towns, ill from the effects of an excessive amount of clembuterol in beef liver. Clembuterol is a growth hormone, which increases muscle growth. It is related to anabolic steroids, and is one of the drugs most frequently found in Olympic athletes who fail doping tests. When given to animals, it increases a farmer's profit, because it takes less time and feed to grow a cow to marketable size. Its use is against both Spain's laws and those of the EC.

Clembuterol can be used in amounts significant enough to affect bovine growth without being detected by a person who eats the meat, although the experience of many unfortunate athletes has demonstrated that anabolic steroids pose a threat to human beings in the long run. The 233 Catalans who have been hospitalized with shortness of breath, racing hearts, and headaches after eating calf's liver were the victims of an exceptional greed, which had led two slaughterhouses to use extremely large amounts of clembuterol to fatten their cattle before the kill. The dosage was so high that the animals' livers retained a toxic quantity, which was passed on to consumers even after the liver was cooked.

While only two slaughterhouses have been implicated in the poisonings, the press reports that police investigations have uncovered a well-established mafia in the livestock industry that manufactures and sells clembuterol. Farmers and veterinarians, perhaps worried about eventual prosecution, have come forward, repentent, to testify that there was widespread clembuterol use throughout Catalonia's cattle industry. Twenty thousand pounds of clembuterol have been confiscated, and twenty-six people arrested. Among them are the veterinarians on duty at the two slaughterhouses where the cattle, overloaded with clembuterol, were inspected and approved for human consumption.

When news of the clembuterol poisonings broke in the press, the sales of liver fell through the floor, and beef sales in general diminished drastically. People all over Spain have seen some pretty horrible examples of what unscrupulous food producers will do for a little extra profit, and they try not to take any chances.

One of Spain's worst public health disasters of the century happened in 1981. More than twenty-five thousand people from a wide area around Madrid were poisoned by something they ate. Over one hundred fifty of them died almost immediately. Thousands more were suddenly and permanently disabled, central nervous systems damaged beyond repair. The common afflictions included impaired respiratory function, or limbs becoming too weak to use, or fingers that contracted and stiffened into claws. These effects were permanent.

The disease first came to the public's attention on May 6, 1981—when an eight-year-old became the first person to die from it. Thousands were stricken in the weeks that followed, but by the end of May the government still did not know what was causing the epidemic, and had no answers for an anxious public. Finally, on June 10, it was announced that the cause of the illness had been established: adulterated cooking oil.

A widespread scheme had been uncovered whereby the manufacturers of cooking oil were buying cheap rapeseed oil intended for industrial use and mixing it with cooking oil. The adulterated product was then sold by men going door to door or selling it at markets from their cars. Many people in poorer neighborhoods bought their cooking oil from these ambulatory vendors because it was cheaper than buying oil in stores.

The case against the cooking oil was not airtight, because not all those who consumed adulterated oil got sick, and not all those who got sick had consumed the oil. To this day, there are people who believe a tomato pesticide, an organophosphate used too near harvest, was the culprit. Nevertheless, by the end of the investigation twenty-one people involved with the cooking oil scam were convicted, including four owners of companies who were each condemned to thirty years in prison.

By this year, over seven hundred people have died from the effects of the poisoning. Thousands more will pass the rest of their foreshortened lives in poor health. The legal consequences are still not wholly resolved, and the government has not still not decided how much, if any, compensation it will pay the victims. Meanwhile, affected survivors are paid a disability pension between $400 and $650 a month. Their haunted eyes, hollow faces, wheezes, wasted muscles, and twisted hands serve as a constant reminder to those who see them of just what poisoned food can do to a human body.

Over this past decade, what Spaniards eat has changed partly due to caution, partly due to a new consciousness about health food and things like cholesterol, and partly due to the invasion of fast food. Ten years ago, when people came into a bar late in the afternoon and wanted a little something to eat, something to tide them over until the 10 P.M.

supper hour, they ordered a *tapa*. This is a small plate of something, and can range from olives to sausage to anchovies to shrimp to octopus or any one of a hundred items. Each cafe has its own choices displayed on the bar. While those made with eggs or mayonnaise can be a public health hazard in themselves, tapas are one of the great culinary delights of Spain. Barcelona is not considered prime tapas territory—that distinction is accorded to Madrid and Seville—but there are plenty of places to get a toothsome tapa. A glass of sherry and a tapa is a great late-afternoon pleasure, a break that provides a delicious lift.

These days, customers can choose between tapas and a package of Ruffles potato chips. The Roof-lays, as they're pronounced in Spanish, come on a plate in a colorful, aluminum package, the self-same package that can be found all over the world in bars from Texas to Taiwan, Paris to Prague, with nothing changed but the language. That, and the price. A small bag of Ruffles in a Barcelona bar costs almost a dollar. While it might be true that Ruffles are subjected to more rigid quality control than a tapa, there is something sad about the sight of a Spaniard sitting at a bar, squared off to open a pack of potato chips on a plate, a taste imported from the New World. The enslaver enslaved, caught and captured.

Consumer cuisine has made other conquests on Barcelona's restaurant scene. Among the fast-food brands represented are McDonalds, Burger King, Kentucky Fried Chicken, and six Domino's Pizza outlets. The owner of one of the Domino's franchises said he was doing a big business among the Catalans, and that pizza was the best fast food to be selling in Barcelona.

"A lot of people here have told me they think the burgers and chicken are dirty, they're not interested in it. They don't like the way it looks or tastes," said Mike Storm, who was himself an Olympian, having competed in the 1984 pentathalon in Los Angeles. "On the other hand they love our pizza because we use all local, fresh ingredients.

"What I make here are not like the Domino's pizzas you eat in the States, with hamburger meat that is more preservative than meat. We use all natural ingredients, and none of our products contains preservatives. People in Barcelona really pay attention to what they eat. I don't think of this as a restaurant, I think of it as a manufacturing facility for high-quality catered dinners."

Storm, a Harvard Business School graduate, spent two years flying back and forth between Barcelona and the States, crunching numbers and scouting the territory before finally committing to this venture. Now he's wondering why he waited so long. He opened his first Domino's Pizza store three months ago, and sales are far ahead of what he had projected. His business is on a corner in the Horta neighborhood, a long way from the center of town, a place where no tourists are likely to be found. It is a typical, densely packed Barcelona residential neighborhood, and Storm estimates that within a mile's radius there are two hundred fifty thousand potential pizza eaters.

"Madrid's neighborhoods are also very dense, but I chose to come to Barcelona because in Madrid the idea of eating dinner at home is a little shameful," said Storm. "Madrileños like to go out and have a good time, and to be at home is kind of a failure to them.

"People in Barcelona like to go out too, but they have an incredibly strong tradition of home and family in Catalonia, and they like to eat together. These are people who like the idea of calling out for a pizza, and eating it around the television."

Home delivery of pizza caught on in Barcelona beginning in the late 1980s, and Storm has plenty of competition. The five other Domino's franchises in the city are outside his "service area," but there are fifty or sixty other take-out pizza stores that aren't. At night, the city's streets abound with their delivery boys whizzing around town delivering pies on their *motos*.

Storm started with ten such motor scooters, and he has just bought four more. There is competition, he said, but much less than there would be for the same number of potential customers in the States. By 1996, he plans to have forty Domino's Pizza parlors across the length and breadth of northern Spain, and estimated he would have a potential clientele of almost twenty million people.

Despite the success of pizza delivery services, fast food has enjoyed only limited acceptance in Barcelona, appealing primarily to the young, and those with little time to prepare food. It has not done much to change the overall eating habits of the Barcelonese or to reduce business at the city's markets. There is a deep tradition of Catalan cuisine, based on that same profusion of food that is offered for sale in the Boqueria. Vegetables, beef, pork, and seafood are all used extensively, along with the ubiquitous garlic and olive oil, to create a large and savory body of

dishes. (Catalans, like most Spaniards, do not like hot, picante food, although the growing number of ethnic restaurants in the cities is very
slowly changing that.)

The two big meals in the day are *la comida*, the largest, eaten somewhere between 2 and 4 P.M., and *la cena*, supper, served after 9 P.M. In
between, come stops for a bite in the middle of the morning, a *tapa* in
the late afternoon, sandwiches, and pastries whenever the urge strikes.
Cafes all over the city offer a midday comida according to a fixed-price
menu. Nowadays, $8 will buy you a choice among four or five different
dishes for a first course and again for a second, along with bread, a glass
of wine, dessert, and a cup of coffee.

Many traditional Catalan dishes are found on every neighborhood
restaurant's menu: *espinacs a la catalana*, for instance, spinach sauteed with
pine nuts and raisins, or *mongetes amb botifarra*, white beans and the tasty
botifarra sausage. There is a Catalan recipe for almost every food en-
countered in a market, and the cuisine can be sampled in restaurants ranging from a corner cafe to a place that has been taking two or three hours
to get a customer through a midday meal since the eighteenth century.

A good place for seafood is the wide street at the edge of Barceloneta, the Paseo Nacional. Across from the port, it features the reincar-
nation of a number of the small restaurants that were razed along the
beach during the city's Olympic renovation in 1990. Another great place
to go for Catalan cooking is outside Barcelona in one of the old farm-
houses, called *masias*, that have been converted into restaurants. There
are a number in the Collserola hills just outside the city. After an excellent meal, people can take a walk through the countryside.

In addition to the standard and expansive year-round repertoire
of Catalan dishes, some mark the season. One flavorful example is the
calçot, an oversized green onion available only in late winter. These are
grilled until charred on their thin outside skins. Then they are brought
to the table, six or eight on a plate, along with a special kind of thick
sauce, called *romesco* in Catalan, which is made from a combination of
tomatoes, almonds, and garlic. The calçot is dipped in the sauce, and
stuffed into the mouth—messy and delicious. They are only available in
February and March, and everyone has their favorite restaurant or cafe
for eating calçots while they last.

Winter's first days are accompanied by the appearance on many street corners of little huts where chestnuts and sweet potatoes are roasted on charcoal braziers. When spring comes, these disappear and the *horchaterías* open. An *horchata* is a cold, sweet, thin beverage, like a watery almond milkshake, which originated in Valencia. Down come the metal shutters, up all winter, and once again passers-by can stop in to pay about $1.75 for a tall, cold glass, which is also sold in liters to take home.

What Jews did and did not eat during the Middle Ages, and how they prepared it, set them apart from their Gentile neighbors. Jews were routinely accused of macabre eating practices, particularly around Holy Week, a favorite charge being that they kidnapped and ate Christian babies. Another common allegation was that they stole the sacred host from churches and ate it in blasphemous rituals. What was true, of course, was that the medieval Jews kept kosher. Every aljama had kosher butchers, and non-kosher products were not for sale in the Jewish barrio.

Food played a major role in the Inquisition, and a great deal of attention was paid by the inquisitors to what conversos had or had not eaten, when their guilt was being deliberated. Among the accusations leveled at conversos was that they refused to eat pork or seafood, or that witnesses had seen them keeping kosher.

There are a number of such instances recounted in Yitzhak Baer's two-volume work, *A History of the Jews in Christian Spain*, widely regarded as an authoritative text on the subject. He writes about a woman named María González, for instance, whose husband was identified by another converso, under torture, as someone who regularly supplied kosher meat to Jews. Her husband fled before he could be hauled in front of the Inquisition, and the authorities relaxed María González in his stead. In another instance, a converso named Ferdinand Husillo confessed that he regularly visited Jewish homes and ate kosher food there. He also admitted he had practiced the Jewish ritual of mourning by sitting on the floor and eating eggs and fish. He, too, was relaxed.

It was not only what a person ate that could get them killed by the Inquisition, but also what they did not eat. Many conversos came to the attention of the Inquisition when a nosy neighbor or false friend noticed that they never ate shellfish or swine. Conversos were routinely fed pork and shrimp to see whether their conversions were holding. By extension, the consumption of these foods became an expression of Catholic faith.

While there were differences between what Jews and Catholics ate in the Middle Ages, they shared basically the same cuisine, made from mostly the same ingredients. In fact, the Catalan cuisine was one of the few things the Sefarad took with them when they left Catalonia. In those disastrous four months in 1492 between the time the edict of Expulsion was announced and put into effect, the Jews had to sell just about everything and were able to carry only a few possessions to their new homes in foreign lands like North Africa, or Turkey. But they took language and a lot of recipes.

This Catalan food was bred in the bones of the Catalan Sefarad. For centuries after the Expulsion, their descendants were eating these same dishes, and their recipes were passed directly down through generations. Medieval Catalan recipes are still being prepared by Jews in places as far apart as Istanbul and Buenos Aires, dishes like stuffed tomatoes with stuffed peppers, and a chard puree with bechamel sauce.

"The food my family ate in Turkey in 1900 was almost entirely Spanish cuisine," said Alberto Arditti. "And not so much Spanish as Catalan, dishes you can still get in Catalonia today. When I first came to Barcelona in 1924, I lived in a *pensión*, a good pensión, where they provided meals as well as a room, and those meals were very familiar to me. I had no trouble getting used to the food here, because I had been eating it all my life."

Jews, like everyone else, endured food shortages and rationing, during and after the civil war. "There were many bodies in the streets," Arditti said. "People starved. I, like many others, survived, but there were also those who died of hunger, and those who died in the fighting.

"For food, I had the advantage of not being a smoker. I would trade tobacco coupons for a certain number of kilos of potatoes, and I would take half the potatoes to the *aceitero* and trade them for some cooking oil. You survived, but you didn't have much. It was something, and you weren't going to die of hunger. Don't talk about kosher. In those days you ate what you could."

It was easier to keep kosher during the Middle Ages than it is now.

In the medieval aljama, any food shop would be kosher, but now there is only one kosher butcher in the city, in a shop across the street from the synagogue on the Calle Avenir. The butcher shop has been open since 1954, the year the house of worship was built. People go to the synagogue to buy their boxes of *matzoh*, the unleavened bread eaten during the Passover season. There, a secretary sells boxes from a stack in a corner of the director's office.

The 1992 congregation is usually defined by its members as conservative, neither as strict and rigorous as orthodox Jews, nor as liberal and lax as reform Jews. Many members of the congregation keep kosher in their homes, to a degree, but that may mean no more than refraining from putting pork or shellfish on their tables. Outside the home is Barcelona, a city where the most delicious plates of these animals are regularly set before a person and it is not easy to abjure them.

Carlos Schorr is an engineer, born and raised in Barcelona. His father was an Ashkenazic Jew who came to the city in 1927 from Poland. Carlos has served on the executive board of the congregation and been a part of the Jewish community all his life. He said many people claim to keep kosher, but that few do so in a strict, Biblical sense.

"We have all styles represented," he told me. "There are those who adhere strictly to the rules of kosher, but I doubt they would even amount to ten percent.

"Then there are the people who keep kosher at home, a kind of 'folkloric' kosher, and they come mostly from North Africa. In the street they eat what they want. If they are eating in a restaurant that makes a good paella with shrimp, that's what they'll eat. At home, with their children, they keep kosher, but even the kids eat what they want when they're outside. I think probably thirty percent of the congregation falls into this category. The rest do not make any effort to keep kosher."

For a lingering sense of what the world of cabarets along the Parallel felt like in its heyday, eat a late supper at one of the little cafes around El Molino that specialize in serving, around 1 A.M., the people who come in to get a little something when the evening's first show ends. These places fill up with Runyonesque characters, faces battered by a lifetime of hard knocks, voices hoarsened by decades of cigarettes and cognac or *anis*. Among the late diners are men with their women's makeup still on, dancers, chanteuses, comics, bookies, hustlers, agents, grifters, and a shoal of slightly sinister folks who take their sustenance from these waters.

Immediately after Franco died, cabarets became even more popular than they had been while he was alive, according to Adrián Tanquía, who owned the Barcelona de Noche during the 1980s. With no one coming to censor their scripts, the shows became more and more extravagant and suggestive. There was work up and down the Parallel for transvestites, and many straight Barcelonese spent part of a Saturday night at a cabaret to enjoy some risque entertainment in the new, more open Spain.

"A lot of middle-class people came regularly," said Tanquía, when I talked to him one evening over a beer at a bar in the barrio chino. He was an Argentine who had first come to Barcelona as a dancer in the early 1970s, while Franco was still alive. When he acquired the Barcelona de Noche in 1982, people were still enjoying the first flush of freedom.

"Everyone was still learning about liberty. People would go to an opera at the Liceo and then come to our club afterwards, dressed in their evening clothes. They liked it because it was a transgression of their social norms. Salvador Dalí often came in, we frequently had celebrities. We had room for four hundred fifty, and it was full a lot of nights."

It was not long, however, before total access to serious pornography made the cabarets seem awfully tame. Their floor shows paled in comparison to the live sex shows available for about the same price at places like the Cafe Bagdad, a Parallel music hall that converted to hardcore porn with the advent of democracy. The old-fashioned cabaret spectacle ceased delighting people, they were no longer satisfied with suggestion, nor drawn by the mix of dance and bawdy humor. The costumes of spangles, sequins, and plumes left the new generation cold. The audience that continues to come to the clubs along the Parallel is not a young one, and it is being winnowed by death each year.

"The Barcelona de Noche was a real music hall in the old sense, and after the transition to democracy there was no more mystery," Tanquía told me. "The idea of coming to see transvestites, of watching men in women's clothes wasn't as attractive and exotic as it used to be. What we did at the Barcelona de Noche was to mix parody, music, and beauty. It was a magic place in the heart of the Parallel."

The Barcelona de Noche is gone, expropriated by the ayuntamiento for a small plot of grassy park, as part of an effort to open up the old city to some light and air in preparation for the Olympic crowds. When I talked with him, Tanquía was still haggling with the municipal authorities over the compensation he was to receive. Most of the other cabarets have also disappeared from the Parallel, victims of the sexual revolution.

Cabaret has not entirely disappeared from Barcelona's nightlife spectrum, however. La Belle Epoque is a theater with comfortable banquette seating and a cabaret stage show. About $40 buys two drinks and a show, which runs a couple of hours. It includes a half-dozen extravagantly staged dance pieces featuring the eight house danseuses (four of whom are natural women, four of whom are not) along with a comedian who comes on midway through the program. Plus Dolly Van Doll, the Belle Epoque's owner and mistress of ceremonies. The stage is equipped for many kinds of special effects and there is a four-member house band.

Dolly Van Doll invited me to interview her one night in her dressing room before the evening's show. She was born in northern Italy, but left home as a teenager to pursue a life in cabaret. Compactly built and sturdy, she had started life as a man, but has been a woman for twenty years. The night we talked, she was wearing a robe and sitting at a dressing table in front of a long, high mirror, with light bulbs around its edges. She put on her makeup and talked to me in the mirror. I watched as an attractive and unadorned, blonde Italian woman with a fashionable, short hairstyle, transformed herself into a heavily made-up, bewigged, bejeweled, brassy, and glittering creation in a white gown with a deep cleavage. The tango-like strains of "Hernando's Hideaway" drifted up into the room from a trumpet on the club floor below. Occasionally, she stopped doing her delicate work with rouge, glitter, colored pencils, and lipstick to get up, cross the room, and look down through a small window to count the crowd.

She did not want to discuss the change of gender she had undergone many years before. "Ninety-five percent of the people who come here have no idea of any of that part of my life. I never wanted to exploit it. People come here because they appreciate me now and the entertainment we provide them, and the beautiful atmosphere of La Belle Epoque."

Van Doll opened the Belle Epoque in 1981, and it was immediately successful, drawing crowds of both Barcelonese and tourists. It is located in an upscale neighborhood, on Calle Muntaner near the Avenida Diagonal, far from the more dubious neighborhoods around the Parallel. However, Van Doll is no stranger to the Parallel—from 1972 to 1976, she was a co-owner of the Barcelona de Noche, before Adrián Tanquía bought it.

"The club was a wreck when my partner and I took it over in 1972," she told me in a husky voice and charming Italian accent. "We completely redid everything, even the bathrooms and dressing rooms, and I created a show that was a success. The place was full of people in tuxedos and evening gowns. We turned it into a very popular nightspot."

Just before the socialists came to power, she opened La Belle Epoque. "Everything changed so fast after Franco died, it was almost impossible to believe. There we were at Barcelona de Noche, we were about the most erotic thing going on, and within three months after he died you could go to a club and see bestiality—three women onstage with a burro. That's how it was.

"My club has always been dignified, I wanted to present things that were artistic and beautiful. I have never allowed pornography here, this is not what we do. Things may be more open now under the socialists, but when Franco was alive the times were better for theaters like La Belle Epoque, or Barcelona de Noche, because there was more audience for the shows we put on."

The end of the dictatorship paved the way for today's sex shops and porn palaces, and it spelled the beginning of the end for most of the city's cabarets, along with many so-called "waitress" bars. These were places where men came to meet women, buy them drinks, talk with them, and see what developed. The women stayed behind the bar and, thus, were classified as legal waitresses, not illegal prostitutes.

By now, of course, there are no laws regulating the presence of single women on either side of a bar, and they are free to sit in front of the bar and sip something while waiting for a man to come in and approach. The number of bars, however, where that is done professionally is declining steadily. Pepe, a Barcelona native, owns such a bar in an upscale neighborhood not too many blocks from the Belle Epoque. Life under Franco was more diverting, he said.

"I'm not saying I supported Franco, or that I support the socialists," he told me one night at his bar. "I've never had any interest whatsoever in politics. But, in Franco's day, encounters between men and women had mystery, elegance, grace. And there was a happiness, an *alegría* that isn't there anymore."

In the last years of the dictatorship, from 1972 to 1975, things were clearly changing, Pepe said. In those years, he owned a place that was registered as a sports club, but actually was a sex club. It was open twenty-four hours a day, with a restaurant and bar, as well as a sauna, jacuzzi, mini-disco, and three rooms with waterbeds and pornographic videos. He paid money to the police to be left in peace, and the two hundred–plus members of his club paid an enrollment fee, and monthly dues after that.

When the dictator died, Pepe branched out, and started a partner-swapping club that, according to him, was an excellent business. People arrived with their spouses or partners, and switched off with someone else for a roll in one of the beds on the premises. To manage a club where people come to go to bed with someone else's husband or wife— there are a half dozen such clubs now—requires the skills of a diplomat, Pepe said.

"That's a hard kind of club to run. It can be stressful. In order to have it work you have to keep it subtle. You have to keep an air of respect between people, which can be difficult after they've been fucking each other's spouses."

He decided to sell that operation, because he was getting older and wanted something less demanding. That something was the waitress bar at which we sat and talked. There were four nicely dressed women also there, two with older, well-dressed men beside them. I had watched these middle-aged men in coats and ties come through the door, cross

over to the woman of their choice, and order drinks. Conversation between the pairs was quiet, there was occasional laughter, but nothing
raucous. Drinks were about $20 apiece. Pepe told me he made the entire
price of the man's drink, and half the woman's. She kept the other half,
and also got a salary.

"The only thing I do in here is serve drinks," he said. "If they want
to do anything else, they'll have to do it somewhere else. When I started
this place there were probably three hundred other bars like it in
Barcelona. Now, there are probably about fifty left. Most of them have
closed, and more are closing all the time.

"Men used to go out at night, meet each other for a few drinks and
a good time. Now they stay home and watch television. Their wives are
all working and telling their husbands what they can and can't do.
Young men used to make a habit of coming to places like this, but no
more. Now it's an aging crowd and less of them each year. I got this
place in 1981, and I had thirty women working here. Now, there are
seven."

Pepe looked to be in his mid-fifties, with thinning brown hair and
a slight paunch. He sat at a corner of the bar all night long, with a Coke
in front of him; a gold bracelet on one wrist, a watch with a thick, gold
band on the other. He was casually but expensively dressed. All the time
he was talking to me, he seemed entirely absorbed in our conversation,
but he did not miss a thing that was going on at the bar, interrupting
himself every so often to issue an instruction to the barman.

"For me, this life is all right," he said. "I had a heart attack eight
years ago, and all I want is a quiet place like this where I can work without too much stress and still keep food on my family's table. But, I'll tell
you one thing: democracy has not made life in Barcelona any more fun.
On the contrary. Where's the mystery? Where's the grace? The fun is
gone. These days we're free. But free for what? Free to criticize Franco.
Who's dead.

"And, free to live in a teats-and-ass democracy. Big deal."

CHAPTER SIX

Old Plagues & New

Tuesday, February 18

It is twilight, crepescule, almost dark, the last of the day's light dying in the air. I'm walking on the Calle de la Merced, a narrow cobblestone street near the port, with the central post office at one end, and the Cathedral of Our Lady of Mercy, for whom the street was named, at the other. It is one of many streets in this part of the barrio gótico that date from medieval times and still feel like it. A pedestrian gets a visceral sense of what it would have been like to be alive then, walking down a fourteenth-century street at dusk.

I am coming back from the post office, full from a highly satisfying pit stop at one of the dark old bars along this street that sell plates of crusty bread and strong cabrales cheese, accompanied by glasses of cider. There are three or four of these places in the space of a block. They are like bars in a Brueghel painting, with huge casks mounted up on sturdy racks, ancient beams running across high ceilings, shadowy recesses where toothless, florid customers sit drinking at rough wooden tables. The cider can only be considered properly aerated and acceptable after the bartender has poured it over his shoulder from the bottle, through the air and into a glass held in his other hand behind his waist. The cheese is as pungent as only good cabrales can be. Hams hang from the blackened wooden ceiling beams. These places are redolent of age, cheese, and spilled wine soaked into wood.

I am walking along in the cold, clear air, savoring the aftertaste of the cheese. A skinny young man, with a mop of black hair fallen over his eyes, is squatting on the sidewalk, with his back against the wall of the cathedral. His head is bent in utmost concentration, teeth closed down on the corners of a dirty red bandana wrapped tightly around his bicep as he coaxes up a vein, thin syringe poised and ready in his other hand; a needle into a forearm vein, oblivious to passers-by. Here, against the wall of the Cathedral of Our Lady of Mercy, is a retail consumer, an end-user in one of the oldest and most profitable multinational industries, the drug trade.

There was virtually no drug trade nor drug problem in Spain during the years when Franco kept the nation isolated from the rest of the world. It was not until the technocrats began opening the country's markets and borders to the outside that the seeds of a drug problem were sown. The technocrats were the younger generation of middle-class executives who began to shape economic policy for Franco in the 1960s. They allowed an import market to develop; made it much easier for foreign companies to invest in Spain; and began an aggressive campaign to capture tourist business. While the technocrats remained loyal to Franco and, above all, to the Catholic church, they felt Spain had to change, or else it would join the ranks of the perennially underdeveloped nations of the world.

For twenty years under the dictator, the economy had deteriorated, staying afloat thanks only to the remittances from foreign countries sent back by immigrant workers. It was not until 1954 that the average yearly wage inside Spain even returned to its pre-civil-war level of twenty years before. The economy was in desperate need of change, and the technocrats applied some drastic free market measures. Their success was tremendous, and resulted in what were called "the years of development," from 1961 to 1973. Average income quadrupled during those years. The number of people in the country with refrigerators grew from four percent to sixty-six percent. In 1959, one in every hundred Spaniards owned a car. By 1973, it was one in ten.

Tourism fueled Spain's growing economy. In 1953, about 700,000 people visited the country, according to figures from the National Institute of Statistics. Twenty years later, in 1973, the number was fifty times higher to about 35 million. Spanish tourism's best year was 1988, when some 54 million visited. There is widespread optimism that 1992 will surpass that with both the Expo in Seville and the Olympics in Barcelona as drawing cards. Spain needs a good tourist year, because in 1991 the Gulf War and the rising price of goods and services combined to keep visitors away, and only about 35 million came, about the same as two decades earlier. The future of tourism in Spain is uncertain. Other sunny shores are much cheaper, in Greece and Portugal, for instance, and they are drawing away many of the people who tanned themselves on the Costa del Sol.

For many years, however, Spain was the undisputed European favorite among tourists. They were initially attracted in the 1960s by aggressive promotions, focusing on the cheap prices and the beautiful weather. In addition to the vacationers who came for a couple of weeks of sunshine at low prices, many thousands of older people, mostly from high-tax, cold, wet countries like England, retired to Spain. Most of them settled on the southern Mediterranean coast, pumping a lot of money into the construction and service sectors, and bringing a lot of foreign exchange with them in the form of monthly pensions. With what was an extremely modest sum in England, a retired couple could live nicely in a flat by the sea on the Costa del Sol.

Tourism was one of the first spots of color in Franco's dull grey regime. Many Barcelonese remember the excitement and titillation of seeing bikini-clad tourists from northern Europe on their beaches. The Spaniards living inland read about them in the newpapers and the gossip magazines. Spanish women were forbidden by law to wear bikinis, but it was not practical to try and prohibit French or Swedish women, for instance, from donning as little as possible. They had, after all, paid substantial sums of money to come for the sun, and the pleasure of feeling it on as much of their bodies as was minimally acceptable. There were other countries competing for tourist revenues by offering sun at cheap prices, such as Yugoslavia and Italy, where there was no objection to women wearing bikinis, and the Spaniards had to agree not to legally harass foreign women who chose to do so.

"For people of my age who lived through the 'tourist' boom, those foreign women were really something," said Jaume Riera, the director of the archives of Aragon, who was born in 1941. "There was a widely accepted image of Swedish women as lascivious, easy, blonde, and beautiful. When you told your friends, 'I met a Swede,' it meant you had met a foreigner, the kind of attractive woman who would wear a bikini and be easy to win. It's an archetype that my generation had.

"Men and women reacted differently, of course. Men wanted to meet such a woman, and the presence of these foreign women in Spain was exciting to them. However, Spanish women felt that the foreigners offered unfair competition."

Once those bodies were allowed to blossom on the beaches, there was no turning back. Spain rapidly became Europe's favorite vacation spot, and the sleepy fishing villages along the Mediterranean became one of the most developed stretches of coastline in the world. Spaniards saw lots of people who appeared to have better lives than they did—people with more money, more leisure time, and more freedom to make their own choices about their private lives. Often, these foreigners were people who might be doing the same kind of work in their countries as the Spaniards were doing in Spain, but they seemed to be enjoying life a lot more.

John Hooper puts it well in his book, *The Spaniards:* "The development took place in an environment which had not changed all that very much since the eighteenth century—a world of thrift and deprivation which had its own strict moral code. Overnight, its inhabitants were confronted with a new way of life in which it seemed as if the men had more money than they could cram into their wallets and the women walked around virtually naked."

In the early 1970s, tourism generated more revenue than anything produced in the country. It also generated its share of controversy.

Conservative members of the Spanish church and government worried about the effect of tourists on morals at home, while those Spaniards who had been in exile since the end of the civil war accused the tourists of sponsoring the Franco dictatorship with the foreign exchange they brought to Spain. Both sides were, in their way, right.

Almost everyone in Spain was touched in one way or another by tourists, or the revenues they generated. Young people, in their teens and twenties who still had most of their lives ahead of them, were particularly affected. They wanted to join with the rest of Europe in its march toward the good life. If Spain has been reconquested by North American consumerism, tourists were the shock troops.

Those bikini-clad bodies on the beaches seemed to be a symbol of a wider, more exciting reality. For the young in particular—notably those living in the cities and beginning to have a little disposable income—freedom from the old ways was symbolized by getting high, as well as wearing bikinis. They took to smoking hashish in a big way. While the eminently respectable leaders of today's Socialist party may not all have experimented with drugs during their student days in the late 1960s and early 1970s, it's a good bet they at least knew plenty of people who did. Many of those who started getting high in their early twenties, are now professionals in their mid-forties who still indulge in a toke from the occasional *porro*, the tobacco-hashish joint of choice for cannabis-smoking Spaniards.

The socialists initially adopted a tolerant attitude toward drugs when they came to power. On April 26, 1983, they passed a new law allowing people to have a cache of drugs no larger than what could be defined as "for personal use." In fact, it was reported that minutes later a handful of socialist legislators smoked a porro with some reporters in the congressional gardens behind the Cortes in Madrid. The consumption of drugs in public was not a criminal offense. It was no big deal to see someone roll a porro and pass it among friends in a bar. Someone squatting against the wall of a cathedral, shooting up, was certainly guilty of bad taste, but was not breaking any laws.

"The socialists decided to treat the consumer of drugs, the habitual consumer, as somebody who might need help and have a health problem, but not as a criminal," said Eugenio Madueño Palma, a reporter for *La Vanguardia*, who has written extensively about drug use in Barcelona. "The traffickers were regarded as the criminals."

"In 1982, when the government first began dealing with the drug problem, they followed the Dutch model. But now we are following the American model. That's the way many, many things have changed here, actually."

The socialists' original attitude of tolerance quickly became a political liability, an Achilles heel that allowed the main opposition party, the Popular Party, to claim the socialists were encouraging drug use. Conservative members of the Popular Party blamed a big rise in drug-related crimes on the new policies, although supporters of the depenalization measures responded that the rise was merely the continuation of a trend that had begun long before personal possession was tolerated. In many neighborhoods which formerly had been poor but relatively safe, there were people selling heroin on the streets, and others were coming into the neighborhoods to rob and steal so they could buy it. By 1991, three out of every four crimes in Barcelona were drug-related.

"The general direction the government has now taken on drugs indicates that consumption will no longer be tolerated," said Madueño, when we talked over coffee one afternoon, in a cafe close to the *Vanguardia*'s newsroom. "Addicts will be treated as criminals, not as people with health problems. No one wants to see a junkie shooting up in public, so the government has made it illegal. This means that junkies who don't want to be arrested will be forced to inject themselves somewhere that no one will see them, and this also means that if they have an overdose, they'll be dead before they're discovered."

Street dealers in Barcelona are frequently gypsies, or immigrants from underdeveloped African or Asian nations. The wholesalers and traffickers who rake in the real profits from the sale of drugs in Barcelona are often Catalan, or Spanish, or Colombian. These people are wealthy and usually unconcerned with local law enforcement, which contents itself with prosecuting the visible and impotent street marketeers.

The revenues from drugs have risen in a spectacular curve. Soft and hard drugs constitute an immensely profitable business all over

Europe, regardless of where the drugs are finally sold to a user at the retail level. Drugs are estimated to generate over $100 million annually in Spain, although no one can put a precise figure on the traffic. In 1991, according to a study by the German government, over $2.5 billion in drug money was invested (laundered) in EC countries. Spain certainly gets its share, and a number of Spanish banks have been implicated in international sting operations. With immense sums of money involved, the struggle to prevent drug use and drug-related violence through legal prohibition, North-American-style, is doomed to fail, according to many observers. The only thing prohibition accomplishes, they say, is to guarantee that profits will remain enormous.

"The only things that the legal persecution of drug addicts do are raise the price of drugs and the criminal revenues from them, and cause a lot of crime and delinquency," said Moisés Broggi, president of Barcelona's Royal Academy of Medicine.

"Prohibiting drugs does not have any advantages for anyone except big-time drug traffickers, and this is true all over the world. Life is hard, and many people need a way to lighten that. Some people will always use drugs. What we need is education, widespread propaganda campaigns to discourage people from using addictive drugs. The money that we spend on the apparatus of persecution should be spent on education."

I spoke with Broggi, eighty-four, one afternoon in the book-lined study of his home, where he served us each a strong demitasse of espresso, a snifter of remarkably smooth, ten-year-old Spanish cognac, and a slim Davidoff cigar from Switzerland, which he said he smoked one of each day, after his midday meal. A short, dapper man with grey hair, glasses and a relaxed manner, he was a surgeon until his retirement. He began his medical practice in Barcelona in 1931. Drug addicts in those days, he said, were treated by physicians. Drugs were cheap, and addicts were not "persecuted" by the law.

"In every culture there are people who are going to use drugs, and it is ridiculous that in our culture we have legalized two of the most harmful—alcohol and tobacco—while outlawing other, less harmful ones. What we need is a worldwide effort to depenalize these drugs and put them, and the people who use them, under medical supervision.

Prohibition has not, cannot, and will not work, but there are many powerful interests who do not want to see the current state of affairs changed."

In elaborating an EC-wide policy, the European parliament voted 171 to 135 against even considering decriminalization—although this would have allayed serious concerns that when border controls are lifted next year, drugs may be easily distributed from one country to the next. (In January, citizens of any member country may legally cross the borders of another without being interrogated, much as if they were traveling across the United States, rather than going from one sovereign nation to another.) Depenalization would, of course, render such concerns redundant. It might also allow Europe to cleanse itself of the dirty, untaxed, and immense profits realized by drug traffickers.

Besides decriminalization, there are, basically, only two other general approaches that authorities can take to the problem of drug abuse. These are outright legal prohibition, accompanied by vigorous law enforcement measures along the lines of the North American model; or what is called "harm-reduction" strategy, such as that adopted in Hamburg, Germany, and Liverpool, England. In these cities, municipal authorities provide community centers for addicts where they are able to obtain clean needles, counseling, medical services, showers, free coffee and a cheap lunch. Proponents of harm-reduction maintain that drugs are not going to disappear, and that the social service system needs to maintain a minimum of contact with addicts, teaching them how to be less of a danger to themselves and others.

AIDS prevention is one of the strongest motives for this type of approach. With a prohibition-based public health policy, people who do not want to comply with abstention rules remain unreachable and unteachable, often having sex for money, and/or sharing needles. If it is too late, and they are already testing HIV-positive, there will be no one to counsel them.

In Barcelona, the public health policy of the city's socialist administration tries to strike a balance between prohibition and harm-reduction. While general drug use becomes more and more the province of law enforcement, the social service infrastructure allocates most of its attention and resources to the city's hard-core users, primarily as a reaction to the rising incidence of AIDS (SIDA, in Spanish, an acronym for *Sindrome de Immunodeficiencia Adquirida*).

The technical director of the municipal drug plan is Pilar Solanis, a Catalan physician in her mid-thirties. Short, with dark brown hair, Solanis has a lot of energy, and she is a heavy smoker. She rocks back and forth in the chair behind her desk as we talk, gesticulating, and she tells me she became interested in drugs and public policy while she was a doctor with the public health service. Some of her patients were addicts, and she began to be curious about the things being done to deal with drug problems. She came to work for the municipal government, and helped to elaborate and implement its drug program.

"We have an older population of heroin addicts, people who have been using heroin since the end of the 1970s and through the 1980s, who are in bad shape physically, hygienically, and socially. We have to do what we can to reach these people for two motives: to help them and for the protection of the public. These people have grave health problems like AIDS, or tuberculosis. There are probably 150 people here like that.

"Our policy with these people is to concentrate on assistance, not prevention. For nearly two years we've had maintenance programs with methadone available for this population. You can't tell these people, 'Give up drugs.' We offer a substitute they can take by mouth, in a hygienic method. They won't need to steal to support their habit and since they have to come in each day to get their dose, we'll be able to help them with their other health problems."

In Barcelona, and all over Spain, it is heroin that people mean when they talk about hard drugs. Cocaine has yet to raise the same level of concern among citizens or the authorities. Nevertheless, the amount of cocaine confiscated by Spanish police quadrupled between 1989 and 1991, from 1,852 kilos to 7,573, according to government figures. Much of that was only passing through the country on its way to the rest of Europe. Spain is the largest gateway to the EC for cocaine coming from South America, according to a United Nations study last year. There are a number of Colombians living in Spain who are connected with the international distribution network of Colombia's cocaine cartels. They have a lot of money to spend, and they find life congenial.

Cocaine still has an image in Barcelona of being a party drug. It is popular among the sleek, monied young who fill Barcelona's designer bars and snort lines in the bathrooms. They see it as perfect for staying out until 6 A.M. on the weekends, drinking and dancing, and its use is climbing sharply in urban areas. It is regarded as a drug of the well-to-do, much as it was in the United States before the advent of crack.

"Over the past two years we have studied the patterns of cocaine use in Barcelona," said Solanis. "Consumption is definitely growing rapidly, but from a recreational point of view. It is still something the elite do on the weekends, usually in combination with alcohol. Furthermore, these people go to private centers if they have problems and not to our public treatment facilities, so we can't accurately know how many people have abuse problems with it.

"So far, Barcelona does not appear to be a good market for crack, and we hope it stays that way. Very, very little crack has been seen here."

Saturday, February 29

This once-every-four-years date falls on a weekend, rarer yet, and I go to eat a midday paella, that marvel of saffroned rice and seafood, at the Can Costa, the last standing example of what was once a long row of old beachside restaurants in Barceloneta. The Can Costa's dining room looks right out across the beach to sea, but the place is under the Damoclean sword of the bulldozer. It is condemned to be demolished, exactly like all the other restaurants that had once been on both sides of it. In their places are piles of rubble, broken concrete blocks, pieces of rebar sticking up through slabs of wall lying at the edge of the beach. Only the Can Costa interrupts a mile-long vista of sand and palm trees.

I take the metro from Ensanche to Barceloneta, and sit across from a short, older, grey-haired woman dressed in widow's black. She has a deeply lined face, and square, work-chapped hands with short, broken nails, big capable hands that lie clasped in her black lap. She is wearing black leather shoes, and her feet do not quite touch the floor of the subway car. On her thick, third finger she wears an old, gold wedding band. It looks more part of her flesh than an adornment, as if her finger is a tree trunk that has grown, over many years, around a golden girdle of wire. Tears are slowly leaking from beneath her closed eyes, down the seams that lie like valleys along her nose, they drip off her chin. I do not know what to say, and say nothing. She is still sitting there when I get off at Barceloneta.

The kitchen is right inside the front door of the Can Costa. The first thing customers see when they come in are pots and pans, and piles of fresh seafood waiting to be ordered and cooked. The delectable smell of things frying and steaming hits me full in the face as I come through the door and a plate of delectable, flash-fried tiny squid, called *chiperones*, is passed underneath my nose from the cook to the waiter. I continue back to the tables overlooking the beach, and after a brief wait I am at a table. It's 3 P.M. and the place is full. The meal begins with mussels in a marinara sauce, *mejillónes a la marinera*, and then a paella, punctuated by the sight of tankers and yachts passing along the blue horizon, across the sea outside.

Later, full and satisfied, I walk over to the docks where Barcelona's fishing fleet ties up and sells its catch. Saturdays and Sundays, most of the boats stay in, berthed and tied, nets piled in their sterns, and there is none of the hustle and bustle of a normal day. The smell of fish and bait still hangs over the place, along with the odor of sea, diesel fuel, and hosed-down concrete—the same olafactory bouquet of any fishing port in the world. Signs of life are few. There is a small coastguard of cats, looking hungry; a handful of strolling couples admiring the boats; and a few dark-skinned immigrant workers, men who may not have the proper identification and documents for wandering very far from the boat on which they are working. These men sit on the piles of nets in groups of two or three, chatting, and smoking cigarettes. A thin, unshaven, tired-looking man about my age comes out of a cabin on one of the boats to hang laundry on a clothesline strung from bridge to bow.

I wait for the metro back, standing on the Barceloneta platform in front of one of the big Wanted posters with the faces of the two Basque terrorists on it. The poster is grimy and torn at one corner. Police have still not found the pair, although they struck again on February 16, gunning down a pair of men, army band members, in broad daylight on a street near a military barracks in Barcelona's toney Pedralbes district. (Five men had also been killed in Madrid two weeks before when a car packed with more than eighty pounds of explosives, along with nails, bolts, and lengths of chain, was detonated on a crowded street as a military van passed by, killing its occupants.) The citizens of Barcelona are feeling a little anxious, despite press reports that crime in the city during 1991 was down two percent from the year before, attributable to an increased Olympic police presence.

A week ago, Mayor Maragall met with FBI agents in New York during an Olympics promotion trip. He assured them the Games would be totally secure. When he spoke to the press in Washington, the mayor told them that the security plans for the Games had predicted just this kind of upsurge in terrorist activities. He warned that it could worsen during early spring, but expressed absolute confidence that there would be no disruption of the Olympics. "Terrorism may squeeze the Games, but it will not suffocate them," he said.

At the same time as the mayor was in the States, the Spanish Minister of the Interior, José Luis Corcuera, announced that the government would begin implementing the next phase of its Olympics security plans sooner than anticipated. Immediately, in fact. Prime Minister Felipe González reiterated that the government would not be blackmailed and would not, in any way, negotiate with the terrorists.

More police than ever appear in the streets. At the same time, Barcelona's best hotels are already totally reserved for the nine days of the Games, at prices averaging fifteen percent above normal. If the government is not able to establish clear and complete control of ETA before the Games, a lot of those reservations are going to be jeopardized.

Saturday, March 14

The terrorists certainly have not slowed down the pace of Olympic construction, which continues unabated. Slowly but surely, the impending Games are entering the life of the city. On the occasional sunny Saturday or Sunday, people have begun making their way up on the newly constructed escalators from the Plaza España, alongside the National Palace, to the Olympic Ring on top of Montjuich. Here, within a few hundred yards of each other, are the venues for track and field, gymnastics, swimming, diving, water polo, wrestling, and weight lifting.

Once atop Montjuich, people visit the stadium and walk around the broad plaza beside it. There are lots of couples with a kid or two, the parents sit on the low walls while kids kick soccer balls and chase each other around. Mothers distribute sandwiches and fruit to their families. Young couples wheel baby carriages and stand near the base of the eight-hundred-foot telecommunications tower, an oddly-curved and tapered needle looming over the site and the city, the tallest structure on Montjuich.

At one end of the plaza is the Palau Sant Jordi, or Saint George Palace, a huge covered indoor arena with seventeen thousand seats. Designed by the Japanese architect Arata Isozaki, it has the soft lines of a toadstool cap, and will be the site of gymnastic events during the Games. It has already served as a venue for everything from basketball games to a Michael Jackson concert.

People walk over to the stadium, enter through its concrete runways and gaze down at the field, imagining the green turf peopled with track and field competitors. The stadium was built in 1929 on a massive and imposing scale for the International Exposition. I am surprised to see goal posts at either end, but this is where the Barcelona Dragons are playing professional American football in the international World Football League, which is going rapidly bankrupt.

The vista from Montjuich is fantastic. In one direction I look across the high dome of the National Palace, and beyond it are the rooftops and steeples of the city. In the other direction is the sea, stretching out beyond the city's cemetery, the village-sized settlement of walls, niches, and crypts that sits prominently atop one end of Montjuich, looking out to the Mediterranean.

Long known for the dead, Montjuich has been brought to life by the Olympics. Many of the couples wandering around would never have dreamed of spending a sunny afternoon up here before. Now the crest of the hill is crowded with citizens. The Games are giving the Barcelonese parts of their city back—and they'll keep them long after the end of the Games.

Does God pervert justice? Or does the Almighty pervert the right? If your children have sinned against him, he has delivered them into the power of their transgression.

🐌 *Job 8:3*

The faithful are given to viewing calamity as a response from God to their wickedness, their all-too-human frailty. When things go badly wrong, people think, What did I do to deserve this? As much as this is so now, it was even more true during the Middle Ages, when scientific explanations were not at hand. When natural disasters occurred—floods, droughts, and epidemics—they were invariably seen as evidence of God's displeasure. This was as true for Jews as for Catholics. Even when Catholics rose up in the towns, assaulting the ghettoes and slaughtering Jews, the people of Israel blamed themselves, declaring that God had withdrawn his protection from His chosen people as retribution for their evil ways and lack of faith. In like manner had Adam and Eve been expelled from Paradise, Sodom and Gemorrah burned to ashes, the world flooded, and the first and second temples in Jerusalem destroyed.

Catholics held disease and disaster to be retribution not only for their own sins, but for allowing Jews, the descendants of the very people who had murdered God's only begotten son, to continue dwelling among them. One of the signs of God's displeasure was the plague, which made regular appearances during the Middle Ages. Often, the Jews were actually accused of poisoning wells with plague-infected potions in order to kill Catholics—never mind that the plague buboes appeared on the bodies of Jews and Gentiles alike.

Not everyone saw the plague as divine retribution. Some few, mostly doctors and apothecaries, held that the outbreaks of plague were due to natural causes, mal-aspected conjunctions of astrological alignments and weather conditions corrupting the air, the soil, and the water. Those who could afford to do so, left the cities and towns when plague struck and camped in the countryside for months on end, believing the relative cleanliness would protect them. Although the quickest to flee were, indeed, likeliest to be spared, rats and their fleas often followed right behind, and the countryside was frequently no safer than the town.

We have no first-hand written description of the terrible plagues in Barcelona during the centuries when Jews lived there, but there is a detailed plague diary from the year of 1651, which was kept by a Barcelonese named Miguel Parets, a tanner and well-respected small businessman who had even served on the city's Council of One Hundred. His wife and three of his children fell ill with the plague and died, along with an estimated third of Barcelona's forty-five thousand residents. His diary was translated into English from Catalan by James Amelang, and it records that those who managed to flee the city had it little better than those who stayed behind:

> And they were so afraid and so tired of hearing and seeing so many misfortunes that in order not to be within the city nor to see so many travails, they left to live in huts on Montjuich mountain . . . taking their families with them and making huts out of dirt and sticks or timber and branches . . . .
>
> But this way of fleeing did them little good, for they ran the same risk, except that the air outside was better and more healthy. Neither did they continuously witness as many deaths, as many travails, as many privations as they had in Barcelona, which was enough to break the hearts of stones, much less of people. Thus, those who were outside of Barcelona in the area around its walls were only far enough away not to see and hear all these things, but for the rest they were in as much danger from the plague as those inside the city.

Those left behind the walls of the city faced conditions as terrifying as anything the mind can imagine: widespread and random death, the web of society falling completely apart, no way to protect the family whose members died daily, streets filled with bodies left for the carts to come and get, shops closed, people staying in, terrified behind their ever-locked doors.

We can assume it was much the same in the Middle Ages, except that by Parets's time there were no Jews left to blame. They got plenty of blame, however, when the plague struck in 1348, one of the worst epidemics in Spain's history. The spring of 1348 saw the appearance of the disease all over Catalonia and Aragon. Historians were not sure if it had arrived by land from Perpignan in France, where it was raging, or by sea, disembarking at some Spanish port with passengers, crew, and rats. What was certain was that this particular epidemic was especially ferocious and fast. So rapid was its appearance and strong its devastation, people believed it must have come from poisoning. There were the usual rumors that Jews had contaminated the wells.

In Barcelona, increasing numbers of people fell ill and died. Royal officials tried to protect their Jews by banning inflammatory sermons or public speeches, but to no avail. Whether they were infecting the water or simply calling down divine wrath by their presence among God's true believers was of no great importance—they were responsible. Jews had to worry twice as much, not only about dying of plague, but also about the antisemitic hysteria of the Christians, who were already half-crazed with fear and grief. That spring of death, Barcelona had the worst anti-Jewish riots the city had ever seen.

On a Saturday—May 17, 1348—a Sabbath day in the Jewish neigh-borhood, a funeral procession of Christians, one of many during that plague, came through the Plaça Sant Jaume, and found itself at the edge of the call. Some of the members of the funeral cortege, joined by a group of rabble rousers, descended on the Jewish quarter. Money-lenders, in particular, were targeted for abuse, and the crowds always found the promissory notes they were holding and burned them.

Some Jews were murdered, others had their homes destroyed, shopkeepers had their businesses looted and torched. This was, perhaps, the first time that Barcelona's Jews had seen such naked and unsheathed hatred from their Gentile neighbors, and it was, although they did not know it, the precursor to the complete destruction of the aljama that would follow forty-three years later.

Outbreaks of violence at Easter season were always a threat during the Middle Ages, but once the season was weathered, life usually re-turned to a more normal and tolerant relationship between the Gentile and Jew. It was not an excess of Holy Week fervor that ultimately de-stroyed Barcelona's large Jewish community, but a wind of antisemitism that blew across almost the entire Iberian peninsula in 1391 and fanned a fire smoldering since the plague riots of 1348. This time the flames would leave nothing but ashes.

In 1391, almost all of Spain's aljamas experienced attacks by Gen-tiles that were unprecedented in their ferocity. Some historians estimate that over fifty thousand Spanish Jews died at the hands of Christians dur-ing 1391, and at least a thousand are thought to have been killed during the riots in Barcelona. Many more are said to have converted.

The wave of mob attacks began in the kingdom of Castile, in June, sweeping over Jewish communities in Seville, Córdoba, and Toledo. On July 9, the aljama in Valencia was sacked and an estimated two hundred fifty Jews killed. Most of those who survived were forced to convert in order to stay alive. The trouble moved relentlessly toward Barcelona. A letter dated July 26, 1391, from the king of Aragon to the municipal authorities in Barcelona, thanked them for preventing a mob from reaching the aljama.

However, the king could not protect his Jews for long. Rioters killed about a hundred Jews on August 5, and the aljama was burned and looted. Mob violence continued sporadically over the next six days. Many Jews were forced to choose between conversion and death. By mid-October, Rabbi Yehuda Cresques wrote from the court at Zaragoza: "Today, already, there is not one person in Barcelona who can be known by the name of Israel."

A few Jews straggled back to their old Barcelona neighborhood, but the last of them packed up and left for good in 1396. After that, there is no record of any Jewish resident in the city. In 1424, the king of Aragon, Alfonso V, put the seal on the absence of Jews in Barcelona. He decreed that Jews could never again settle there, and that Jewish visitors to the city were not allowed to stay more than two weeks, during which time they had to wear a circular yellow badge on their clothing.

In the years between the end of the Second World War and the construction and inauguration of the synagogue on Calle Avenir in 1954, Barcelona's Jewish community settled in, adjusted to life under Franco, and began, cautiously, to assert its presence. Very cautiously.

In June 1945, a law was passed confirming Catholicism as the state religion. The law also specified that other religions would be permitted to exist in the country, but would not be accorded official recognition. Their members (and this included Protestant Christians) were permitted neither to practice in public, nor advertise their presence, nor proselytize in any manner. All aspects of life were strictly controlled by church and state. To be anything but Catholic was to be a second-class citizen, permanently excluded from the dominant culture.

When Barcelona's Jewish community wanted to open a synagogue in 1945, the municipal government denied them permission. The matter reached the ears of Jews living outside Spain, and political pressure was applied first on Madrid, and then on Barcelona's mayor. Permission was granted in December of that year, and a piso was rented by the congregation. There was worry and, often, trouble. In Franco's Spain, any meeting, even in a private apartment, of more than three people was illegal, and the begrudging exception granted by the city did not exempt the Jews from petty, semi-official harassment. People remained cautious.

"Until 1947, the entire community was pretty much an underground one," Barcelona engineer Carlos Schorr told me. "When people got together for a religious service, it was in more or less a clandestine manner. They had to get permission from the police each time. There were instances when the police came in and disrupted the service.

"I also remember there was a party one time—it was a holiday, Chanukah or Purim—and the Jews had organized a social dance. Some young men from the Falange, Franco's party, showed up. They were dressed in their uniforms with blue shirts. They came in and started hitting people. The Jewish kids got in a big fight with the Falangists."

Most of the Jews in those years owned small businesses, and they had the same chance to fail or succeed as their Catholic neighbors. There were, however, a number of careers in which their religion would have been a handicap, if not a total impediment.

Carlos Benarroch, for instance, found only limited opportunities in Franco's army. Benarroch is a Sephardic Jew, born in 1914 in Melilla, one of two cities on the northern coast of Morocco that still belong to Spain. His family could trace its roots back to Sefarad ancestors. Franco organized his initial revolt against the Republic among the soldiers he commanded in North Africa, just as Benarroch was coming of cannonfodder age in Melilla. He fought under Franco during the civil war. "I might very well have gone to officers school, and had a career in the military, but Jews were not allowed to be officers in the army."

Benarroch has lived in Barcelona for almost thirty years, and has served a term as vice president of Barcelona's congregation, he told me over coffee. He is a handsome seventy years old, his skin is the golden color of caramel, and his silken, snow-white hair curls over the collar of his dark suit jacket. "Catholic officers couldn't even marry a Jewish woman if they wanted to advance their careers. That was also true for other professions. Marry a Jew and you lost your career, unless the woman converted.

"There wasn't anything written in the law prohibiting Jews from practicing certain professions, but it was understood. Jews could be lawyers, or doctors, or businessmen, or have a small factory, and be left alone. They could occasionally be professors in a university, but they would never be head of a department."

The first place Benarroch lived when he came to the Iberian peninsula was Almería, in southern Spain, just across the Mediterranean from his old home town in Morocco. In Almería, he took a job in business and fell in love with a Spanish girl, a Catholic.

"I did not ask her to marry me, although we loved each other, because I wanted to marry a Jewish woman so that my children would be Jews.

"I finally did meet and marry a Jewish girl, and when we had a family, I decided to move to Barcelona. Mine was the only Jewish family in Almería, and I wanted to come here so my children wouldn't have to grow up with only Catholics."

It was not easy to raise Jewish children during the Franco years when the church was in charge of youth at school, at play, and at prayer. Religious studies were mandated in all schools, public and private, although non-Catholics were, according to the law, allowed to request an exemption. Many parents never talked about their Jewishness to non-Jews. They found it difficult to request such exemptions. Many did not want to give their young children any idea that they were different but, on the other hand, they did not want them subjected to Catholic instruction either. The stereotype of the Jews as evil and as outsiders was reinforced by that instruction, and Catholic schoolchildren grew up hating the myth of the Jew, especially since few knew one personally, at least not consciously.

"My parents hid the fact that they were Jewish during the Second World War when they saw how friendly Franco was with Hitler, and they continued to hide it afterwards," said Julia Behar Algranti, a psychology professor at the University of Barcelona whose parents came to the city in 1932 from Smyrna, Turkey. "We were a very insulated family."

When Behar was a young girl in Barcelona's grammar schools during the 1950s, there was always the unsettling sensation that she was different from her classmates in some unspoken fashion. "I knew we weren't Catholics, but I didn't know what it was we were. I knew that I couldn't go to Mass with everyone else, but I didn't know why. At the age of eight, all the girls but me had beautiful white dresses for their first communions. That was really important then, and I couldn't take part. It was painful and confusing."

Things were not much better a decade later when Mònica Adrian went to grammar school in the 1960s. "Each day, we went to chapel, and each day we had religious studies. My parents did not want to cause problems. They told me, 'You go to chapel with the rest, just don't do what they do.' A priest at the school told me I had to be baptized, or I would be living in sin. I was eight, and all the other girls had already had their first communion, and the priest told me if I died suddenly I would spend eternity in purgatory.

"Later, I went to another public school, and it was worse," continued Adrian, now director of the Baruch Spinoza Foundation. "My parents, who were not practicing Jews, asked for an exemption for me from prayers and religious studies. The professors were all Falangists and soon all the students knew I was a Jew. The other kids wouldn't sit next to me. They thought I killed babies and drank blood. For them, Jewish meant something bad and they avoided me. When you're that age, all you want is to be popular, and it was hard for me. I began spending a lot of days in the park instead of at school. I'd leave home as if I were going to school, but I wouldn't."

"After three years of that, my parents realized what was going on and sent me to the French School here, a private school with students from all over, where I didn't feel unique or different. Many of the Jewish kids in Barcelona went there, and it was then that I began to get involved with the community and make Jewish friends."

Since 1972, Barcelona has had a school for Jewish children under fifteen, but it is attended only by those from the most devout families. Others prefer their children to mix in public school, even if it means dealing with the prayers and devotions, and still others opt for secular private arrangements such as the French School.

Tuesday, March 31

My heart can take on any form
It is a monastery for Christian monks

A temple for idols
And for the Kaaba of the pilgrims
And for the tablets of the Torah
And for the book of the Koran.

❧ Ibn al 'Arabi, Tarjuman as-Ashwaq
(Thirteenth century)

Today is the quincentenary of the Expulsion decree, and King Juan Carlos spoke in Madrid's only synagogue at a "reconciliation ceremony," also attended by Chaim Herzog, president of Israel. The king, wearing a *yarmulke*, said: "The history of Spain is full of lights and shadows. . . . We now have the responsibility to make this encounter and this country a real meeting place for generations to come."

The Madrid government has resisted pressure to repudiate the Expulsion order officially, declaring that a law passed in 1868, guaranteeing religious freedom in Spain, made it null and void anyway. (Of Spain's seventeen autonomous governments, only Catalonia's has issued a formal apology to Spanish Jews.) However, the Minister of Justice has announced he will sign an agreement before a month goes by with representatives of Spain's Muslim, Protestant, and Jewish communities granting them the same religious liberties and privileges as those already being enjoyed by the Roman Catholics.

There are an estimated 40 million people in all of Spain. Some 300,000 are practicing Christians who are not Catholics, 250,000 are Muslims, and fifteen thousand are Jews. Now, they and followers of other religions will have the right to be represented in the armed forces, prisons, and hospitals; to maintain parochial schools that share equal rights with the Catholics'; and to have their clergy and places of worship receive the same tax breaks and favored status as the Roman Catholic church.

"These agreements turn the page on a history of intolerance over the past five centuries," said Minister of Justice, Tomás de la Quadra. "The religious minorities that have enjoyed long periods of peaceful and prosperous coexistence in Spain will recoup their equality."

If it was difficult to be a Jewish, Protestant, or Muslim child suffering through a Catholic education during the Franco years, it was worse being gay. "I was from a typical middle-class Barcelona family and went to a school with a lot of religion. I was very Catholic as a child," said Jordi Petit, who was in grammar school during the early 1960s. "I had a very repressive religious education in which the sexes were completely separated in different schools, the girls with nuns, and the boys with priests. When I began to confess to the sin of homosexuality at the age of eleven, the confessor talked to me about the fire of Sodom and gave me large penances to perform. That was when the church began to lose me.

"Mine was the last generation to be marked by the guilt of sexual repression, by a Catholicism of that sort. People from my generation are now in power. People between thirty-five and forty-five years of age, judges, mayors, and the leaders of the country grew up during those years and under those conditions."

Petit has a trimmed, brown beard and is a small man, therefore his name Jordi Petit, which is a *nom de guerre*, adopted in 1969, when people involved in the struggle against Franco took a pseudonym. He has since made some peace with the system, and works with the human services department in the municipal government of a Catalan town just outside Barcelona. He has been out of the closet and one of the spokesmen for the gay community for many years, he explained to me, while we drank beer upstairs at the Cafe Zurich—a popular, overpriced cafe, which, owing to its central location across from both the top of the Ramblas and the Plaza Cataluña, is a popular meeting place.

"Under Franco it was not only a homosexual act that was against the law, but just *being* homosexual," said Petit. "Don't forget, those were the days when people had no rights. The police could do what they wanted. There was no possibility of protesting it.

"Life for homosexuals was terrible in those days. They had no information, no support. They were constantly being told they were breaking the laws of God and man. Many couldn't accept themselves. Many killed themselves. Many others, still children, were taken by their parents to psychiatrists in the hope that their sexual persuasion would change. It was a dark and terrible epoch. People had to connect in the streets, in a certain few places on the Ramblas or the Paseo de Gracia.

"When Franco died, there was a transition period of a few years, during which there was an offensive of the democratic opposition. This included many protest marches, which resulted in all sorts of new fashions among the more progressive elements in our society.

"Heterosexuals started to live in groups, for instance, in cooperative arrangements in apartments in the city or houses in the country. It was trendy to speak of bisexuality and swapping of partners, and to try alternative lifestyles. Women also began to change their roles and assert themselves, many simply as women who were talking about feminism and others as lesbians."

For the average heterosexual resident of Barcelona who was not so progressive, homosexuals were like Jews: they were hard to differentiate from anyone else. The same cannot be said for transvestites. People saw them on the evening news and in the newspaper, marching and protesting. And so transvestites tended to be what straight Barcelonese thought of when they conjured up a homosexual in their minds, according to Petit.

"Some lesbians and gays began to object to the prominence of transvestites in the explosion of sexual liberties. There were always transvestites in the front rows of the marches. But a lot of gays did not want to be identified with or represented by men who wanted to dress as women. For a long time, uneducated people thought of all gays as transvestites."

The sexual energy which exploded among heterosexuals when Franco died was at its most dynamic up until the socialists came to power. After 1982, Petit said, an economic crisis and a certain fatigue combined to break up the communes, and make it less fashionable to be bisexual or have an alternative sexual lifestyle. The pendulum swung back somewhat toward living in more conventional family structures. For gays, however, the band played on a little longer, until AIDS began to take its toll in the middle 1980s.

When the first cases of AIDS were reported in the States, many Spaniards believed it was nothing more than Yankee propaganda, the Puritan spirit trying to scare people back to the dark ages, Petit said. "The number of cases of AIDS stayed relatively small here for a long time, and still it is relatively small. It didn't have the sudden impact here that it did in the gay community in the United States. Most gay men didn't know anyone who had died.

"Sexual behavior is a little different here. Among men in Mediterranean countries anal sex, for instance, is much rarer than in Anglo-Saxon countries. AIDS was slower to spread here, subsequently people were slow to recognize the problem, and sexual habits were very slow to change. However, behavior has now altered. Almost everyone practices safe sex. If you go into a sauna, or the dark rooms at discos, everyone is using a condom."

The latest studies seem to support this conclusion. Intravenous drug use had passed homosexual contact as the leading cause of new HIV-positive cases by the late 1980s. There had also been a dramatic increase among heterosexual teenagers and young adults. In fact, Jordi Casabona i Barbara, the director of the Catalan government's program for the prevention and control of AIDS, has often said in interviews that if people between the ages of twenty and thirty-nine would learn to drive more carefully, AIDS would be the largest killer of young Catalans.

"In fact, with the new law requiring that seatbelts be worn both in and out of the city, if the incidence of AIDS in this age group keeps rising as it probably will, in two or three years AIDS *will* be the number one cause of death," Casabona told me.

Between 1990 and 1991, the cases of AIDS recorded in Catalonia jumped thirty-four percent, from 809 cases in 1990, to 1,090 the following year. This is about on par with the States—in Boston, Massachusetts, for instance, a big city analogous to Barcelona, and a state with about the same population as Catalonia, there were 970 cases last year.

Of 1,592 full-blown cases of AIDS studied in Barcelona between 1981 and 1991, 816 were heterosexuals injecting drugs, and 522 were gay men. Almost seventy-five percent of them were between twenty and forty years old. Catalonia now has the highest proportion of AIDS of the seventeen autonomous regions in Spain, and is home to about twenty-thousand HIV-positive people.

Both hospitalization and medication are covered by the national health insurance system, a cumbersome plan which costs Spaniards a lot of taxes to maintain, and which works slowly. But, it works. Citizens are covered for healthcare expenses, including visits to doctors, major medical bills, and prescriptions. AIDS patients require frequent treatment at hospitals, and Casabona said attempts are being made to set up an outreach program that will both cut costs and allow patients to remain at home.

"One of the keys to controlling and reducing the number of affected people is to educate everyone about the disease, whether they are afflicted or not," said Casabona. "The government is doing what it can to make information available. There is some marginalization of people who are infected, but not much. There have been cases where parents did not want their children in school with an infected child. I am sure there's *some* discrimination against someone when it's known they have AIDS, out of ignorance about it, but I don't think it's widespread."

The Spanish attitude toward illness makes frank discussion of AIDS, or any other sickness, uncomfortable for many. People do not talk about their diseases, and even deny them right up until they die. For instance, the spectacular flamenco singer Camarón de la Isla is being treated for lung cancer, but refuses to say he has anything more serious than "pneumonia," although his large public knows he is dying at the age of forty. When the great cinematographer Nestor Almendros died of AIDS, *La Vanguardia* blamed complications from an unspecified illness. The king's father, Don Juan de Borbón has been a residential patient in a clinic since losing his larynx to throat cancer, but the details of his illness are never publicly discussed.

"People here do not generally talk about these things," said Casabona. "In the United States, if the president falls ill there are drawings in the paper illustrating how the disease affects his body. You would never see that here."

CHAPTER SEVEN

High Passions

Monday, April 20

It is the day after Easter Sunday. I am back in the city following an intense out-of-town Holy Week, and the signs of spring are everywhere, although it remains unseasonably cool. The plane trees along the curbs are leafing out, tables appear on the sidewalks in front of cafes, the iron shutters are gone from the fronts of the horchaterías, bathing suits and windsurf boards are in shop windows, and ski equipment is on sale cheaply, if you can find it at all.

What the mountains are to Barcelonese in the winter, so are the beaches during the summer. There are miles and miles of them, both north and south of the city, and everyone has a favorite. Many people buy or rent pisos in some small town near a beach within an hour's drive of the city and go there for weekends and summer vacation.

Those who cannot afford a summer rental or who do not even own a car can still go to the beach. They just take the metro to Barceloneta and spend the day on the sand. Officials insist that the sea at Barceloneta is clean enough to swim in safely, but only some Barcelonese take them at their word and guidebooks continue to advise tourists to go a little ways outside the city to swim. The water off Barceloneta might not be all that clean, but the beach is perfectly adequate for sunbathing, making it a favorite among the elderly and many of the city's poor.

Along the highway to the town of Castelldefels, just south of Barcelona, are miles of windblown, weatherbeaten campgrounds under short pine trees, go-cart tracks, tennis courts, discotheques, and cinderblock apartment buildings full of summer rental units. Castelldefels has a feeling of the Mississippi Gulf coast about it. A long, flat, down-scale beach, working-class, with good restaurants, sun, and swimming. Packed in the summer, it empties out during the winter, shutters go up over the windows of the pizzerias and discotheques, if only to come loose and spend the grey, cold months flapping and banging in the winter winds.

For those who want a "better" beach, the resort town of Sitges lies a mere twenty minutes further south. With a population of some eleven thousand, Sitges is frequently named the best gay resort in Europe, and has a worldwide reputation for tolerance. There are said to be more gay bars in Sitges than in Barcelona or even New York. The annual Carnival Week parades in Sitges are famous throughout Spain for the extravagance and elegance of the transvestites who lead them, putting what was once a fishing village in a class with New Orleans and Rio de Janeiro when it comes to celebrating Mardi Gras. The beaches of Sitges are divided into gay and straight, as well as nude and clad.

Many people take Easter week off, and because it fell in the last half of April this year, lots of Barcelonese had hoped it would be warm enough to take their first trip of the year to some seashore. Unfortunately, no. It was so cold, in fact, that lots of Catalans put the ski racks back on their cars and headed for the mountains. Catalans are unusual in traveling during this holiday. In most parts of Spain, it is a time for staying at home and participating in the events surrounding Easter. Holy Week, in many places, calls up a religious fervor that takes some bizarre forms, but not in Catalonia, where it is celebrated as the most solemn of the year's religious holidays, without lots of fanfare. I decided it would be a good time to get out of town. My only problem was deciding which way to go.

Lots of people go to Andalusia to see the renowned processions that wind through the streets during the days and nights preceding Easter Sunday. These are carried live on national television. In Granada and Seville, men parade under the weight of large floats bearing lifesize statues of the Virgin Mary, her hand outstretched in benediction. Each float is built on wooden rails and eight men, four to a rail, carry it on their shoulders through narrow, cobblestone streets. In front of and behind the float come groups of men dressed in shiny, black, satin robes, pointed hoods with eyeholes covering their faces—to North American eyes, they look like Ku Klux Klansmen in black instead of white. But they are robed and hooded in penitence, not in violence, parading in anonymity through the streets to fulfill a pledge made during the year to the Virgin in exchange for some favor granted. Also accompanying the procession are a score of women, wearing black dresses and mantillas in their hair and holding tall, white, lit tapers. Throngs gather on the sidewalks and cry out in adulation to the Virgin.

It was Aragon, however, where I most wanted to see Easter celebrated, because they do it by drumming the Passion. I accepted an invitation to visit my friends Pilar and her husband, Fernando, who live in the small Aragonese city of Alcañiz, some four hours west of Barcelona. In the towns around Alcañiz during Holy Week there are numerous processions, as well as a tradition going back to the Middle Ages of frenzied drum playing, beginning on the stroke of midnight heralding Good Friday.

Two kinds of drums are played: a snare, which is used by about nine out of every ten drummers, and a big bass drum, beaten with a mallet wrapped in leather. The drums are expensive—$250 for a snare, $400 for a bass—but every family owns at least one and frequently each member has his own drum, even miniature snares or bass drums for the toddlers. Traditionally, only men and boys have played the drums, but recently a number of towns have permitted anyone to play.

Calanda, about fifteen miles from Alcañiz, has become something of a tourist attraction for its drumming. (This was the birthplace of Luís Buñuel, the Spanish filmmaker, who left Spain after the civil war and became a citizen of the world.) Each year, thousands of people who do not live in Calanda go there for the spectacle.

But, I wanted to drum, not to watch. And, I did not want to do it in front of a lot of people standing on the sidewalks of Calanda with video cameras. I borrowed a snare drum from Pili and Fernando and they took me to La Puebla de Híjar, a town of some three thousand people not far from Alcañiz. When we arrived about 11 P.M., it appeared every resident was awake and milling around the town square preparing for the midnight march.

The half-dozen bars around the square were doing a booming business. Part of the tradition is to get there early enough to have a drink in each place, warming up for the long, cold night ahead. People were two or three deep at each bar doing just that. They gathered in the square as the hands of the clock on the town hall, illuminated by the Good Friday full moon, moved toward midnight.

The people of La Puebla de Híjar stood there waiting, their breath rising in cold puffs in front of their faces, the chrome of their drums polished and gleaming at their belts in the moonlight. They shuffled from one foot to another trying to get warm, drumsticks poised in their hands. It was a cold, cold night, and everyone was dressed in layers of clothing, but none of the men wore gloves. Many of the drummers would play almost continuously for the next eight or nine hours, well into the sun of the coming day. They played until their hands bled, and kept on playing. Dried blood on the skin of a drum was a sign of strong faith, and blood was never wiped off, but allowed to dry on the drumskin. Later the next day, when men asked each other if they had drummed the night before, it was de rigeur to hold out a hand, palm up, displaying bandages over raw flesh where blisters had been raised, broken, and rubbed raw as the owner of that hand had drummed on, oblivious, through the night.

Midnight came in the plaza, and the drumming began. The air filled with the pounding of drums, and people moved off through the narrow streets. Almost immediately, the marchers began breaking up into dozens of small parades. Groups clotted and dissolved on the sidewalks. People drummed with one group for a bit, then moved on to another, unceasingly playing the same rhythm, one for the snares, another—a complementary one—for the bass. Each town has a slightly different rhythm, although everywhere it is a simple four lines of beats and pauses, and back to the beginning.

Simple, and powerful. And I could not get it. Even with the assistance of quite a few cognacs, I had trouble getting loose enough to slide into it. For the people of La Puebla de Híjar, however, it was a rhythm they had known all their lives. Come Easter, it was second nature. It pushed them on, let them go, and allowed them to rise above themselves. All around me, people were drumming right on time without thinking about it, in perfect unison, the rhythm as familiar to them as a nursery rhyme, something they had been hearing since their mothers first brought them out bundled up in swaddling clothes while they walked through these streets in time to the Good Friday drums.

"After you've been drumming five or ten or fifteen hours, it's better than any drink you can imagine," Fernando told me, before we got there. "You get tremendously high."

Sad to relate, it did not happen to me. I remained disappointingly grounded, although I walked around and around the little town, drumming with different groups of people for almost four hours. I had to concentrate too hard just to keep up with the rhythm, and could not lose myself as we paraded through the cold, moonlit streets. However, it was easy to see that others were feeling a touch of ecstasy.

Folks made an occasional pit stop, piling their drums in a corner of a cafe to have a cognac, or glass of wine, or coffee with a shot of rum in it. The doors opened repeatedly, letting in chilly blasts along with someone who would stand in the doorway and drum for a moment, before unharnessing his instrument and coming to the bar for a quick warm-up.

There is no scriptural basis for playing the drums as Easter approaches. People have a variety of explanations, as I heard in the bars of La Puebla de Híjar. The religiously inclined speculate that the drumming started as a mournful accompaniment to religious processions, or perhaps to hasten the resurrection. Others assured me that the tradition has pagan roots and is a rite of spring, that the drums are beaten to signal the awakening of the world, to rouse the dormant fertility in all things, to sound the alert that another season of fruitfulness is upon us. Then, there are those who claim that the esoteric theorizing of both camps is nonsense, a lot of hot air to cover up the fact that the whole thing is nothing more than an excuse to drink a lot, stay out all night, make noise, and go through the macho exercise of seeing who could play the longest and bleed the most. People drummed all through the Easter weekend I passed in Alcañiz. There was not a moment in the early morning or late at night when I could not hear the sound of at least one snare drum being played close by, keeping the city's particular rhythm around the clock between Good Friday and Easter Sunday. Even today, back in Barcelona, the rhythm keeps popping up in my mind like a song vaguely remembered.

Pope John Paul II, himself, has experienced a drummed Passion in Aragon. He visited Zaragoza, Aragon's capital, during the Good Friday weekend of 1984. In the wee hours of the first morning he was there, the Pope was awakened by the drumming. The story goes that he came out on the balcony of the Episcopal Palace and addressed the drummers below: "You Aragonese know how to pray, how to sing, how to dance, and with these drums you're able to wake the dead."

Sounds like fun, all right, unless you were a Jew in the Middle Ages, one of those direct descendants of the Christ-killers, in which case the rituals of Easter Week would have been enough to put the fear of God into you. The robes and the hoods of the penitents, and the drunken mobs of frenzied Christians driven by the drums and crowd madness, must have been terrifying. Spring represented the most anxious time of the year for the Jews. It is easy to imagine the nervousness with which they must have viewed the approach of Holy Week. They laid low inside the alja-mas, commemorating their own springtime holiday, Passover. How sad and ironic it was to celebrate the deliverance from bondage and slavery in Egypt, only to find themselves, thousands of years later, at the mercy of Christian mobs.

Alcañiz, itself, had a sizeable Jewish community in the Middle Ages, and over the centuries it was subject to the occasional assault. One of the worst Easter seasons on record there was in 1412, when the city was visited by Vincente Ferrer, a populist court politician and preacher of antisemitic harangues. He traveled over the length and breadth of Iberia, stirring people up against the Jews, and he also wielded tremendous political influence in Aragon.

Wherever he chose to go and preach, he was accompanied by a

band of flagellants and penitents, scourging themselves as they walked. Such was their reputation, writes Baer in *A History of the Jews in Christian Spain*, that Jews fled their homes and towns at the news they were coming.

That spring of 1412, Ferrer worked the Gentile citizens of Alcañiz into a fever pitch and, at the same time, pressured the authorities to make life hard for the Jews in the hope of converting them. He recommended a series of drastic laws prohibiting Jews from engaging in most professions, taking away the legal autonomy of the aljamas, and forbidding any contact with Christians. After Ferrer left Alcañiz that summer, the town's Jews sent a letter of protest to the king of Aragon, claiming that the regulations he had inspired the local authorities to pass were insufferable. The climate was such in Alcañiz, they wrote, that they were afraid to go out in the streets.

The Jews of Alcañiz got no relief, and simply had to bide their time until, little by little, the malevolence subsided to its quotidian. As for Ferrer, he moved on and was beatified after he died for his tireless travels on behalf of the gospel. He is the patron saint of the city of Valencia.

The relationship between the citizens of Barcelona and the church is a long and complicated one. Certainly, following Isabella and Ferdinand's rise to power and the Expulsion, the Catholic church single-handedly determined cultural norms for almost five hundred years. The church rarely exercised its control with compassion. Generally, it allied with the businessmen, factory owners, landowners, and the royal court, and brought their sympathies to bear on decreeing how lesser people should live their lives. What's more, during all those centuries, Rome was always willing to dispense God's favors to the chosen. In the Middle Ages, the rich could buy penances. (It's still pretty much that way, although less defined. The daughter of the prince of Monaco has her first marriage annulled by Rome, while a young, working-class Catalan woman in a disastrous union is stuck with it for life if she obeys her priest.)

There has long been tremendous working-class resentment toward the church and its clergy, boiling over during civil uprisings. In 1909, for instance, during Barcelona's Tragic Week, a general strike turned ugly and rioters attacked churches, convents, and Catholic schools. They opened tombs at monasteries and convents, pulled out the skeletons in their shrouds, and danced with them in the streets.

This anger was worse during the Spanish civil war, when Republicans executed nuns and priests. Some of the women were violated before they were killed. Franco's forces portrayed themselves as fighting a holy war to defend and save the church from destruction at the hands of aetheistic communists, Freemasons, and Jews. "Our war was not a civil war, a war of party, or a military coup, but a Crusade of the men who believe in God," said Franco in a 1940 speech.

On the civil war's final day, Pope Pius XII sent Franco a jubilatory telegram from Rome. Once the Republicans were overthrown, the Catholic church was back on top, and the division of duties between church and state was once again clear: the state would run the machinery of government, while the church would be responsible for the education of Spain's children, and the rules governing the social behavior of its adults. In another of his speeches, Franco said: "In the history of Spain it is impossible to divide the two powers, church and state, because both always concur in fulfilling the destiny assigned by Providence to our people."

Just as both the Jewish courts and the courts of the Inquisition looked to the state to carry out their judgments during the Middle Ages, so Franco's government served the church, passing its moral proscriptions into law and enforcing them. For people who grew up before Franco died in 1975, this meant that many aspects of their lives were controlled by the church. From the most profound and intimate family decisions about contraception, abortion, divorce, and the like, to censorship of films, books, magazines, and television, the church determined what people would do and see, how they would live their lives, and with whom.

When Franco died, there was a peaceful revolt of individuals against the church that eclipsed, in its way, any of the sporadic violent rebellions against ecclesiastical control that had come before it. A 1991 Catalan government study concluded that twenty-nine percent of Catalans between fifteen and twenty-nine defined themselves as aetheists or agnostics, another twenty-five percent as not having any particular religion, and only thirty-five percent as Catholics.

"There is not a lot of religious practice, even among those who say they are Catholics," said Joan Carrera Planas, the auxiliary bishop of Barcelona. "Probably only twenty percent of that group in Barcelona are religious, and there are a lot of working-class neighborhoods where the number of people who go to church on Sundays doesn't even reach five percent."

Carrera is one of two auxiliary bishops in Barcelona, directly beneath the bishop of the diocese in the ecclesiastical order. He has an office in a beautiful medieval building of massive stone walls and arched windows, just across the Calle del Obispo (Bishop's Street) from the cathedral and close by the Plaza del Rey. Our appointment was at noon, and the cathedral bells marking the hour resounded off the stone walls.

Carrera is middle aged, substantial, with bifocals, short salt-and-pepper hair brushed stiffly back, and a ready smile. He describes himself as part of the "progressive" wing of the church, which had been vocally opposed to Franco's excesses during the last years of the dictatorship. He admits that the number of practicing congregants has fallen off, but remains hopeful. "While the number of people regularly attending church is very low, there is another category that is very high, and that is those who don't go to Mass on Sunday but do come for baptism and First Communion for their children. I would say this includes ninety percent of the people in Barcelona."

In post-war Europe, at least four countries—Ireland, Portugal, Italy, and Spain—were under the dominion of the church. But during the following forty years, all of them but Ireland have separated church and state. Many people still think of themselves as Catholics, but they rarely go to confession or mass, and tend to believe the church has no business interfering with private decisions. Ecclesiastical authorities recognize that things have changed—at least temporarily.

"These days, the church must convince people to believe, without imposing belief on them," said Carrera. "This is more difficult, slower, less spectacular. But, perhaps in the end these believers have a deeper faith because they have chosen freely to be part of the church. This is our path now, this is our pastorate in a democracy."

Thursday, April 23

It is the day of Saint George, the dragon-slayer; Sant Jordi to the Catalans and the patron saint of Catalonia. The custom on Sant Jordi's day is
to exchange gifts with a loved one: women receive a rose wrapped with
a stalk of green wheat in a sheaf of paper imprinted with the yellow and
red Catalan flag; and men receive books. This is the day that really marks
spring in Barcelona.

Because the saint's day has fallen so shortly after a late Easter, it is
not an official holiday. People are technically at work, but the city is in a
fiesta mood. It has been one of April's rare warm, sunny days and at
least half the women in the world—in the metro, in the streets, in the
markets—are holding a rose and a green stalk of spring wheat. Roses and
stalks of green wheat are everywhere—people roam the city selling
them, raising money for charitable groups, or just for themselves. The
men all carry a book in their hands. Bookstores put a tableful out on the
sidewalk, the Ramblas is lined with booksellers in temporary stalls, and
there are nearly as many books as roses for sale.

This is also the only day of the year the Catalan government opens
its fifteenth-century building in the Plaça Sant Jaume to public tours. Of
course, it is the Catalan taxpayers who pay year 'round for the building—the seat of Catalonia's government for five centuries—and for the
salaries of the bureaucrats and politicians of the Generalitat who work
there. A lot of people take advantage of the annual opportunity to see
how their money is being spent, and today there was a long line around
the plaza.

On the side opposite, the equally historic Barcelona city hall
houses the municipal government, the ayuntamiento. It is, at least, open
for tours on Sundays. Otherwise, these corridors of power are off limits
to citizens. Members of the public cannot just walk in and wander, or
even get past the front door, without satisfactorily explaining the precise
nature of their visit to a police officer.

Tonight is clear and pleasant, a real spring evening as befits the
night of Sant Jordi. I go to see a film at a cinema on the Ramblas. On
the way to the theater, I pass through the subterranean walkway that
connects the Plaza Cataluña with the top of the Ramblas. There is an

excellent trio of long-haired, rock-and-roll musicians set up in the hub of the underground passageway. It provides a small theatre-in-the-round, with a domed stone ceiling and superb underground acoustics. The group has somehow tapped into an electric current. They are nicely amplified, and cooking. The trio consists of a drummer with a good-sized set of traps, an electric bass player, and a guitarist who plays a mean electric guitar, and also sings in Catalan. They are young, each with dirty, stringy blond hair held back by bandanas, each wearing a T-shirt and pair of jeans, each with skinny, muscular arms. They are playing hard. The lyrics to the songs are in Catalan, but the music is pure, driving rock and roll. A big circle of people has formed around them, passers-by who have been grabbed by the music, people swaying back and forth, tapping their feet. In the front of the circle is a balding, middle-aged man wearing a brown corduroy sportcoat and dancing by himself, putting a 1,000-peseta note ($10) in an open guitar case between each number. He is, apparently, an Italian, because as he dances he occasionally shouts, "Magnifico, magnifico!" Lots of people in the circle are holding a rose and a wheat stalk, or a book.

The film I see, a comedy called *El Rey Pasmado* (*The Amazed King*) is an excellent period piece set in the fifteenth century. Directed by Spain's Imanol Uribe, it is based on a novel by Gonzalo Torrente Ballester about a young king, Philip II, and his single-minded obsession to repeat the rapture of his first sexual experience. It is rated PG-13, despite a number of scenes with attractive naked women.

The theater on the Ramblas where I watch *El Rey Pasmado* is a two-screener, and on the other side is showing *The Silence of the Lambs*, a Hollywood film about a psychopathic killer who likes to bite his victims and the female agent who stalks him. It is rated R—not recommended for anyone under eighteen unaccompanied by a parent—although there is not a naked breast or buttock in the whole film.

This is the sort of thing many Catalans find obscene: the warped sexuality of violence so familiar to the United States. They find the puritanism of the States mystifying, and do not understand how naked breasts, or love-making, can be considered the equivalent of violence and murder.

Breasts appear with great regularity in Barcelona, in advertising (both in print and on television), in films, and on the beaches, where many women, young and old, choose to sunbathe topless. This, in a country where, twenty-five years ago, for unmarried people to publicly kiss with passion was a misdemeanor in real life and unacceptable in the movies.

While Franco lived, the church ruled on every cultural offering, from books to films to the floor show at the Barcelona de Noche. Censorship had been stoically endured as long as most people were too poor to care, but as the economy began to develop in the 1960s, it was increasingly resented. Barcelonese would fill up their cars with their friends and take the two-hour drive north to the small French city of Perpignan for a weekend of watching uncensored films, or those that were wholly barred from exhibition in Spain. As late as 1971, censors prohibited 108 foreign films from being shown, and allowed another 130 only in substantially edited versions.

Movie theaters in southern France catered to the Catalan trade, and films banned in Spain frequently had long runs in French towns like Perpignan. Travel agents in Barcelona arranged weekends there everyone knew were just to enjoy the films, books, and magazines—pornographic and otherwise—that were forbidden at home. Busloads of Catalans spent the weekend going to as many movies as they could see, films such as *Last Tango in Paris, The Exorcist*, or *A Clockwork Orange*.

How quickly everything changed, how long ago those clandestine weekends seem. This year, the publicly owned telephone company, Telefonica, decided to allow private businesses to rent lines for phone sex. The people who set up the first of these 900-number operations are getting rich fast, because Spaniards have taken to phone sex in a big way. In just four months, the original five companies have become more than fifty. That same increase took five years to occur in England, where phone-sex lines were introduced in 1986.

The change in people's behavior is all the more astonishing considering how deeply the church has affected the history of Spain, what a church-in-the-bones country it has been for five hundred years, how much doctrine has been written, and how much blood spilled in the name of the Son. After all that history, people are still ready to lose themselves in the pleasures of this world, with little thought of the next.

Last fall, Pope John Paul II addressed a papal letter to the Spanish priesthood and the faithful, warning them that the nation was becoming "neo-pagan." The letter exhorted the flock to resist the rising incidence of birth control, abortion, and divorce. The Pope insisted that his harsh words were spoken out of love, but the Barcelonese expressed resentment in the newspapers the next day. While they may not go to church regularly, and while they support a woman's right to make up her own mind about abortion and birth control, they still think of themselves as Catholics, worthy of grace.

Curiously, while the number of believers is down and the church is finally separated from the state, there is one thriving sector of Spain's organized Catholic population: the shadowy and immensely powerful Opus Dei, or the Work of God. Founded and headquartered in Spain, it has chapters in an estimated eighty countries. Its members are fundamentalist Catholics, about ninety-eight percent of them lay persons.

"I am not a sympathizer with Opus Dei," said Joan Carrera. "They are very traditional, and a number of them participated in the Franco regime. They are like the early Jesuits, in the sense that they believe society should be a hierarchy headed by their aristocracy.

"They have a large base of economic resources, while at the same time the progressive part of the church has become disorganized and ineffective. Members of Opus have become well situated in the Vatican. It is a movement of order, of a severe discipline, and for that reason can be dangerous. I hope that in time, like the Jesuits, they will mature."

Opus was founded in Spain in 1928 by a priest from Aragon named José María Escrivá de Balaguer y Albás. Its theology places heavy emphasis on penitence, and many members are said to flog themselves on a weekly basis, while some wear a garter of thorns under their trousers. Their names are not revealed outside the organization and all dedicate a substantial portion of their incomes to it. After the civil war, the organization grew rapidly and, under Escrivá's direction, began to concentrate its efforts and its funds on higher education. Opus Dei members began appearing in important posts in Spain's universities. Many of Spain's business and industrial elite trusted their sons to Opus for their education. It was not long before graduates were moving out into public and private positions of influence in the country. To what extent Opus members are in power in Spain today is not known, but most people believe they continue to play a significant role in shaping local and national policies.

Escrivá died in 1975, and on May 17 Pope John Paul II will beatify him in a Vatican ceremony, vesting him with sainthood. This has aroused considerable controversy in the worldwide Catholic community. Escrivá was a man who insisted that he be provided with only French mineral water to drink when he visited America, and had Spanish melons flown to him for his dinners around Europe, according to a former associate. Hardly the stuff of sainthood. Both of the obligatory two miracles he is reported to have performed seem somewhat questionable. Vatican-watchers told the press this points up the degree to which Opus's power has spread to the Holy City. Pope John Paul II is a strong supporter. A number of Opus members have been brought from Spain to serve in the Vatican hierarchy. No wonder Escrivá's is one of the fastest beatifications on record.

When they returned to Barcelona in the twentieth century Jews behaved in a generally circumspect manner, and were never so discreet as at Easter. It was no wonder. A lot of the old Gentile habits still lingered.

"I can remember as a child, in a small Catalan village, that on the Saturday before Easter Sunday, the boys would be taken upstairs in the church," recalled Barcelona attorney Jordi Oliveras. "They had empty cardboard boxes laid out on the floor, and they gave us sticks and we beat the boxes, and that game was called 'Killing the Jews.' Of course, what did I know? I had never met a Jew. A Jew was something mythological, more like a dragon than like another human being."

In other towns, people came out on their balconies and beat on pots or pans, calling out, 'Kill the Jews! Kill the Jews!' The collective notion of the Jew as the incarnation of evil was deeply ingrained in the religious education of most Spaniards. They never connected the image of the Christ-killers, objects of hatred worthy only of being beaten and humiliated, with the few, if any, actual, living Jews they might have met in their lifetimes. They regarded killing the Jews with the same holiday delight as that with which North Americans hunt Easter eggs or believe in Santa Claus, or eat a big meal at Thanksgiving.

"Holy Week," said ninety-one-year-old Alberto Arditti and grimaced, shaking his head, sunk comfortably back into the cushions of his broad sofa. He laughed ruefully as he recalled how it was. "On the Saturday of Glory, the day before Easter Sunday, there was not a piso on this block where a woman didn't come out on the balcony beating on a pot and calling, 'Kill the Jews, kill the Jews.' How do you think we reacted?"

He had another laugh, nodded his head, and made a show of opening his mouth wide and closing it tight. "We kept quiet. Holy Week was something else here. You didn't see any Jews outside, certainly not going around identifying themselves to anyone as Jews. There was a level of fanaticism in those days that is hard to believe now. You couldn't blame the people. What did they know? It was the fault of the church. Generally, we identified ourselves as French or Turkish, or wherever you had come to Spain from, and that was that. It was enough, because it never occured to people that you might be Jewish. They never imagined they were looking at an actual Jew."

Thursday, May 6

The Olympics are only seventy-nine days away, as I am informed by the newspapers, which have been counting down daily since I got here. Apart from construction getting closer to completion, however, and the occasional cab driver who wants to practice pidgin English (painstakingly and expensively learned over the past years in anticipation of the wave of dollar-spending tourists expected to flood the city during the Games), there is little indication of excitement.

When the impending event does come up in a conversation, it is usually about whether to go on vacation before competition gets underway on July 25, or after it is finished on August 9. Many Barcelonese who would like to see the Games and be here for the excitement are dubious about giving up any of their August vacations to do so. There is something fundamentally unappealing about the idea of spending a block of vacation time at home. On the other hand, the Games are a once-in-a-lifetime occasion. Folks are in a quandary, but they will have to act quickly if they want tickets for the big events. Seats in the stadium are already sold out for most days of track and field competition.

A lot of the world's news gets told by the media here with an Olympic twist. Magic Johnson is HIV-positive, but we're assured it won't affect his Olympic play when he arrives with the U.S. basketball team, a.k.a. the Dream Team. War rages on in the Balkans, but the Croatian basketball team is practicing in the lulls between shellings. Skinheads are becoming an increasing threat in Germany, and tennis great Boris Becker—engaged to a dark-skinned woman—says his own country should be banned from the Games.

Then there are the odd bits of Olympic news that surface from time to time. For instance, the Banyoles city council is still standing firm and refusing to take El Negro off exhibit (the threat of a boycott seems to have pretty much lost steam, and no African country has announced such a move). A plan to move Barcelona's prostitutes out of town is rumored, but the city says nothing has been decided.

And, strangest of all, it turns out that in addition to stringent doping procedures for all the athletes, women will be tested to make certain that they are, in fact, women. A small scraping of skin will be taken from the inside of each woman's mouth, from the pocket of the cheek, and tested for gender. Simply checking the athlete's genitalia does not serve as sufficient proof that a woman is not overloaded with male hormones. What's going on here, sport or science fiction?

That things have come to this pass may surprise me, but it doesn't surprise Maria Louïsa Fernàndez Gàlvez, the Barcelona lawyer who has helped more people change their legal gender than any other lawyer in Spain. Many of her clients had begun their transformations by being transvestites, she said, but the difference between transvestites and transsexuals was as vast as that between make-believe and reality. The transsexual is someone who does not want to pretend to be a woman, but is willing to do whatever is necessary to become one.

To do a good job of dressing up like a woman, a transvestite need only spend an hour or two, but to actually have a sex change involves years of saving money, undergoing hormonal treatments, and enduring major surgical procedures. Most transsexuals begin life as males. Generally, a Spanish man who wants to change into a woman goes to a well-known surgeon in Madrid, and can expect to spend about $15,000 by the time he achieves his goal. For the smaller number of transsexuals who begin life as women, Switzerland is the nearest place to find qualified surgeons who can change them into men, and the eventual cost of the process is about $65,000.

"The need that compels someone to go through all of this has nothing to do with how restrictive or permissive a society is. It is something they feel inside," Fernandez told me in her office. Despite her chunky size, she was light and graceful on her feet as she moved around her office, talking. It was a plain, unintimidating office, with a large, round table where she liked to come out from behind her desk and sit while talking to clients.

"To have a sex change is something that people only do when something internal obligates them to do so," she said. "There is an overwhelming sense that they were born in a body with the wrong sex, and it is always something they became aware of early in their childhoods. Mothers will often relate how at three years old their sons were already putting on their sisters' clothes, and asking for feminine things to wear. This is something that does not have to do with the sexual permissiveness of a society, but with how someone is. The desire to change sex is not something that only appeared in Spain after Franco died.

"Paradoxically, although homosexuality was against the law, it was really easier to legally change your gender while Franco was alive. You simply went to the person in charge of the local civil register and swore that a mistake had been made when your sex was inscribed on the birth certificate. You didn't need a lawyer or anything, and the procedure cost almost nothing. This is what people did if they left the country, had a sex change, and came back."

When the socialists came to power in 1982, the whole process of changing facts in the civil registry was modified, requiring people to go before a judge first. Numerous judges in Spain were not inclined to look favorably on the case of a man who had become a woman, and wanted a corresponding change of name and legal status.

"I began doing this kind of law by accident in 1985," Fernandez said. "A person showed up one day at my office, a transsexual woman—someone who was born a man—and asked me if I could help her change her legal identity. It was very early in my professional career, and I got interested in the subject and how it was dealt with under the law.

"It was not until 1983 that being a transsexual was decriminalized. There was no precedent established for how to treat these people. I had the first case that reached the Supreme Court where the sex change was recognized as legal. Since then, I've had about thirty cases involving the law and transsexuals. It has been quite gratifying to help create a small body of law that wasn't there before, and to see that most of my transsexual clients live in a couple relationship, and are happy with their lives. Two couples have even adopted children."

CHAPTER EIGHT

Tailpipes & Reactors

Wednesday, May 20

It has been a wet, windy spring with frequent showers, the rainiest spring in twenty-five years, according to *La Vanguardia*. The days when there is no rain are unseasonably cool. The news media has begun to speculate on what a rainy Olympics might be like, although the meteorological forecasts continue to call for a dry July—not surprisingly, since Barcelona normally has months of uninterrupted sun and hot weather during the summer.

On the days when it has not been raining, I've frequently taken a walk down into the old city through the working-class neighborhoods around the San Antonio market. It's a walk that takes me by the small stone church of St. Paul, built in the twelfth century, a downtown church from medieval times with a domed roof, rounded in on itself with the ponderous dignity of a very old turtle.

A block away lies the dusty Plaza de Folch y Torres. Retired men gather here in the mornings to play petanca on sunlit courts they have outlined with the toe of a shoe in the dirt of the plaza. There is sunshine, but it is weak and the air is cool. Most of the petanca players are wearing sweaters or light, poplin jackets. Some of these grandparents are serving their working families as day-care providers. The toddlers play on the plaza's one or two pieces of modest playground equipment or kick a soccer ball in the dust, while the old men sit on a bench, keeping one eye on the children and the second on the petanca court. At midday, which, in Spain, means around 2 P.M., their daughters or daughters-in-law get off from work for two or three hours and come by the plaza to pick up the kids and take them home to feed them their comidas.

I watch as one white-haired grandfather, in creased grey slacks and a clean white shirt, turns over a little girl to her mother. He clowns for his tiny, curly haired granddaughter, who looks back at him over her mother's shoulder. The old man puts his thumbs in his ears and wiggles his fingers in front of her steadfast gaze. He jumps up and down in a spry hop, and wriggles his fingers in his ears again. He does not speak, nor shout, but I seem to hear him calling, Remember me, remember me. The child watches him casually over her mother's receding shoulder, without nearly enough focus or attention to imprint his likeness on the long years ahead.

In the late afternoons, the plaza and surrounding cobblestone streets fill up with schoolchildren and adolescents. School hours are from 9 A.M. to 2 P.M. and again from 4 to 6 P.M., so after school there is still a little daylight. Despite the cool spring weather, the kids shed their clothes a lot faster than their seniors. As the light fades into shadow on any afternoon in the narrow back streets, the kids are wearing shorts and kicking soccer balls, shouting their oncoming-car advisories—*Coche! Coche!*—just like children playing football in the streets of any U.S. city learn early on to do. The voices of kids in Barcelona carry the same urgent note, a warning that the enemy is approaching, as a broad Mercedes Benz or Volvo comes lumbering, racketing down a tiny street, sucking up all the space. Adults on the sidewalk and children at play both have to stop and put their backs to a wall so as not to be clipped by a passing wing mirror.

In 1960, there were one hundred twenty thousand cars registered to the residents of Barcelona, and by 1970 that number had tripled. Now, there are close to a million. For most of the years Franco was alive, people drove only SEATs, manufactured by the state-owned automobile industry. The most popular model was the SEAT 600, a low-priced, tiny, squared-off car, engineered to fit in the narrow streets of the cities and villages without driving passersby to the wall. While the SEATs were perfectly serviceable vehicles for daily routines, they were not designed for high-speed weekend trips on a four-lane *autopista*, Spain's equivalent of the interstate highways.

With Spain a fully-fledged member in the union of multinational consumers, cars are no longer built to fit the streets. Instead, the streets are widened to accommodate the cars: Mercedes, Volvos, BMWs, Peugeots, Renaults, and Citroens. Many of them are sleek, fast cars, with the same dimensions as mid-sized cars being sold in the States. Barcelonese keep on buying them, despite the fact that a new car in Spain is more expensive than in northern Europe, and considerably more expensive than in the States. A sub-compact Citroen, for example, a bottom-of-the-line, basic model, costs about $11,000 in Barcelona, and even for that comes with only a one-year warranty.

In a densely populated city with extremely narrow streets and a constantly increasing number of cars, there is bound to be a shortage of parking places. People often spend as much time driving around the crowded neighborhoods of Barcelona looking for parking, as they do making their journeys. It sometimes seems as if most of the traffic on the congested streets consists of drivers in search of a place to park. Car real estate has experienced the same boom as human housing, and people pay a lot of money to rent or buy parking space near where they live. In fact, according to press reports, Barcelona's parking is the most expensive in Spain. An underground parking lot recently constructed by a Japanese firm just off the Ramblas contains 780 mechanically controlled spaces, each of which sells for about eight million pesetas ($80,000).

"It's the free market, and it's the law of supply and demand," laughed Ramon Ferreiro i Dou, spokesperson for the city's department of public ways. "It doesn't seem so expensive to me. The normal price for a parking place in any area of the city is 3.5 million pesetas [$35,000].

It's a seller's market, and I have to think the price is going to continue rising."

New parking lots are constantly being constructed, many of them underground, but there are never enough. The city is estimated to be short about 230,000 parking spaces already, and municipal officials expect at least 250,000 more cars in Barcelona by the year 2000.

Revised regulations have just been issued that increase the number of parking spaces the city can require for new residential and commercial buildings. At the same time, Mayor Maragall's administration eliminated a municipal regulation forbidding the construction of underground parking lots in older parts of the city, a regulation originally approved out of concern for the foundations of older buildings nearby.

Pollution from automobile emissions in Barcelona is frequently visible in the form of a dirty haze trapped over the city. There are days when the breeze coming off the sea through the streets is brisk and clean, when the clarity of the light and freshness of the air are invigorating. On other days, however, the haze makes each inhalation seem slightly toxic. The vast majority of cars still use leaded gasoline, and lead levels in the air are high. Gas is expensive, shockingly so by North American standards: about $3.60 a gallon for unleaded. 1993 has been designated as the year when all new cars sold in Spain will have to use unleaded gasoline.

"Barcelona has about one hundred square kilometers of space, of which thirty are the Collserola hills where there is no one, leaving only about seventy square kilometers we can use for urban living," said Ferreiro. "In this space are 1,700,000 inhabitants and 800,000 cars.

"The city is bound by the sea and the Collserola, neither of which allow it room for expansion, and that's why it's the third most densely populated city per square kilometer in the world. The pollution here would be much worse than it is, though, if it were not also for the sea and the Collserola. The sea serves as a regulator and the Collserola acts like a pair of lungs, and that is why all the pollution gets cleared out and you have one of those spectacular, clear days. Nevertheless, year round, cars are the worst pollutants of the air in Barcelona."

The actual production of those automobiles is another source of pollutants in the city. Barcelona is often referred to as Spain's "little Detroit" by automotive and business writers because of its high concentration of manufacturing plants. The days are gone when the only one was SEAT's in the Zona Franca industrial neighborhood on the southern edge of Barcelona. That plant has been there since the 1950s, originally producing those little, square SEAT 600s, along with a line of small, simple, inexpensive sedans. Now SEAT is owned by Volkswagen and the cars rolling off the line are a lot bigger and more expensive.

In 1985, Volkswagen bought SEAT from the Spanish government. In 1990, SEAT was the eighth largest company, by sales, in Spain, and the largest in Catalonia, with revenues of $4.3 billion. These days, when people go into a SEAT dealership looking to buy a new car, the salesman is likely to drop his voice (not wanting to be disloyal) and tell them it is not the same SEAT it used to be, but much better: it may still be made by Spaniards, but now it's done with German know-how.

SEAT was joined in the Zona Franca by production plants for Pegaso, the national truck manufacturer that was acquired by Fiat; and Nissan Motor Iberica, which produces trucks, vans, and four-wheel drive vehicles. Nissan began buying into Motor Iberica in 1980 by acquiring a twenty percent share of the corporation, and has increased its holdings to sixty-seven percent.

Nissan Motor Iberica employs over seven thousand people. The corporation has been forced to alter its idea of a workplace and the rules that govern it. Japanese management has had to come to terms with the huge gap between what Japanese workers and Spanish workers will accept as a reasonable production schedule. Workers in other European countries are frequently willing to produce by Japanese rules in exchange for the jobs and revenue generated by Japanese investment, but it did not prove easy to apply the Nissan production model to Spanish managers and workers who are accustomed to a three-hour lunch break and taking a vacation for the entire month of August.

"We try to respect local customs and traditions among the Spanish workers, but we must also introduce the Japanese model if we are to be able to compete successfully and respond to economic conditions. So we try to reach a compromise," said Kiyoshoi Sekiguchi, director general at Nissan Motor Iberica in Barcelona. "The four-week vacation is a very deep tradition here and we have not changed that, but there is only one hour off for lunch."

Sekiguchi laughed. "There is no siesta time. Office hours for managers are eight to five, and there are two production shifts. It takes time, but, little by little, both workers and management are becoming accustomed to doing things in the Nissan way."

There is a huge automobile market awaiting the Japanese in Europe. Next year, trade barriers will begin being lowered for Japanese cars in each of the EC countries, and the timetable, to which Spain is bound, calls for full access by 1999. This will pose a serious threat to Spain's domestic car producers, who enjoy a strong protectionist policy set by Madrid. In 1991, for instance, only fourteen thousand vehicles manufactured in Japan were allowed to be sold in Spain.

Another negative factor in the near future of the Spanish automobile industry is that it is third, behind the nation's chemical and energy producers, in the amount of money it will have to spend in order to bring existing plants up to EC environmental standards by 2002. The Spanish government estimates that auto plants will need to invest more than $1.5 billion to come into line, or be subject to huge fines.

The Spanish government, as well as industry, is also being required to match EC environmental standards, and it's not going to be easy. Northern European countries have been investing public funds, heavily, for over a decade in technologies and strategies for dealing with problems like waste disposal, recycling, and lowering industrial pollution. The EC's environmental regulations reflect those years of investment and progress.

Spain has no comparable programs, however. Before the socialists came to power in 1982, there were virtually no environmental laws, or any environmental public policy. It was not until Spain was admitted to the EC, in 1986, that laws were passed to regulate toxic and hazardous waste. In order to meet EC regulations and timetables, Spanish industry and government will have to look outside the country for the research and the technology to deal with their environmental problems. Spain's Ministry of Industry estimates that the public and private sectors will have to spend $12 billion during the 1990s to avoid EC fines and sanctions.

The easiest aspect of complying with EC norms was to pass the laws mandating them. Spain has pretty much done this now in a substantial body of environmental laws. What is not in place, however, is an enforcement program with any teeth to it. A 1992 study, contracted by the U.S. Consulate in Barcelona, concluded: "Spain is about ten years behind the U.S. in environmental enforcement. Besides lack of experience in enforcement, the Spanish environmental authorities are understaffed and lack the appropriate technology to monitor its environment. In most instances Spain has the regulations, but simply can't enforce them, or doesn't. The main reason for Spain's cautious approach to environmental enforcement is the country's unemployment rate—seventeen percent in late 1991."

Barcelona and Catalonia are, like much of Spain and the rest of Europe, highly dependent on nuclear energy for electricity production. Initially, the socialists were opposed to relying on the commercial nuclear plants, but their stance has softened over the years. Three of the country's nine plants are in Catalonia.

"The socialists have halted work on some reactors and scrapped plans for others, but at the same time, reactors have been opened across the country, and this means the socialists have chosen an energy policy of Russian roulette," said Jordi Bigas, the editor-in-chief of a well-established environmental magazine called *Integral*, published in Barcelona. "In addition to the danger from an accident, the policy is an economic disaster. There have been years when up to thirty percent of Spain's foreign debt has been for the technology for these nuclear centers, primarily being bought from firms based in the United States.

"To pay for this, the government wants profits from these plants and is not disposed to support any research into alternative, renewable energy sources like the sun or the wind. This is beginning to change here, but we are far behind other countries like France, Italy, and even Turkey."

In 1989, the Vandellos I plant in Tarragona, an hour south of Barcelona, came close to causing the most serious nuclear accident in western Europe, as serious as Chernobyl's, according to Bigas. "The reactor's refrigeration broke down and a fire started, and they were on the verge of a catastrophe. If that had happened, you and I would not be sitting here right now. When the fire broke out at the reactor, the workers fled. They thought it was all over. Fortunately, at the last minute, the refrigeration system began to function again of its own accord."

It is impossible for public interest groups to obtain data about the day-to-day functioning, or malfunctioning, of the plants. In fact, the only jurisdiction over them is by the central government's Council of Nuclear Security with headquarters in Madrid, which sends inspectors from plant to plant on a regular basis.

"The records of these inspections are considered 'reserved information.' Unlike the Nuclear Regulatory Commission in the United States, they are not available to the public," said Bigas. "There are no offices of the Council that are open to the public, even in Madrid. Every six months a report is made about the nation's reactors to the Cortes, because the Cortes funds the Council, but the reports are general, and more specific information is not provided."

Public access to environmental information in general does not exist in Spain as it does in the States. While industries with hazardous waste stored onsite in Catalonia are required to report to the Catalan government, the public has no access to their records. In 1990, an estimated thirty percent of the industrial firms in Catalonia obliged to report the wastes they produced did not do so. There is not much incentive to comply with the regulation, because in the unlikely event a company is cited for its failure, the fine will be under 200,000 pesetas [$2,000]. In a heavily industrialized center like Barcelona, this kind of laxity is particularly disquieting. However, people do not seem particularly disturbed, nor even concerned.

"In the late 1970s and early 1980s, it was not hard to bring out a lot of people for a march against nuclear power. But not anymore," said Miguel Angel Diez Hidalgo, president of the Barcelona chapter of an environmental group called the Association for the Defense of Animals and Nature (ADENA). "People just won't come out. They have become resigned that, in the long run, the politicians will do what they want."

Environmental awareness has always been higher in northern Europe than in the Mediterranean countries, where depressed economies often made putting bread on the table (and paying the rent on a place to put the table) a difficult proposition. People did not have time left over to worry about the environment. This, added to the Spanish inclination to consider one's own interests first and foremost, has resulted in a population with little environmental consciousness.

"People are not interested in doing anything that is not the most convenient for them," said Diez. "They will not work for the environment on a weekend, they will not turn up for a protest, or a march. You can't throw in the towel for the environmental movement here, but things move very slowly."

Friday, June 26

Late in the afternoon, I am waiting in a *tabac*, which is not only where tobacco products are bought, but also the only place to acquire stamps outside of a post office. The older man in front of me is buying a box of cigars. He is short, thin, dressed in a soft, dapper, grey suit, balding with a fringe of silver hair. He is debating between Partagas and Cohibas, two of the finest brands of Havanas.

The proprietor is in no hurry to pressure the guy into making a decision so he could get on to selling me 83 cents' worth of stamps for a letter to Tennessee. A box of twenty-five Cohibas costs over $400, and even a box of Partagas will set the customer back $50. In the end, the smoker settles on buying two boxes of Partagas, and happily forks over a 10,000-peseta note, the equivalent of a $100 bill.

Cigars, and tobacco in general, have addicted large numbers of Barcelonese since Columbus's first voyage back to a Jew-free Spain in 1493. He brought three members of the Solanaceous plant family never before seen in Europe with him: hot peppers, tomatoes, and tobacco. Five hundred years later, Barcelonese smoke anywhere and everywhere, and are astonished by the increasing legal restrictions on people's rights to do so in other parts of the civilized world. France and Italy moved to prohibit smoking in public places in 1992, but there is no such legislation pending in Spain. North America is regarded with particular dismay by smokers in Barcelona, many of whom have the impression that in the States it is illegal to smoke outside your home.

Smoking sections in restaurants and other buildings in Barcelona do not exist. Guests do not ask nonsmoking hosts if it is all right to smoke; they ask for ashtrays. Go figure: Spain has the highest percentage of smokers in Europe, as well as the longest average lifespan—a fact Spanish smokers are not loathe to reiterate. Nevertheless, at the beginning of this century, lung cancer was nonexistent in Spain and today it is the leading fatal cancer in men. The legislative handwriting is on the wall about smoking in public places, but Spaniards are determined not to read it for as long as possible.

Some Barcelonese speculate that sensitive U.S. Olympic athletes, accustomed to entirely smoke-free environments, may have their performances adversely affected by the tremendous amount of passive smoking they will be doing, unless they stay in their rooms during the entire time they're not competing.

What appears more likely to affect them, however, and all the other athletes, is having to compete in the rain. The weather is staying wet and cool. People are increasingly nervous about the uncharacteristic days, beginning to worry that the Games will be rained out—even if there hasn't been a rainy July in living memory—that they will turn out to be hoodooed, hexed, jinxed. Spaniards are a little skeptical of their own abilities to carry off global media events, and many wonder if the result will be international shame instead of fame.

(As if to confirm such skepticism, less than two months before the World's Fair, Expo '92, was set to open in Seville in mid-April, the Spanish-built Pavilion of the Discoveries burned to the ground. It had taken over three years and $20 million to construct, and was dubbed the jewel of the Expo in the press. The building was completed and had a sprinkler system. Unfortunately, the system was not operational. People nodded when they heard, as if this was news they had been expecting.)

One thing that *is not* going to interrupt the Olympics is terrorism. Even though police have still not apprehended the two terrorists whose filthy, torn, and tattered Wanted posters are still up on some Barcelona walls, ETA's power to strike has been undone. Over the course of the spring, the French police have arrested a number of high-ranking ETA members living in southern France, people who were directing both the group's terrorist attacks and its finances. ETA has been left without access to funds or strategists.

For many years, the group has been partly directed from southern France, which harbors substantial sympathy for the Basque cause. Many refugees from the civil war settled there, and, during the dictatorship, any group opposing Franco inside Spain had their stamp of approval. In addition, the area around Bayonne and the Biscay Bay was part of Basque country during the Middle Ages, and the cause of the separatists arouses some sympathy. While there have been a number of pacts between France and Spain about cracking down on the fugitive terrorists, they haven't really done so until now.

House after house was raided, their occupants arrested and brought before magistrates in handcuffs or belly-chains. The French tolerance for ETA has ended, and with it has gone most of ETA's capacity for coordinated terrorist action inside Spain. Already, ETA is in such disarray that it appears doubtful the group can ever rebuild its former strength. The mayor's assurances to the FBI look like they are going to be kept.

While the Barcelonese may not be acutely concerned with the pollution of their air, or the nuclear power plants that generate their electrical energy, many of them do have to cope with a disaster in their living environment that strikes much closer, literally, to home. Buildings in many neighborhoods of Barcelona are prone to a structural weakness that can cause them to crumble.

On November 11, 1990, the first apartment building to collapse from "aluminosis" came down. Suddenly, without warning, a five-floor apartment building in the working-class neighborhood of Turo de la Peira collapsed, killing one person and seriously injuring three others. It happened as a result of high-aluminum cement being used in construction rather than Portland cement.

Until it was banned in 1977 (decades later than in most other European countries) Barcelona's builders used it because it set much more quickly. Construction could proceed more rapidly, at a higher profit. Almost all of the residential buildings affected by aluminosis were built between 1950 and 1970 to accommodate the great influx of workers coming to Barcelona from other parts of Spain. At the beginning of the 1950s, Barcelona had 1.3 million residents. Twenty years later, that number had grown by half a million, and the number of residential units in the city had doubled. Block after block of apartment buildings were put up by speculators and developers, who sold the pisos to workers as fast as they could get them on the market. These were apartments in large complexes, the sorts of polygons of new worker's apartments that rise in squared-off buildings on the outskirts of any large city.

In 1973, a man writing anonymously in the bulletin of the Barcelona neighborhood of Vallbona described his complex of apartment buildings: "The rooms are so small that the beds are almost too close together to pass between, and there is humidity in the ceiling, in the walls, in the floor that ruins the furniture . . . all our homes are rotting; the dust of the streets when it is dry and the mud when it rains, you have to walk a long way every day for a bus or a train; all of this is killing us little by little . . ."

These were the homes that people who came from Andalusia, or Estremadura, dreamed of when they moved to Barcelona—the piso and enough food on the table and, later, a television and a car. Who would have imagined that within twenty years their dream homes would be tumbling down around them? The building that collapsed in the Turo neighborhood was just the first chapter in a long nightmare for the city's residents. Aluminosis is a disaster on both an individual and community level that will affect Barcelona for years to come. Twenty-five neighborhoods and about fifteen thousand residences have now been identified as having aluminosis. Two thousand of the pisos are in buildings so badly affected that they will have to be torn down rather than repaired.

It was the administration of socialist mayor Pasqual Maragall that inherited the problems of these buildings, while the sons and daughters of those who constructed them inherited the wealth. Because the cement was legal, and because the companies that sold it to builders always provided literature describing aluminous cement and the ways it should be used, its manufacturers refuse to accept any responsibility for what happened.

A building with aluminosis continues to weaken until it eventually collapses, usually around thirty years after it was built. The identification of buildings in Barcelona with aluminosis has been ongoing since 1991. Repair is not easy, or cheap. The cement involved in the structural supports has to be replaced, so temporary supports have to be installed.

Current public policy is that buildings put up under public contracts with aluminosis will be repaired, or replaced if necessary, at public expense. In the case of buildings put up by the private sector, local and federal governments will jointly compensate people for fifty percent of the cost of repairs.

However, politicians in Spain have a reputation among the citizens for coming forward and saying the right thing, but being notoriously slow to suit action to words, particularly if that action involves writing a check. People cannot afford to wait years to make the necessary repairs to their homes if they want them to continue standing, so they pay for them if they can and hope the government will someday keep its word.

The six-floor building put up by Barcelona's Jewish congregation in 1954 on the Calle Avenir has meeting rooms, a library, administrative offices and two actual synagogues on different floors, each with its own altar, holy Ark, and scrolled Torah therein. Unfortunately, the building also has aluminosis, and its structural soundness is seriously compromised. Religious services are carried on around steel, floor-to-ceiling supports, protecting the building from collapse.

The condition of the synagogue mirrors, in some ways, the condition of the congregation to which it belongs—coming apart at the seams. There is a deep division among Jews in Barcelona about what the city's Jewish community and religious life should be like. It is an old debate, recently intensified by new arrivals.

When the Second World War ended, Barcelona's Jewish community consisted of refugees from the length and breadth of Europe, each country represented in relatively small numbers. Mostly, it was made up of central and eastern Europeans and Turks. Many of the Jews who had come to Barcelona as refugees during the war continued on to North or South America, or to Israel. By 1954, however, the community was stable enough to buy the Calle Avenir site in an upscale neighborhood. By law, they had to build it to look like any apartment building, with no external sign or decoration that would mark the fact that it contained a Jewish synagogue.

Over the years that followed, there were two waves of Jewish immigration that changed the character of the community. The first was a large number of Moroccan Jews who began arriving in the early 1950s, and continued coming for about fifteen years. As Morocco struggled for and achieved independence, the stable, ancient Jewish communities in the Spanish protectorates of Ceuta and Melilla began feeling the pressure of the new Muslim government. Many Moroccan Jews crossed the straits of Gibraltar for Spain. Their influx changed the nature of the Barcelona congregation from Ashkenazic (European) to Sephardic (Jews descended from the Sefarad, as well as those from the Middle East or North Africa).

"Until the Moroccan Jews began arriving, the life of the community was more important than the customs and traditions of the religious practice," said Barcelona engineer Carlos Schorr. "Up to that point, the community was more cultural and social than it was religious. People attended services for the most important holidays, but it was the community life that mattered most.

"The Moroccans, however, came from a long, established tradition of an intensely lived religious life, which overshadowed the communal and social aspects of being a Jewish community."

The community acknowledged this difference in 1954 when it put the two synagogues in the Calle Avenir building. The synagogue on the ground floor is the more orthodox, and has a balcony for women and girls, whereas that on the second story is all on one floor (even so, the women generally sit in the back). With the two synagogues, the community paradoxically managed to function as one, housing both factions under the same roof until the late 1970s. That was when large numbers of Jewish refugees began arriving from Argentina, fleeing their homeland's military dictatorship.

"People were leaving Argentina simply because life there had become too hard—not just for Jews, but for all middle-class people," said Benjamin Glaser, forty-nine, who was one of the early immigrants from Buenos Aires in 1976, and one of a small number of Argentine Jews who had joined the Barcelona congregation. "It was a situation of chaos in economic and social terms, and a time when the authorities were beginning to impose a harsh repression. You began to see police stopping and arresting people in the street."

The standards the Moroccan immigrants had used to define and hold together the community revolved around the synagogue and religious practice. These clashed with the values brought by the Argentines who had been accustomed to a liberal ideal that put more emphasis on the social and communal life than on religious traditions. Their notion of Judaism was too relaxed for either of the groups that worshiped in the two synagogues in the building on Calle Avenir.

Those Jews who arrived in Barcelona from Buenos Aires were in for a double shock, according to Glaser, an architect and partner of Carlos Schorr. Not only did Argentine Jews share an openness with other Argentines that was not to be found among Catalans, but they also felt rejected by Barcelona's Jewish community.

"The immigrants had to suffer two traumas right away," Glaser told me. "The first was to be treated as a *sudaca* by the Catalans. They might live here, but they would be excluded from the lives of the Catalans, who are totally different from the Argentines in their attitude toward daily life. This was very surprising to us.

"However, many Argentines expected better treatment from the Jews. They figured it would be an advantage to be Jewish because there would be a community waiting for them, and it was astonishing to discover this was not the case."

What the Argentines found was a conservative community, that placed little value on the type of intellectual achievements many of the immigrants brought with them and even less on their ideas about what it meant to be Jewish. There was an almost instant friction between the two groups, and very few of the Argentine Jews joined the congregation.

"The Jews from Argentina accuse us of being too old-fashioned and strict," said Carlos Benarroch, descended from Moroccan Sefarad. "That's not really true, but we are more traditional. Here, we want our children to grow up as Jews.

"I don't know how it is in New York, or in Buenos Aires, but here we demand a minimum amount of Judaism in order to conserve identity. To us, the Argentines don't seem to want to do this, not even to have a small amount of traditional practice."

Tuesday, June 30

The Olympic fever is, finally, noticeably rising.

Journalists are beginning to arrive. The press center in the Plaza España is up and running, a doctor is on call there around the clock, and the elaborate Olympic database has come on line at dozens of terminals scattered throughout the immense media facility, which will accommodate some five thousand working journalists less than three weeks from now, each bearing large, laminated press credentials around their necks.

The bars and restaurants around the Plaza España are full of foreign tongues. The Ramblas sports more than the usual number of television crews carrying expensive video cameras on their shoulders, trailed by assistants with boom mikes, looking for interviews and local color.

Unfortunately for them, Barcelona has lost a lot of its local color during these last few weeks. The municipal government announced that all licenses and permissions to work the Ramblas were off, null and void during the Games. Officials did not want the usual hoard of beggars, buskers, street musicians, mimes, jugglers, shell-game hustlers, and fire-eaters asking tourists for their time and change.

In addition, the city's prostitutes, transvestites and women alike, were told that during the Games they would have to ply their trade in the Zona Franca, zona nowhere, a warehouse district on the edge of Barcelona. The Ramblas was off-limits, as was the well-worn stroll behind the stadium at Camp Nou, within walking distance of the fancy hotels along the upper end of the Avenida Diagonal where heads of state would be housed.

Security plans called for the entire Camp Nou area to be closed to vehicular traffic during the Games. No one would be allowed to drive through, so there would be no customers, municipal officials told the hookers, assuring them they would be allowed to come back when the Games were over. There were a lot of prostitutes who did not believe they would be allowed to return, but they were not given much choice.

The branch of city hall with administrative responsibility for street-walkers is, logically, Ramon Ferriera's department of public ways. No one forced the prostitutes to do anything, he told me. "We didn't move anybody, anywhere. It was done in mutual agreement with the city police. That area absolutely had to be closed for the Olympic family. There will be police everywhere. If the cars can't come in and these ladies and gentlemen are there, how will they make any money?

"Our offer to them was the Zona Franca. And we told them that when the Games were over and the cordon was lifted, they could come back. They accepted the offer. That's all. Simple. Nothing complicated or sinister. We are not trying to prohibit streetwalkers in Barcelona. Cities have good things and bad, but however you see prostitutes, cities always have them, they are a part of a cityscape.

"Catalans are not like Americans. As long as something does not molest us, we are inclined to let it exist. And, do not forget that we are a world port, and when the first Phoenician sailor came, you can be sure there was a lady here waiting for him with an hour of her time for sale. Our job is not to prohibit prostitution."

The authorities, apparently, do not feel comfortable with an entirely sanitized Ramblas, and have left a little color, granting permission to a few regular street performers to work. Among them are a living statue of a nun, a knife-thrower, and a flamenco dancer. The dancer is Antonio Barranco, fifty-seven, who dances three hours in the middle of each day on the Ramblas, calling himself Lola Capullo. Tall, thin, angular, dressed in the traditional flamenco outfit of black boots, sharply creased black trousers, white ruffled shirt, black vest, and a black wide-brimmed hat, he gracefully dances on a large, round piece of half-inch plywood. He has a small, cheap, portable tape player and a cassette of flamenco music with the volume cranked up as far as it will go. His booted toes and heels pound the wood, while his hands curve in the air above his head, and keep time by clacking castanets. He has closely cropped hair, and round, firm breasts that would be the envy of many a twenty-five-year-old woman. They are, of course, silicone implants, part of a larger plan, which he has never had the money to complete.

Lola Capullo was an early and enduring hit with the media. Because Barcelona is not a flamenco city, it is hard for a randomly roving journalist to encounter it here, but for many foreigners it is the music of Spain and makes a great audio backdrop to a piece. Whenever a camera or sound crew happens on Antonio Barranco, it is love at first sight. Along with Gaudí's Holy Family Cathedral, and the fountains in the Plaza España, Barranco has become a signature shot for the city, and during the Olympics he's a sure bet to be flashed on television screens around the world.

"People are always coming up to me on the Ramblas and asking if I'm a man or a woman," he told me, when I visited him one afternoon deep in the barrio chino where he was living. "I shrug. What can I say? Both. Neither. I could never be either one."

He showed me pictures of himself as a handsome, young man during the 1950s. "For my mother, I was a man. She didn't want to know anything about my other life, so I sent her pictures like these."

Other pictures, taken after his implant surgery, showed him reclining on a bed in scanty lingerie, breasts revealed, looking thoroughly the attractive woman. The pictures were taken by his wife.

"For the sake of appearances, I married twenty-eight years ago. My wife knew all about me from the first day. I hid nothing. She's had her life, I've had mine. But, we've been through a lot together."

They were still going through a lot together when I met them. They were renting a room in an apartment, living there with a chihuahua puppy. They were allowed the use of a tiny kitchen and a small parlor that was in deep shadow at midday. The place had tall ceilings and stained plaster walls, from which the paper had long since peeled away. The walls, and the ceiling ten feet above us, were criss-crossed with cracks. He gestured around himself with despair when he showed me the small room with its two narrow, iron beds where he and his wife were staying. They paid 2,000 pestas [$20] a day for it. His short, plump wife, who said she was suffering from asthma, sat on one bed and sewed up a tear in a ruffled white shirt. She sat with her back against the wall, short legs stuck out across the bed in front of her, and the chihuahua puppy beside her on the frayed grey blanket. Above Antonio's bed was a picture of Jesus holding a bleeding, scarlet heart. A half-dozen flamenco dancer's hats, round with stiff brims, red and black, were hung on nails along one wall.

Antonio and I sat talking at a battered, wooden table in the parlor, which was scarred with cigarette burns. "My father and my brother were both homosexuals. My father kept his homosexuality hidden. We lived in Andalusia and we were dirt poor. We didn't go to school. I taught myself to read and write. At the age of thirteen, in 1948, I came to Barcelona to look for work."

He found it, working as a bell-hop's assistant and substitute elevator operator in a starched uniform and round bell-boy's cap, at a fancy hotel on the Plaza Cataluña. "After less than a year on that job, there came an evening when the police stopped me in the street and said, 'You're a queer.' And I said, 'So?'"

"That was my first time in jail. They sent me to the correctional institute for minors. That's where you went until you were twenty-one. I was in and out I don't know how many times after that: for fifteen days one time, a month the next—on and on and on. My mother couldn't understand why I kept getting into trouble. 'Why don't you go into the military?' she asked. So I decided to join the Legion."

He showed me a black and white photo, yellow-brown with age, of himself in the uniform of the Spanish Foreign Legion. "In the Legion, I was eventually prosecuted for being a homosexual. I did three years' hard labor, a pick and shovel. They sent me all over: Valencia, Barcelona, and Ceuta. It was horrible. They ruined me. Three years at hard labor. I was never a real human being again. After it was over, they threw me into the street with my head shaved. I wasn't even a person, anymore. I came to Barcelona."

Even under Franco, Barcelona was slightly more liberal than other parts of the country. The clubs along the Parallel were thriving, and Barranco found work as a dancer. From 1960 to 1964, he worked at Barcelona de Noche. It was a precarious existence, however, and his trips to jail continued. Finally, he left the country for Italy, and did not come back until after Franco died.

Tears welled up in his eyes, spilled over and rolled down his cheeks. His voice broke. "The Olympics will make me famous all over the world, but so what? I have nothing but sorrow. My life has been hard, too hard. Every time I had something I lost it. Now I have nothing. Nothing.

"I had my own home in Genoa, Italy, then I came back to my homeland to live in a democratic Spain. I had a house on the coast in Torremolinos. It was taken away from me by trickery because I'm a homosexual. They have left me with nothing, and the socialist government did nothing to protect my rights.

"The only thing they have not been able to do to me is take away my dancing. I've always loved dancing and I'm on the Ramblas dancing for at least three hours each day that it's not too wet or cold. When I'm dressed up, on the Ramblas, and I hear the music I forget everything and I dance. At fifty-seven, I can still dance two or three hours without realizing it. When I dance, nothing hurts, my head doesn't ache, and I forget my suffering."

CHAPTER NINE

Olympic Grace

Sunday, July 26

The last week of June brought some intermittent blue skies and bright sunshine. People broke out their summer wardrobes, began going to the beach on weekends, and thinking about vacation. It looked as if summer had finally arrived, but then it started to rain. And rain. No one could remember a summer with such miserable weather. Climatological records showed it was the wettest first two weeks of July since 1941, and only twice this century had the average temperatures been cooler. The idea of rain during the Olympics began to loom seriously, one of the few contingencies for which the planners of the Games had not been worried enough to plan. What if it rained during the opening ceremony, scheduled for the outdoor stadium atop Montjuich on the evening of July 25?

It did not. The weather for last night's inaugural ceremony was excellent and the evening went off without any serious problems. At least none I could see from my bar stool. I watched the whole thing on television at the cafe around the corner from my piso, the same seat I frequently occupy to watch el Barça's soccer games. Last night, the regular patrons paid somewhat less attention to the events on the small screen than they do if Barcelona's eleven are on the field at Camp Nou.

Things got warmed up when King Juan Carlos and Queen Sofia made their entrance, accompanied by the Catalan national anthem, followed by the Spanish national anthem. The order of the anthems was the evening's big coup for Catalan nationalists. Catalan politicians have mounted an aggressive, expensive campaign in the past few weeks to identify the Games with Catalonia. Huge, five-story-high Catalan flags hang down the fronts of buildings from the roofs. Flags to drape across balconies have been given away to anyone who will display them. They are everywhere.

This has been bitterly resented by non-Catalans. The sight of King Juan Carlos and Queen Sofia entering the great stadium and walking slowly toward the royal box to the strains of "Els Segadors" provoked intense reaction on both sides of the debate over Catalan independence. A loud discussion immediately broke out along the bar.

"That's a typical Catalan thing to do, to play their anthem first, and I don't care who hears me say it," a middle-aged, balding man said in Spanish from the end of the bar, shaking his head in disgust and sipping from his snifter of anis. "Madrid has spent far more on these Games than the Catalans, and everyone knows it. If Cataluña was a country there would never have been enough money for the Olympics to be here. Even they'll tell you that. It's an insult to the king and queen."

On the other side of me, a young man with black hair slicked back, wearing a shiny suit and narrow tie sang along with "Els Segadors" and cheered when it ended. "All the foreigners that are here don't know a thing about Catalunya," he said in Catalan, loudly enough to be heard by us all. "The Games are going to put us on the map of the world. People are learning that Spain and Catalunya are two different things."

The televised ceremony moved on to opera.

I live close to the headquarters of ONCE, the national institute for the blind. Each day all the city's lottery ticket sellers, an army of them, go there in the morning to get their tickets and in the evening to turn in the day's receipts. The neighborhood has a lot of people moving through it with canes or seeing-eye dogs. Four middle-aged, visually-impaired people, two men and two women, were sitting at one of the tables, the same place they sit almost every evening at dusk. When there are soccer games on telelvision, they halt their ongoing conversation and stare sightlessly into the middle distance, listening closely, cheering, commenting occasionally on el Barça's play. Last night it was the opera that got their attention, including performances by José Carreras, Montserrat Caballé, and Plácido Domingo.

That was the aural highlight of the ceremony. Other than opera, its high points were visual. Next up was the Fura dels Baus, one of Barcelona's two world class theater groups that work in large, open spaces. They used two thousand people to mount a colorful spectacle depicting the birth of Barcelona on the coastline of the Mediterranean. The Fura dels Baus had the sighted patrons mesmerized at the bar.

Then there was a procession around the track at Montjuich stadium, of the ten thousand Olympic athletes parading behind their flags. It took a long time for all the delegations to pass around the stadium in alphabetical progression. Once done with the circuit, they stood in the middle of the field, where the numbers of athletes got larger and larger. They milled around chatting with each other, generally oblivious to speeches by Mayor Maragall and Juan Antonio Samaranch, the former Francoist who is now president of the International Olympic Committee. Likewise, attention at the bar began to flag, another round was ordered, people went to the bathroom. Then, a casual statement by the announcer informed us that the evening's nearly three hours was costing $18 million. The middle-aged man sitting next to me swore viciously.

"The Olympics—you can have them," he muttered. "They need to be spending some of that money on giving old people a decent pension, and on getting some hospitals. Too much money spent on buildings and sports, and not enough on people.

"My daughter's in the hospital right now, and I can tell you it's hard to find a bed. When you do there's no air conditioning, and that kind of heat is not only uncomfortable, it's bad for the health of people in the hospital. This is not worth $18 million," he said, gesturing toward the television.

The fifty-five thousand spectators in the stadium were reacting with considerably more enthusiasm, applauding the end of the speeches.

The spectacle drew us back, as a Catalan archer stood spotlit in the night, in front of the hushed crowd, aiming an arrow of flame into the bowl of the huge, gas Olympic torch towering above the stadium. He drew back his bow, to everyone's relief the arrow hit its target, the flame lit, and the Olympics began.

Reuters Press estimated that as many as three and one-half billion people, two thirds of the world's population, watched the opening of the Olympics on television. These are the most representative and international Games since Rome in 1960. Iraq is here, less than eighteen months after the Gulf War, as is Cuba, with Fidel Castro at the head of its delegation. The competitors who have come from South Africa were not even born the last time their country was allowed to send athletes to the Games. This will be the last Olympics for the team composed of the former athletes of the Soviet Union, which is calling itself the Unified Team. In 1996, these athletes will be representing the newly independent nation states from which they come. There is even a group competing from the former Yugoslavia, where war is raging, although the athletes have no flag, nor national anthem, and are not being allowed to participate in the opening and closing ceremonies.

While it was not visible from my bar stool, the inaugural was less than absolutely perfect. One person died of a heart attack—the father of a U.S. swimmer. And, there was a problem with the Iranians. In the procession around the stadium, each country's delegation walked behind a volunteer from Barcelona who carried that nation's flag. There was last-minute panic when the Iranian delegation, all men, refused to walk behind the female volunteer who had been designated to carry the flag of Iran. Someone from the Barcelona Olympic Committee hurriedly found a male volunteer, and substituted him to placate the Iranians.

Today, a spokeswoman for the International Olympic Committee responded to a question about the incident at a press conference. She told reporters that although the IOC supported applying sanctions against those countries guilty of racial discrimination, and would continue to do so, sanctions would not be applied in cases of obvious gender discrimination.

Neither Judaism nor Islam is known for an enlightened attitude toward women and their roles in the world. Both are staunchly patriarchal in their notions of God and family. While Jewish women do not have to go about veiled, like many of their Muslim counterparts, they are not allowed, under traditional Jewish practice, to sit with men in the House of God. They have to gather upstairs, farther from the holy scripture, the Torah. Likewise, Muslim women do not pray with their men. They can enter the periphery of the mosque, but they do not go into its heart to pray.

However, even during the Middle Ages, both Jewish and Muslim women could divorce their husbands if they were being mistreated, and receive some form of alimony. Catholic women, on the other hand, are free to worship in the cathedral with men, but are bound to their husbands for life. This is not just a religious injunction in Spain, but was the law of the land right up until the Republicans began their brief term of governing the country in 1931.

Shortly after they came to power, they passed a set of laws that dealt with women's rights. These included extending the vote to women, as well as assigning them equal status with men in the home and the workplace. Both civil marriage and divorce became legal and equally accessible to men and women. In 1935, the Catalan Parliament, controlled by Republicans, passed a law that formally declared the equality of men and women. In 1936, abortion was legalized.

This entire body of law was revoked as soon as Franco and the Falangist party won the civil war in 1939. From that point on, a wife could not legally take a job, start a business, open a bank account, get a driver's license, or take a trip without her husband's approval. Women could not work at night, and they were strongly discouraged from pursuing any kind of career. The law under Franco that governed the rights and roles of women was based on one fundamental and oft-stated Falangist tenet: "The husband must protect his wife, and she must obey her husband."

Adultery for both sexes was a crime, but for the man it was only illegal if he committed it in the family home; if he left his family and went to live with his mistress; or if his indiscretion was so great that his affair was considered public knowledge. For a woman, any adultery, anywhere, was a crime, and punishable by a prison term of up to six years.

As John Hooper pointed out in *The Spaniards*, the fact that a woman could be charged with desertion—a crime—if she left the family home for even a few days against her husband's wishes, meant that a woman who was being physically abused could not take refuge outside the home without her husband's consent. And, if she did leave, she would probably have to do so using public transportation, because without her husband's signed permission, a woman could not get a driver's license.

Paradoxically, the years when this disenfranchisement was at its height were those when Spanish men were leaving family and homeland in record numbers to work at menial, hard labor in some other country. The women stayed behind with total responsibility for running the household on a daily basis. They had no time to consult with their husbands when the need for immediate action arose. These were, effectively, single-parent households where the women made all the decisions, the only contribution of their husbands, a regular check in the mail, if that. The men might manage to get home twice a year— at Christmas and for a week or two during the summer. As likely as not, when they went back to France to work the fields, or Germany for their non-union construction jobs, the wives they left behind were pregnant, again.

María Moron (pronounced Mo-roan) was a child during those years, in a village in southwestern Spain. Currently the director of a private think-tank focusing on women's issues, Barcelona's Centre Estudis Dona i Societat (Center for the Study of Woman and Society), Moron remembers the years of her childhood as having been lived among a community of women, a matriarchal daily life enclosed by a patriarchal society.

"Here in Barcelona, perhaps it was a little different during those years, but in the small village where I grew up, one of the things that helped women support this situation was that everyone in the community knew one another, and helped one another out," she told me one afternoon in the center's modest offices in the Ensanche district. "Although their husbands were gone, women did not have to face their daily lives by themselves. At the beginning of the 1960s, for instance, when money was scarce and women sometimes couldn't buy what they needed, the other women in the village shared with them.

"Small farmers who had olive groves would harvest the olives with one pass, and then leave the second pass to single mothers in the village who could come and get enough olives to take to the aceitero and get ten or fifteen liters of olive oil. Women got by. They raised a cow, and pigs, kept chickens, planted gardens, and sold a few vegetables, some chickpeas or potatoes. There was no health coverage in those days, but there were some old people who still remembered how to prepare herbal medicines for things like colds and fevers."

While women had to keep their families going on a daily basis, they were also programmed from birth to shun independence and independent thinking, and to defer to men in all matters. To step outside those boundaries could mean being lost in this world, and damned for eternity. Women were taught to be ashamed of their sex, of its weaknesses, and to gladly accept their inferior position. Girls who reached their adolescence as recently as twenty years ago grew up in a world where to be a woman was to be a second-class, disenfranchised citizen.

"When I first began to meet American women, the thing I admired most about them was that they were not afraid to speak out at their workplace or in a classroom," my friend Carmen, a biochemist, told me. "They were not bothered by the fact that they might be saying something that was wrong. Here, both sexes are taught that if we speak out about something we might be proven wrong, or rejected, and that it is better to keep our mouths shut. We are taught not to call attention to ourselves, and that is particularly true for women."

In fact, under Franco, the idea of a woman pursuing a career in the sciences was unthinkable. From the cradle they were groomed for a career as a housewife, tending home and children, while men went into the world. The state constantly reinforced these expectations and behaviors, most often through the Feminine Section of the Falangist Party, which was the organization entrusted with responsibility for the women of Spain, for controlling the way they thought and lived.

The founder of the Feminine Section was Pilar Primo de Rivera, daughter of Miguel Primo de Rivera, whose government had preceded the Republic. In a speech in 1943, quoted by Carmen Martín Gaite in her book, *Usos amorosos de la postguerra española* (*Amorous Customs of Postwar Spanish Women*), Pilar Primo de Rivera said: "Women never discover anything: they certainly lack the creative talent to do so. That is something reserved by God for the masculine intelligence. We are not able to do more than interpret, for better or worse, what the men make."

Teenage girls were indoctrinated each day with fear of the masculine sex. Nothing was so frowned on as a woman who tried to usurp some part of the masculine role for herself. There were parts of Spain where women could not wear pants. Jordi Petit remembers driving with his parents in 1963 on vacation from Barcelona to Andalusia.

"We stopped one morning at a market in a village, and my mother was wearing slacks, the kind women were starting to wear in Barcelona in the 1960s," he told me. "The women in the market stoned my mother, picked up rocks and threw them at her. We had to run to the car to escape. Here on the coast of Catalonia, things were a little more liberal because people were used to seeing tourists, but the women who lived in places more inland were raised in an incredibly conservative environment."

Girls were taught that the world was full of temptation, and they must always struggle against their bodies. They were not allowed to wear pyjamas, they wore nightgowns. When they changed for bed, they were taught to pray during the undressing and dressing, so they would not pay attention to their momentarily uncovered flesh.

Men were not subjected to equally rigid standards. For young men, it was accepted practice to lose their virginity to a prostitute, which served the dual purpose of releasing some of their pubescent hormonal energy, and also provided them with the experience they would need when it came time to find a mother for their children, and claim their own flowers of Spanish maidenhood. These blooms were on display every Sunday afternoon in the village square or urban plaza. There eligible girls promenaded hand in hand, while the young bachelors watched them from a cafe. Men were taught to see women in one of three molds: mothers, whores, or wives. And from childhood they were groomed to enter a society in which the men were dominant, and never found themselves on common ground with a woman.

There was no church-burning when Franco died, but there was an active dismantling of the structures of the church from around peoples' lives, particularly by women. By the late 1960s, as feminist movements grew in the United States and much of northern Europe, Spanish women began to resist their traditional roles, and nowhere were they more determined than in Barcelona, the closest metropolis to the rest of Europe.

"Once women took the first step, they found themselves in the process that produces consciousness," said Moron, a blonde woman, in her early forties. "For a woman who finds a way to have her own life in a situation where she was previously bound to circumstances that destroyed both her and her marriage, the process is irreversible. She's not going back to being a housewife under the dominion of her husband.

"Don't forget that Spanish women had been taking care of things without their husbands for years, when their menfolk were working out of the country. There was a feminist movement here even before Franco died. There were groups of women who went into the street to protest the dictatorship. These were not feminists in the sense that everyone was radical, but rather an organization of women that ranged from radical feminists to housewives. If it had not been for the presence of those thousands of well-organized women, then we wouldn't have even the recognition in society we have today."

Moron ran brightly polished nails through her hair, and lit a cigarette. "I'm under no illusions, though. Spanish women have a long way to go, and the progress they have made hasn't been easy to achieve. The patriarchal tradition here is deeply rooted and resistant to change."

Spanish men, as it turned out, were perfectly willing to see the censorship laws go, and to have naked female breasts in front of their eyes. This was a part of the democratic process to which they were happy to adjust. But, when it came to giving up their dominion in the household, the workplace, or under the law, they balked, both individually and collectively. Women seldom find themselves on an equal footing with men, either in the home or on the job.

"We see the same patriarchal tradition all over the world to differing degrees," said Moron. "Everywhere there is a masculine society where men are the central point of reference. The situation changes a bit under democracy, because women gain protection under the law, which provides sanctions for discriminatory treatment. This, at least, allows a greater degree of participation for women in society. There's a lot, however, that remains unchanged."

Even in those areas of life that are regulated by law, women cannot always get the equal treatment to which they are entitled. The clause prohibiting employment discrimination in Spain does not have the scope of American laws on the same subject. The Want Ads in Barcelona newspapers are allowed to specify gender and age as part of the requirements for an advertised job. A classified ad in *La Vanguardia* is typical: "Attractive girl who can read English, between the ages of twenty and twenty-five, wanted as office assistant."

Women in Spain make about twenty-six percent less money than men for doing the same job, according to the National Statistical Institute. More and more women are entering the work force—currently, they represent just under half. As elsewhere in Europe and North America, the cost of life in a consumer society requires both members in a marriage to have jobs to stay afloat in a sea of credit and debts.

Managerial and executive positions remain almost exclusively the province of men. There are also certain kinds of unskilled jobs that are virtually closed to women, and not just those where heavy manual labor is involved. For instance, waiting on tables is almost exclusively a male profession. Not just in elegant restaurants with white tablecloths and sterling silver flatware, but also in little cafes on the corners serving basic Catalan fare. If you do see a woman waiting on tables, it's usually because she is related to the cafe's owners. (Work as a waiter is, for many men, a lifetime occupation, as the number of older waiters testifies. These are men who have raised their families waiting on tables.)

The socialist party has tried to address women's issues with more than rhetoric, but with much less than what many observers, including María Moron, feel needs to be done. In a policy adopted in 1990, the socialists agreed that twenty-five percent of the people in the directorships of local parties must be women, and that the same percentage would apply to their candidates put up for election. The next year, 1991, the party voted to raise the participation figure to thirty-five percent. By 1992, this had already substantially increased the number of women in politics and government, although their numbers fall off dramatically further up the ranks. Felipe González's press secretary is a woman, but almost all the cabinet ministers are men, and only seventeen of the Catalan Parliament's 135 members are women.

These public gender biases are reflected in the equally important details of private lives. For instance, a 1992 study by the European

Community concluded that Spanish men helped less with domestic duties than men in any other European country. The church, apparently, cannot be blamed for this attitude, because men in staunchly Catholic Ireland are among the most helpful in the home. Eight out of ten Spanish males never perform any domestic duties.

"My wife won't let me help her out at home," one male Catalan acquaintance of mine defended himself when I asked him about the study. "She was raised by her mother to believe that she would be less than a good wife if I had to cook or wash the dishes or do the laundry. What can I say?"

What, indeed.

Friday, July 31

These Olympics are almost as much a competition between multinational corporations as between nations. More than any other summer Games, they are the Olympics of consumption. For the first time, the gold medals are actually made of gold, and they're worth about $5,000. And, for many who win them, the real gold beckons in endorsements, and sponsorship from one or another of the corporations. The multinationals are here in force, company yachts moored prominently in the port. They are here and competing intensely for the logo gold. Olympians such as Nike, Adidas, Visa, Coca Cola, Smirnoff, and plenty of others, battle furiously for maximum brand-name exposure to the global television audience. Many nations are acting much the same way, offering substantial cash rewards to athletes who win medals and bring their countries to the front of the world stage, if only for a moment.

In ancient Greece, wars were suspended while the Olympics took place. Mayor Maragall, mindful of the fact that people will be dying in the war going on between Serbs, Croats and Muslims in Bosnia-Herzegovina while the world watches the Olympics, calls for a ceasefire during the fifteen days of competition. His appeal fails.

The bid to stop the fighting is an admirable effort. The mayor refuses to focus exclusively on how well the Games are running, thanks to six years of his administration planning for these sixteen days. As if, after all the rhetoric and hype, he still believes the Games can have some more important effect on the rest of the world than just being good entertainment and a means for some people to make lots of money. Regretfully, he is wrong. The Balkan war has a demonic energy of its own, and does not stop for blips on the cultural map.

Even if they can't stop wars, the Games are achieving some smaller examples of goodwill. Free physicals are available to anyone in the Olympic delegations, and many people are taking advantage of them. All twenty-three members of Yemen's delegation, for instance, went for their general medical check-ups, and for many of them it was a first. There are lots of people getting their first immunizations, glasses, and dental work.

Many of them have plenty of time to do so, because for the first time in recent years officials have decreed that athletes eliminated in early rounds can continue to receive free bed and board at the Olympic Village on the beach at the north end of Barceloneta until the end of the Games. This has left a lot of athletes footloose and fancy free, and some parts of the city, like the Ramblas, are crowded with remarkably lovely, healthy, young bodies.

Since the Games began, Barcelona has taken on the feel of a real world-class, cosmopolitan, multicultural city. Normally, Caucasian is the dominant racial group here, and Catalan the language most often heard. Anyone without that skin or that language always feels somewhat foreign. Now, people of all complexions from lightest Scandinavian to darkest African walk down the streets, and the sounds of many different tongues, sibilant and harsh, come to the ear. The city is playing its role of host to perfection. Police are not, contrary to what I had expected, greatly in evidence, nor overly intrusive.

The Plaza España is packed with people, night and day. While the sun is shining they come to ride the series of escalators that carry them up to the Olympic stadium, domed gymnasium, and swimming pools atop Montjuich. There are people selling souvenirs and others scalping tickets, crowds of the unticketed walking back and forth. The flame burns high on the torch beside the stadium. People continuously line up to videotape themselves in front of it, a wide cross-section of the world smiling into cameras and waving from the same spot.

There are also many people who get no closer to the Olympics than the Plaza España down below, stopped there by the crowds, satisfied to stroll the sidewalks of the broad Avenida María Cristina leading up to the National Palace, to rub elbows with the polyglot masses.

Television crews from all over the world mill around the Plaza España buttonholing anyone they hear speaking their language, filming the fountains, the people, the palace, the boulevard, and the traffic, all for rapid retransmission to their home countries.

Entrepreneurs have set up on the sidewalks, speaking a variety of tongues, which they use to sell Olympic pins from different countries and past Games. Pin collectors swarm around them five deep, bargaining, swapping, and dealing. The pin hawkers are in the right city—the people of Barcelona are great collectors, and are known for a willingness to collect just about anything. Collecting is a passion nurtured in children by their parents. Barcelonese have taken to collecting Olympic pins with a fervor, although they had never heard of them before now.

Crowds around the plaza do not lessen after the sun goes down. They flock here from all over the city to stand on the brightly illuminated terraces below the National Palace and watch colored jets of water rise and fall in the fountains. The Palace is a huge and astonishing domed building put up for the International Exhibiton in 1929, which looms over one end of the Plaza España. Seven backshafts of light shoot up from its roof like points on a crown. Rock and roll plays on loudspeakers by the fountains, beckoning the continuous stream of people flowing up the steps of the metro into the plaza.

After the nightly detonation of fireworks in the stadium signals the conclusion of another official Olympic day, the very old head off for bed and everyone else goes out to party. The Games have proven to be a windfall for Barcelona's nightlife, during what is normally its slowest period. The city's designer bars are usually empty in July and August when the smart set is on vacation on Ibiza, at Marbella, or some other summer seaside destination. Now, they're doing a brisk business. Some, like Las Torres de Avila, the outrageous, and outrageously expensive, three-story club co-designed by Javier Mariscal who also designed the Olympic mascot Cobi, are rented for the duration of the Games and closed to the public.

"Rich Americans," shrugs José Canal, the club's manager. "We're very happy to oblige them."

The most exclusive club in town during the Games, however, is the discotheque inside the Olympic Village, restricted to people with Olympic credentials. It stays open until 4 A.M. every morning. Those athletes still competing and moving towards the finals in the Games issue public pleas to those who have been eliminated to hold down their partying, and complain that they can't sleep. Nevertheless, the free room and board, and the numbers of young, unattached people, has everyone in a good-time mood, and the discotheque is packed each night.

The only athletes having nothing to do with the Olympic Village are the Dream Team. Michel Jordan and company are staying at the five-star Ambassador Hotel, shunning the Olympic Village, which is not air-conditioned and sleeps two to a plain room. Not for the best basketball players in the world. These guys are the Games' most aggressive marketeers, whenever they appear in public their corporate logos are visible from all angles. They do not so much represent the U.S. as they do Nike and Adidas and Reebok.

It is undeniably hot at the Olympic Village, and it is hardest on the North Americans. Most of the other competitors are not used to air-conditioning. Apart from the heat, life at the Village seems to please most of the athletes. Practically everything there is free. One thing that was not, in the beginning, was condoms. Initially, they were sold from machines for $3 apiece. The complaints poured in—people from under-developed countries could not afford those prices, and a number of the partying athletes raised the issue. Now, officials have announced that condoms are available for free at the on-site, twenty-four-hour pharmacy. It is conjectured that more than fifty thousand condoms will be used during the Games.

In 1990, Spain had the highest per capita sale of condoms in the EC, according to government figures, about 115 million, generating $70 million. There was also a $6 million campaign in 1991 by the federal Ministry of Health promoting condom use, in which over 1.5 million condoms were distributed free. The program drew stinging criticism from the church. The Pope called on Spanish pharmacists not to sell condoms, but sales continue to increase.

This, despite the fact that a generation ago there was a law on the books forbidding the sale of prophylactics. It was generally ignored, and pharmacists sold condoms to men from a box under the counter (one man who remembers using them says they felt as if they were made from "elephant hide"). More sophisticated birth control was harder to obtain, however. Doctors were not allowed to counsel patients about family planning, birth control was not widely practiced, and large families were standard.

The Franco government provided state subsidies for families with more than three children, and the amount paid increased incrementally, so that there was an economic benefit to be gained from having lots of children. I once asked a forty-year-old Catalan friend of mine if he came from a large family? No, he answered, there were only five kids.

By the early 1970s, birth control pills were in wide use. There were many doctors who would write prescriptions for the Pill, only permitted by law for conditions requiring hormonal treatment. The names of doctors who took a broad view of "hormonal treatment" spread by word of mouth from woman to woman. By the time Franco died, birth control was already basically available, particularly to someone with a little money.

Under the socialists, doctors could prescribe birth control pills for any reason, insert intrauterine devices, perform vasectomies and tubal ligations, and freely counsel their patients about birth control. In 1975, when Franco died, Spain's birth rate was 2.72 children for each woman, the second highest in Europe, and surpassed only by Ireland. By 1991, that number was just about halved, with the birth rate at 1.39, the second *lowest* in the world, behind Italy's. In Catalonia, it was still lower, all the way down to 1.23, the lowest birth rate in the world, and below any European region since the years of the Second World War.

Those people who aspire to more than rudimentary survival, who want credit cards and electrodomestic marvels, have discovered that their preferred lifestyle leaves only enough energy for a small number of children. They have neither the time nor the money required of large families. Even with just one or two kids, it is tough to pay for shelter, food, clothes, a car, and everything that everybody sees on television. In this sense is the First World very small: people working hard to buy the same things in one long free-market mall stretching from Barcelona through the San Francisco Bay to Tokyo.

Young Spanish women first began changing their traditional attitudes toward sex and marriage in the mid-1960s, affected by the faint reverberations of the sexual revolution going on in the rest of the First World. Abortions were illegal in Spain, punishable by a stiff fine and a jail sentence for both the abortionist and the pregnant woman. Abortions were available on demand in other European countries—Britain, Holland, and Germany, and thousands of Spanish women with unwanted pregnancies went to England during those years. When a woman told friends she was going to London for a few days, it was assumed she was going for an abortion. There were not only London clinics that specialized in providing abortions to Spanish women, but also those that served women from particular regions of Spain. Spanish law was so strict, however, that women who went to other countries for abortions were liable to criminal prosecution when they returned.

Abortion was one of the issues at the top of the socialist agenda. In the mid-1980s, a law was passed that allows abortions during the first three months of pregnancy in cases where the mother's life or health is threatened. Doctors are generally encouraged to factor in a patient's mental as well as physical health. The socialists have now begun talking about expanding the law to include cases where having the child would cause the mother unwarranted "anxiety."

In cases that fall within the laws permitting abortion, the procedure is free of charge, paid for by the national health system. Even in those cases that do not fall under the categories permitted by law, a woman no longer needs to go to London "for a few days," according to María Moron. "There are private clinics here that will perform clean, safe abortions in the first trimester of pregnancy for $300, even if they are not within the law, and these clinics are generally left alone by the authorities."

Sunday, August 2

Yesterday was the first Saturday of the Games, and more than 500,000 people ascended Montjuich. The moving stairways up the hill from the Plaza España transported eighteen thousand people an hour. Those thirty-eight thousand who were lucky enough to have a seat in the stadium saw Linford Christie, a young Englishman who had left his native Jamaica with his parents for Great Britain at the age of nine, win the 100-meter gold medal, turning in a 9.96-second dash, the second fastest time ever recorded.

Few noted that the date also marked the five hundredth anniversary of the first day Spain was officially without a Jew inside its borders. There were no commemorative events, and the media did not report it. Of course, in 1492 the Expulsion had already been a fact of life in Barcelona for 101 years, where there had been no Jewish community since the summer of 1391.

At first glance, the Jewish community that has returned to Barcelona seems well established, with roots that are already three generations deep in some families. Among many in the community, however, there is a skepticism about the long-term possibilities for Judaism in both Barcelona and the whole of Spain, a sense that the Jews here could, once again, disappear and leave hardly a trace of their passing. This insecurity is not based on the idea that their Catholic neighbors may expel them again, although Jews certainly watch the growing neo-Nazi movement in Europe with dismay. What threatens them is the shrinking of their community.

"In my opinion, there is a definite possibility that Jews could disappear from Barcelona in a century," Jaime Vandor told me one afternoon in his office at the University of Barcelona's department of Hebrew and Aramaic Studies. "It is possible that the number of young Jews will grow successively smaller in the years to come, as it has already been doing for some time, until a point is reached where the community simply is gone.

"I would say ninety percent of the young Jews in Barcelona marry a non-Jew. Maybe not that high a percentage, but the number is high. Many of the Jewish partners in those marriages do not participate in any form in the Jewish community. Among those young people who do want to live as Jews are many who will move to Israel."

The number of births in the community has not kept pace with the number of deaths, casting further doubt on the community's future. One thing that would, obviously, mitigate this trend is the same thing that has served to swell the congregation in the past: a new wave of immigration. The Jews who immigrated from Argentina might represent just the positive numbers the community needs, yet they have not been able to attract or absorb the Argentines.

Some of the younger, more progressive members of the Calle Avenir congregation have decided that such integration is a necessity, and five of them ran in the congregation's 1989 executive board election. The central plank in their platform was a commitment to whatever was needed to open the Calle Avenir congregation to all the Jews of the city. They won a five-year term. They were led by the new president of the community, David Grebler, an articulate, handsome and boyish-looking businessman of Swiss origin who has a lot of energy.

"It's not so much a question of Argentines versus everyone else as it is a division among the three kinds of Judaism: orthodox, conservative, and reform. We hoped to make a new community that would be able to include them all," he told me. "We have failed to do so. Despite our best efforts, we have not been able to bridge this division.

"Our intention was to try and bring all the Jews together in an atmosphere of respect and tolerance. That turned out to be fiction, not reality. In theory, I still think it was an excellent idea, but in practice it has not worked out, and we have not been able to do what we wanted. The problem is that each group feels it has the 'correct' form of Judaism. And the members of each group are not content to practice as they wish and let others do the same, but they each want the other group to change the way they do things.

"It appears that the next step in the history of the Jews in Barcelona will be for each group to hold its own religious services and have its own community life.

"The idea of having that all under one roof has not worked out. Now no one knows what will happen."

Tuesday, August 11

A post-Olympic joke goes:

First Man: "Want to know how long the state of 'Olympic grace' lasted after the Games were over?"

Second Man: "Yes. How long?"

First Man: "As long as it took the hookers to leave the Zona Franca and come back to Camp Nou."

The Games finished two days ago, with a closing ceremony full of pomp and circumstance to accompany the passing of the Olympic banner to the mayor of Atlanta, Georgia, for 1996: spectacular fireworks; a beautiful spectacle built around the theme of fire from Catalonia's other world-class outdoor theater troupe, Els Comediants; and a variety of musical performances including singers Sarah Brightman and José Carreras belting out the Olympic theme song; an all-star flamenco cast; the popular Spanish rock group, Los Manolos; and the jazz duo of North American vibraphonist Bobby Hutcherson and Tete Montoliu, a blind Catalan pianist who is the dean of Spain's jazz musicians.

Tete Montoliu, whose full name in Catalan is Vicenç Montoliu i Massana, is known for not hesitating to express himself frankly, and he was frankly not happy about being on the same bill as the Manolos and an all-star flamenco group. In fact, the only thing he liked about the gig was the check, he told me.

"No one there understood what we were doing, Bobby and I. They received us like we were from another world. They were there to hear the flamenco, or the Manolos," Montoliu said. "I would rather have played at the inaugural ceremony, which was more musical. The closing was too folkloric for me. But, it's okay, we got paid and that's that."

The legendary Lionel Hampton heard him in 1955, when Tete was twenty-two, and called him the best jazz pianist in Europe. Hampton took him out on his first road trip and he has been making a living playing jazz ever since. There was not much work in Spain for a jazz musician under the dictatorship. There were no jazz clubs and the only way to make a living was to travel. Tete played all over Europe and in New York, recording albums—he has cut about fifty now—in a number of different countries.

A fierce Catalaniste, Montoliu is an advocate of complete Catalan independence from Spain. Catalans and black Americans are alike, he says: oppressed. Despite his hostility to the federal government in Madrid, he admits that things did go better for jazz players in Spain when the socialists arrived.

"During the 1950s and beginning of the '60s, the few people who listened to jazz were in Madrid or Barcelona," he told me. "If the democracy has been good for something, it is that everywhere in the country you begin to hear jazz in the streets. Dizzy Gillespie came to Spain and went to every corner of the country. These jazz listeners are a minority, but they are everywhere and they know what jazz is."

By the time Montoliu played at the Olympic's closing ceremony, he was fifty-nine and had a worldwide reputation. He chuckled. "My work has always been well-received in the U.S. I had enough offers so that I knew I could live in the States and play, but I always had to come back to Barcelona, because I've got a problem with pan con tomate. The problem is, I've got to have it."

When the call came from the mayor's office asking if he would play for the closing ceremony, and maybe pick some well-known Americans to play with him, Montoliu thought of his old friend, vibraphonist Bobby Hutcherson, with whom he had been playing in the occasional duo since a house party in Oakland, California, in 1984. "I really like Bobby Hutcherson as a person, he's about my best friend, and musically I think he's a master. When the mayor's office called, I asked them for a million pesetas, and they said yes. Then I asked for expenses, and they said yes again. So I called Bobby in California right away and said, 'Come on. Five thousand dollars, airline ticket and hotel. Come on.' That was good."

Not everyone was as happy as Tete Montoliu with the money they made during the Games. Cab drivers were badly burned by the Olympic torch. In 1991, the city had encouraged cab owners to trade their old cabs in on newer, spiffier models. Over a thousand of the city's ten thousand owners had done so. Cabbies were also offered courses in subjects like English and how to be courteous to foreigners during the year preceding the Games. Many drivers spent the time to take the courses, convinced that if they were prepared to work like crazy, they would make a lot of money.

The Barcelona Olympic Committee betrayed them by putting a fleet of 2,100 courtesy cars on the streets, at the disposal of any member of the "Olympic family," and by restricting traffic around sporting venues to so-called "Olympic traffic," excluding cabs. The committee also provided buses for journalists, so the number of people taking cabs was much lower than predicted. Ten leaders from the driver's union went on a hunger strike, the media began to report the story, and some urgent negotiations with the city ensued. Taxis were allowed into a number of previously restricted areas, but the Games still proved a disaster for most of them, money lost and vacation time wasted.

The entire companionship-for-money industry, usually one of Barcelona's more profitable, also suffered a worse-than-ever summer season. There was more money made in other years from the normal run-of-the-mill tourist than was spent by the Olympic crowd. "These have been the worst nights, financially, of my life," intoned Pepe, summing up the effect of the Games on his waitress bar.

"We had a night when only one person came in and I thought, it can't get any worse than this, and then there was a night when no one came in. No one. Not a single customer."

His bar is in an upscale neighborhood near the Avenida Diagonal, but business was no better closer to the heart of the Olympics. A spot check of the numerous waitress bars around the Plaza España the night after the Games echoed his gloomy assessment. The plain wooden door of the Club María Carmen, for instance, led me into a small room shaped like a flatiron, with a bar running the length of it. It is only two blocks from the Plaza España, and one block from the building where all those NBC staffers, and the people hired to attend them, had worked.

Business during the Olympics was worse than it had ever been, said the bartender, an older woman, short and stocky. There were six women sitting at the bar, barely enough room for a man to stand beside each of them. It was early—10:30 P.M.—and at that moment I was the only man in the place. They all nodded their heads in mournful agreement with the bartender when I asked about the Games.

"For us, the Olympics have been a disaster. Just awful. No one has come in. Every night the plaza has been full of people but it was just not our kind of crowd. The regular bars and cafes have all made lots of money."

Yesterday, with the Games only a day behind them, just about everyone left town, except the poor, the elderly, and the infirm. The city has been left virtually uninhabited, in a mid-August torpor. Shutters are down across shop fronts, and traffic is sparse. A typical August day in a month when the entire city annually goes on vacation.

A few bars are open. A handful of stores. The banks. Among the few groups of professionals still on the job are the prostitutes. As soon as the Olympics were done, they moved back to their beat behind the soccer stadium, and last night they got back to work. Many have lost time and money. Those who have passed the Games working in the Zona Franca are extremely unhappy, because their business was so poor. Now they have to work as much as possible to try and recoup their losses, even though business is going to be slow because everyone else is at the beach.

Many public officials were required to stay on the job through the

Games. Since the beginning of the year, the mayor had also been asking merchants to stay open until the end of the Olympics, rather than begin their vacations at the first of the month. There was concern that visitors not suddenly find themselves in the ghost town that is Barcelona in August. Some storeowners had agreed to stay open.

So, for one reason or another, a lot of Barcelonese were waiting until after the closing ceremony to leave the city, in addition to all the Olympic delegations, almost all of whom had stayed at the Olympic Village until the last minute. Yesterday, more than forty thousand people caught flights at El Prat airport. Vehicular traffic leaving the city was also exceptionally heavy. Cars were packed with families, and enough luggage for two weeks' vacation on the coast, or in the mountains. Barcelona breathed a sigh of relief and exhaustion at Games' end, and everyone seems to have been blown away on the winds of that exhalation.

They all left clutching a favorite Olympic story. Mine was of a twenty-four-year-old Algerian woman named Hassiba Boulmerka who won the 1,500 meter track and field event. Her victory followed years of training in her hometown in Algeria, and Spanish television showed a film of her daily routine. She would run through the streets of her village, chiseled, beautiful face lifted up, dark skin sweaty, deep brown eyes gleaming, black hair streaming out behind her. People shouted insults at her as she passed in her running clothes, many of them fundamentalist Muslims who called her a sacrilege and said she should be forbidden to train or compete. She persisted, and won Algeria's only gold medal.

Wednesday, September 2

This past Sunday, over 200,000 cars were estimated to have entered the city, returning from the August holidays. The lines of traffic coming in from north and south were five miles long, bumper-to-bumper. The next day, Monday, the last day of August, was not much better. It took hours to cover the last few kilometers into the city. Once there, every street, narrow or broad, had cars pulled up to the curb, people unloading suitcases. Many of the returning vacationers were tanned, and some were a scalded, sunburnt pink. Some looked relaxed, and some looked frazzled far beyond what they probably had been when they left. There was no mistaking that August was just about over, and Barcelona was about to start functioning again.

Yesterday was the first workday, the official end of vacation. *La Vanguardia* reported that many markets sold everything off their shelves, right down to the bare wood. People were restocking their larders, and getting back to the real world. The Games were history, and the Barcelonese were going to have to pay the piper, and live without the summer of '92 to anticipate.

The city's projected deficit for 1992, after all is said and done, will be about $2.6 billion, the mayor's office told the press. The budget deficit had first surpassed a billion dollars only five years before, and in 1982 the city's indebtedness had been only about $450 million. The 1992 figure is a high one. In his press conference, Mayor Maragall warned that now would come "the Olympics of austerity," and that Barcelona was going to have to weather some tough economic times in the near future. The conglomerate developing the Hotel des Artes, one of the two, rectangular glass-and-steel buildings of forty-four stories in the Olympic Village has declared bankruptcy on the project, and the building looms there on the beach—stark, ugly, and empty.

Hard times seem poised to strike all of Spain. The nation's unemployment rate has surpassed Ireland's, giving it the highest in the EC, during a year in which each member country is experiencing a rise in unemployment figures. A recession looms on the European horizon, the peseta is shaky on the money market, war continues to rage in what used to be Yugoslavia, and the EC's possibilities of passing the Maastricht Treaty are in doubt—a serious threat to plans for making the Common Market work.

Still, bad news is what people expect to read in their morning newspapers. Away from the pages of *La Vanguardia*, *El País*, or *El Periódico*, things seem to be going splendidly. The weather is beautiful—sunny, but not too hot. The first days back at work from vacation are never too bad, and public stress levels are low. The city has a refreshed, vigorous feeling. As the hour moves toward the end of the day, the outdoor tables at the cafes fill with people catching each other up on the news of their lives, sitting in the late afternoon sun.

Barcelona feels just fine.

# Bibliography

Abraham, Israel. *Jewish Life in the Middle Ages*. New York: Atheneum, 1969.

Amela, Victor M. "1391: el tragico fin de los judios barceloneses." *La Vanguardia (Cultura y Arte)*, November 12, 1991, p.2.

Amelang, James S., ed. *A Journal of the Plague Year*. New York: Oxford University Press, 1991.

Anaut, Alberto. "Sefarad." *El Pais (Suplemento)*, March 29, 1992, pp. 50–63.

Avni, Haim. *Spain, the Jews, and Franco*. Philadelphia: The Jewish Publication Society of America, 1982.

Baer, Yitzak. *A History of the Jews in Christian Spain*. Philadelphia: The Jewish Publication Society of America, 1961.

Benería, Lourdes. *Mujer, economía y patriarcado durante la España franquista*. Barcelona: Anagrama, 1977.

Bonet Mojica, Lluís and Anselm Roig. "Aquel tango de Perpiñan." *La Vanguardia (Revista)*, pp.2–3, Nov. 2, 1992.

Botey, Jaume. *Cinquanta-quatre Relats d'Immigració*. Barcelona: Diputació de Barcelona, 1986.

Castro, Américo. *The Spaniards*. Berkeley: University of California Press, 1971.

Cortijo, Francisco. "Tarjetas En Busca de Un Tipo." *Dinero* 449:28–31, 1991.

Dembo, Richard, ed. "Substance Misuse and the Law." *The International Journal of Addictions.* 25:3A, 1990–91.

Engle, Claude. "Solid Waste Management in Spain." Unpublished background paper for the United States Consulate in Barcelona.

Epstein, Isidore, ed. *The "Responsa" of Rabbi Solomon Ben Adreth of Barcelona.* New York: KTAV Publishing House, 1968.

Escur, Núria. "Sobre La Huella Judia." *La Vanguardia Magazine,* Dec. 1, 1991, pp. 39–48.

Fernandez Suarez, Luis. *Documentos Expulsion de Los Judios.* Valladolid: CSIC, 1964.

Fernández Martorell, Mercedes. *Estudio Antropologico: Una Comunidad Judia.* Barcelona: Editorial Mitre, 1984.

Gaite Martín, Carmen. *Usos Amorosos de La Postguerra Española.* Barcelona: Anagrama, 1987.

Gordon, Diana R. "Europe's Kinder, Gentler Approach." *The Nation,* Feb. 4, 1991, pp.128–130.

Graham, Robert. *Spain: A Nation Comes of Age.* New York: St. Martin's Press, 1984.

Greunke, Gudrun and Jorg Heimbrecht. *El Montaje del Sindrome Toxico.* Barcelona: Ediciones Obelisco, 1988.

Hall, Jacqueline. *Knowledge of the Catalan Language (1975–1986).* Barcelona: Generalitat de Catalunya, 1990.

Harman, Nick. "It doesn't have to be like this." *The Economist,* Sep. 2, 1989, pp.21–24.

Hooper, John. *The Spaniards.* New York: Viking, 1986.

Hughes, Robert. *Barcelona.* New York: Alfred A. Knopf, 1992.

Lisbona Martín, José Antonio. *Retorno a Sefarad.* Barcelona: Riopiedras, 1993.

Lopez de Meneses, Amada. "Una Consecuencia de La Peste Negra en Cataluña: El Pogrom de 1348." *Sefarad* XIX–1 (1959), pp.92–131.

MacLean, Ewan. *Official Responses To Drugs and Drug Dependence,* in *Approaches To Addiciton,* ed. by Joyce Lishman and Gordon Horobin. London: Kogan Page, 1985.

Madueño, Eugenio. *Viaje por El Placer, La Destrucción y La Muerte.* Barcelona: M.C.B. Ediciones, 1990.

Marquina, Antonio and Gloria Inés Ospina. *Espana y Los Judios en El Siglo XX.* Madrid: Espasa Calpe, 1987.

Neuman, Abraham A. *The Jews in Spain* (Volumes I & II). Philadelphia: The Jewish Publication Society of America, 1944.

Orwell, George. *Homage To Catalonia.* New York: Viking Penguin, 1989.

Peiro, Angeles Navarro. *Narrativa Hispanohebrea.* Cordoba: Ediciones El Almendro, 1988.

Riera i Sans, Jaume. *Catalonia and the Jews.* Barcelona: Generalitat de Catalunya, 1989.

Rodríguez, Jesús. "Viaje a Ninguna Parte." *El Pais (Suplemento),* Sept. 27, 1992, pp.25–37.

Roglán, Joaquim. "Tócala de nuevo, tete." *El Periódico,* Feb. 26, 1989, p.4.

Roth, Cecil. *The Spanish Inquisition.* London: Robert Hale, Ltd., 1937.

Rovira, Bru. "El jardín de la droga se desborda." *La Vanguardia (Revista),* Nov. 12, 1991, pp.2–3.

Santos, Carlos. "La Doble Vida de San Escriva (I)." *Cambio 16,* March 16, 1992.

———. "Droga: la prohibición mata." *Cambio 16,* April 27, 1992, pp. 12–26.

"Spain: Mitteleuropa on the Med." *The Economist.* April 25, 1992, pp. 5–24.

Valdéon, Julio. "De La Convivencia a La Expulsíon." *Alef,* Jan. 1992, pp.22–25.

Weiner, Herbert. *9½ Mystics: The Kabbala Today.* New York: Holt, Rinehart and Winston, 1969.